ANYTHING LESS WOULD BE A FIDDLE.

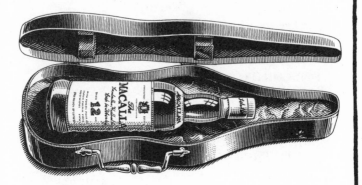

THE MACALLAN'S PLACE AS LEADER OF THE GREAT BAND of whiskies was roundly spelt out the other day in a learned magazine.

The writer mused on the meaning of the term 'Grande Marque', which he concluded, means simply 'Big Name' — and, he went on, 'Rolls Royce, Harrods, The Macallan and *STRADIVARIUS* are all Grande Marques in their spheres.'

So there you have it. Since the season for expansive gestures is now upon us, the gift of a bottle of The Macallan Malt Whisky is surely the most affordable way to make your own GRAND MARK this Christmas.

THE MACALLAN.
THE SINGLE MALT SCOTCH.

Sole U.S.A. Distributor, Remy Amerique, Inc.,
NY, NY Scotch Whisky 86 Proof, 43% Alc./Vol. © 1994

MANHATTAN THEATRE CLUB

IN PERFORMANCE

1995 SEASON

February 6
**An Evening with
PAUL MULDOON**

February 11
**FOR CHILDREN
BY CHILDREN IV**
with Peter Sis

February 13
**MARINA WARNER
and JUDITH THURMAN**

February 20
**GALWAY KINNELL and
HIS ANCESTORS**

February 27
HEART OF THE LAND
Essays on Last Great Places with
Rick Bass, Bill McKibben
and Jill Nelson

March 6
**WAR: ORIGIN &
AFTERMATH**
Readings by Donald Kagan
and Donovan Webster

March 13
**THE IMPORTANCE OF
BEING WILDE:**
100th anniversary of the trials
of Oscar Wilde
With Malcolm McDowell

March 20
NED ROREM

March 27
**THE WEDDING by
DOROTHY WEST**
With Gayle Pemberton

April 3
**AMIRI BARAKA and
GWENDOLYN BROOKS**

April 10
**MELISSA GREEN and
KYOKO MORI**

April 17
**CATCH-22 and
CLOSING TIME
by JOSEPH HELLER**

April 24
**VOICES FROM THE
NUYORICAN POETS CAFE**
Readings by Miguel Algarin,
Paul Beatty, Maggie Estep,
Bob Holman and Adrienne Su

May 8
BRADFORD MORROW

May 15
FIRST FICTION
With Mary Ann Taylor-Hall,
J.D. Landis, Sigrid Nunez
and A.J. Verdelle

May 22
**SHELTER by
JAYNE ANNE PHILLIPS**

FOR MEMBERSHIP and TICKET INFORMATION CALL **(212) 645-5848**.
General Membership: $60. Couple Membership: $100.

**MANHATTAN THEATRE CLUB AT CITY CENTER
131 WEST 55th STREET**

The Paris Review

Founded in 1953.

Publisher Drue Heinz

Editors

George Plimpton, Peter Matthiessen, Donald Hall, Robert Silvers, Blair Fuller,
Maxine Groffsky, Jeanne McCulloch, James Linville

Managing Editor Elizabeth Gaffney

Senior Editor Gia Kourlas

Associate Editors Daniel Kunitz, Elissa Schappell

Poetry Editor Richard Howard

Art Editor Joan Krawczyk

London Editor Shusha Guppy   **Paris Editor** Harry Mathews

Business Manager Lillian von Nickern   **Treasurer** Marjorie Kalman

Design Consultant Chip Kidd

Editorial Assistants

Brigid Hughes, Linda Rattner, Emily Wilson

Readers

Don Ambrose, Rick Hilles, Joseph Mackin,
Margaret Murray, Caley O'Dwyer, David Rosenthal

Special Consultants

Robert Phillips, Ben Sonnenberg, Remar Sutton

Advisory Editors

Nelson Aldrich, Lawrence M. Bensky, Patrick Bowles, Christopher Cerf, Jonathan
Dee, Timothy Dickinson, Joan Dillon, Beth Drenning, David Evanier, Rowan Gaither,
David Gimbel, Francine du Plessix Gray, Lindy Guinness, Christian Hawkey, Fay-
ette Hickox, Susannah Hunnewell, Ben Johnson, Mary B. Lumet, Larissa MacFar-
quhar, Molly McKaughan, Jonathan Miller, Ron Padgett, Maggie Paley, John
Phillips, Kevin Richardson, David Robbins, Philip Roth, Frederick Seidel, Mona
Simpson, Terry Southern, Max Steele, Rose Styron, William Styron, Tim Sultan,
Hallie Gay Walden, Eugene Walter, Antonio Weiss

Contributing Editors

Agha Shahid Ali, Kip Azzoni, Sara Barrett, Helen Bartlett, Robert Becker, Adam
Begley, Magda Bogin, Chris Calhoun, Morgan Entrekin, Jill Fox, Walker Gaffney,
Jamey Gambrell, John Glusman, Edward Hirsch, Gerald Howard, Tom Jenks, Bar-
bara Jones, Fran Kiernan, Joanna Laufer, Mary Maguire, Lucas Matthiessen, Dan
Max, Joanie McDonnell, Molly McQuade, Christopher Merrill, David Michaelis, Dini
von Mueffling, Barry Munger, Elise Paschen, Allen Peacock, William Plumber,
Charles Russell, Michael Sagalyn, Elisabeth Sifton, Ileene Smith, Patsy Southgate,
Rose Styron, William Wadsworth, Julia Myer Ward

Poetry Editors

Donald Hall (1953–1961), X. J. Kennedy (1962–1964),
Thomas Clark (1964–1973), Michael Benedikt (1974–1978),
Jonathan Galassi (1978–1988), Patricia Storace (1988–1992)

Art Editors

William Pène du Bois (1953–1960), Paris Editors (1961–1974),
Alexandra Anderson (1974–1978), Richard Marshall (1978–1993)

Founding Publisher Sadruddin Aga Khan

Former Publishers

Bernard F. Conners, Ron Dante, Deborah S. Pease

Founding Editors

Peter Matthiessen, Harold L. Humes, George Plimpton,
William Pène du Bois, Thomas H. Guinzburg, John Train

The Paris Review is published quarterly by The Paris Review, Inc. Vol. 36, No. 133, Winter 1994.
Business Office: 45–39 171 Place, Flushing, New York 11358 (ISSN #0031-2037). Paris Office:
Harry Matthews, 67 rue de Grenelle, Paris 75007 France. London Office: Shusha Guppy, 8 Shawfield
St., London, SW3. US distributors: Eastern News Company, Sandusky, OH. Typeset and printed
in USA by Capital City Press, Montpelier, VT. Price for single issue in USA: $10.00. $13.00 in
Canada. Post-paid subscription for four issues $34.00, lifetime subscription $1000. Postal surcharge
of $7.00 per four issues outside USA (excluding life subscriptions). Subscription card is bound within
magazine. Please give six weeks notice of change of address using subscription card. *While The
Paris Review welcomes the submission of unsolicited manuscripts, it cannot accept responsibility
for their loss or delay, or engage in related correspondence. Manuscripts will not be returned or
responded to unless accompanied by self-addressed, stamped envelope.* Fiction manuscripts
should be submitted to George Plimpton, poetry to Richard Howard, The Paris Review, 541 East
72nd Street, New York, N.Y. 10021. Charter member of the Council of Literary Magazines and
Presses. This publication is made possible, in part, with public funds from the New York State Council
on the Arts. Second Class postage paid at Flushing, New York, and at additional mailing offices.
Postmaster: Please send address changes to 45-39 171st Place, Flushing, N.Y. 11358.

"The one way of tolerating
existence is to lose oneself in
literature as in a perpetual
orgy."

—Gustave Flaubert,
in a letter, 1858

B·O·O·K·S
& Co.

939 Madison Avenue
New York City 10021

'phone (212) 737·1450

Ploughshares

Emerson College

Tony Hoagland
John C. Zacharis First Book Award

Ploughshares and Emerson College are proud to announce that Tony Hoagland has been named the 1994 recipient of the John C. Zacharis First Book Award for his collection of poems, *Sweet Ruin*. The $1,500 award—which is funded by Emerson College and named after the college's former president—honors the best debut book published by a *Ploughshares* writer, alternating annually between poetry and short fiction.

Sweet Ruin won the 1992 Brittingham Prize in Poetry and was published by the University of Wisconsin Press. In reviewing the book for *Ploughshares,* poet Steven Cramer wrote about Hoagland's work: "His muscular, conversational lines sprint from narrative passages to metaphorical clusters to speculative meditations, and then loop back, fast-talking and digressing their way into the book's richly American interior. Hoagland's is some of the most sheerly enjoyable writing I've encountered in a long time."

Hoagland currently lives in Waterville, Maine, and teaches part time at Colby College and at Warren Wilson's M.F.A. program in writing. He is halfway through a new collection.

The John C. Zacharis First Book Award is nominated by the advisory editors of *Ploughshares.* All first-book authors who have been published in *Ploughshares* are eligible. *Ploughshares* is issued three times a year, and subscriptions are available for $19 ($24 international) from *Ploughshares,* Emerson College, 100 Beacon St., Boston, MA 02116.

The Paris Review

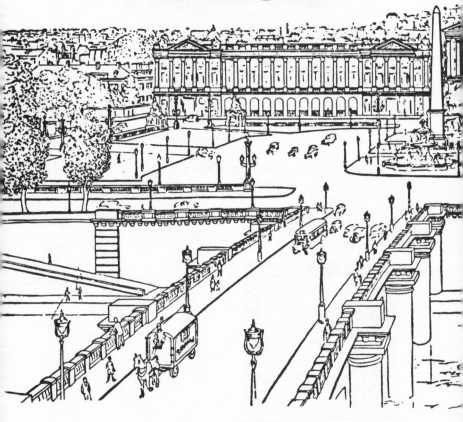

Editorial Office:
541 East 72 Street
New York, New York 10021

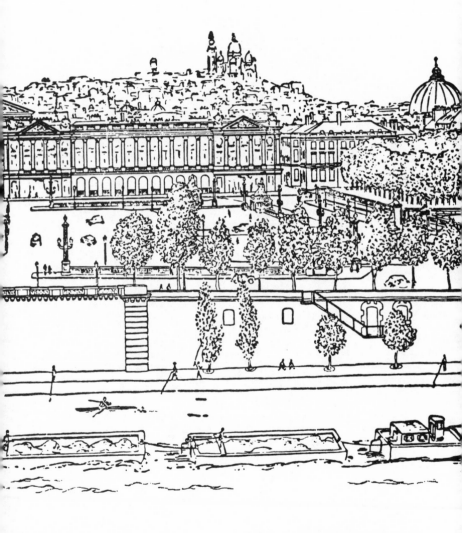

Business & Circulation:
45-39 171 Place
Flushing, New York 11358

Distributed by Random House
201 East 50 Street
New York, N.Y. 10022
(800) 733-3000

Table of contents illustration by Nancy Brett.
Frontispiece by William Pène du Bois.
Cover by Robert Greene. "He Showed Me," 1990.

Number 133

The Djinn in the Nightingale's Eye

A.S. Byatt

Once upon a time, when men and women hurtled through the air on metal wings, when they wore webbed feet and walked on the bottom of the sea, learning the speech of whales and the songs of the dolphins, when pearly-fleshed and jew-elled apparitions of Texan herdsmen and houris shimmered in the dusk on Nicaraguan hillsides, when folk in Norway and Tasmania in dead of winter could dream of fresh strawberries, dates, guavas and passion fruits and find them spread next morning on their tables, there was a woman who was largely irrelevant, and therefore happy.

Her business was storytelling, but she was no ingenious queen in fear of the shroud brought in with the dawn, nor was she a naquibolmalek to usher a shah through the gates of sleep, nor an ashik, lover-minstrel singing songs of Mehmet the Conqueror and the sack of Byzantium, nor yet a holy dervish in short skin trousers and skin skull-cap, brandishing axe or club and making its shadow terrible. She was no meddah, telling incredible tales in the Ottoman court or the coffee-houses by the market. She was merely a narratologist, a being of secondary order, whose days were spent hunched in great libraries scrying, interpreting, decoding the fairy-tales of childhood and the vodka-posters of the grown-up world, the unending romances of golden coffee-drinkers, and the impeded couplings of doctors and nurses, dukes and poor maidens, horsewomen and musicians. Sometimes also, she flew. In her impoverished youth she had supposed that scholarship was dry, dusty and static, but now she knew better. Two or three times a year she flew to strange cities, to China, Mexico and Japan, to Transylvania, Bogotá and the South Seas, where narratologists gathered like starlings, parliaments of wise fowls, telling stories about stories.

At the time when my story begins the green sea was black, sleek as the skins of killer whales, and the sluggish waves were on fire, with dancing flames and a great curtain of stinking smoke. The empty deserts were seeded with skulls, and with iron canisters, containing death. Pestilence crept invisibly from dune to dune. In those days men and women, including narratologists, were afraid to fly East, and their gatherings were diminished. Nevertheless our narratologist, whose name was Gillian Perholt, found herself in the air, between London and Ankara. Who can tell if she travelled because she was English and stolid and could not quite imagine being blasted out of the sky, or because, although she was indeed an imaginative being, and felt an appropriate measure of fear, she could not resist the idea of the journey above the clouds, above the minarets of Istanbul, and the lure of seeing the Golden Horn, the Bosphorus and the shores of Europe and Asia face to face? Flying is statistically safer than any other travel, Gillian Perholt told herself and surely at this time, only slightly less safe, statistically only a little less.

She had a phrase for the subtle pleasures of solitary air travel. She spoke it to herself like a charm as the great silver craft detached itself from its umbilical tube at Heathrow, waddled like an albatross across the tarmac and went up, up, through grey curtains of English rain, a carpet of woolly iron-grey English cloud, a world of swirling vapour, trailing its long limbs and scarves past her tiny porthole, in the blue and gold world that was always there, above the grey, always. 'Floating redundant' she said to herself, sipping champagne, nibbling salted almonds, whilst all round her spread the fields of heaven, white and rippling, glistening and gleaming, rosy and blue in the shadows, touched by the sun with steady brightness. 'Floating redundant', she murmured blissfully as the vessel banked and turned and a disembodied male voice spoke in the cabin, announcing that there was a veil of water vapour over France but that that would burn off, and then they would see the Alps, when the time came. *Burn off* was a powerful term, she thought, rhetorically interesting, for water does not burn and yet the sun's heat reduces this water to nothing; I am in the midst of fierce forces. I am nearer the sun than any woman of my kind, any ancestress of mine, can ever have dreamed of being, I can look in his direction and stay steadily here, floating redundant.

The phrase was, of course, not her own; she was, as I have said, a being of a secondary order. The phrase was John Milton's, plucked from the air, or the circumambient language, at the height of his powers, to describe the beauty of the primordial coils of the insinuating serpent in the Paradise garden. Gillian Perholt remembered the very day these words had first coiled into shape and risen in beauty from the page, and struck at her, unsuspecting as Eve. There she was, sixteen years old, a golden-haired white virgin with vague blue eyes (she pictured herself so) and there on the ink-stained desk in the dust was the battered emerald-green book, ink-stained too, and second-hand, scribbled across and across by dutiful or impatient female fingers, and everywhere was a smell, still drily pungent, of hot ink and linoleum and dust if not ashes, and there he was, the creature, insolent and lovely before her:

                    not with indented wave,
Prone on the ground, as since, but on his rear,

Circular base of rising folds, that towered
Fold above fold a surging maze, his head
Crested aloft and carbuncle his eyes;
With burnished neck of verdant gold, erect
Amidst his circling spires, that on the grass
Floated redundant: pleasing was his shape,
And lovely.

And for an instant Gillian Perholt had *seen*, brilliant and swaying, not the snake Eve had seen in the garden, nor yet the snake that had risen in the dark cave inside the skull of blind John Milton, but a snake, the snake, the same snake, in some sense, made of words and visible to the eye. So, as a child, from time to time, she had *seen* wolves, bears and small grey men, standing between her and the safety of the door, or her father's sleeping Sunday form in an armchair. But I digress, or am about to digress. I called up the snake (I saw him too, in my time) to explain Dr Perholt's summing-up of her own state.

In those days she had been taught to explain 'floating redundant' as one of Milton's magical fusings of two languages — 'floating', which was Teutonic and to do with floods, and 'redundant', which was involved and Latinate, and to do with overflowings. Now she brought to it her own wit, a knowledge of the modern sense of 'redundant', which was to say, superfluous, unwanted, unnecessary, let go. 'I'm afraid we shall have to let you go,' employers said, everywhere, offering freedom to reluctant Ariels, as though the employees were captive sprites, only too anxious to rush uncontrolled into the elements. Dr Perholt's wit was only secondarily to do with employment, however. It was primarily to do with her sex and age, for she was a woman in her fifties, past childbearing, whose two children were adults now, had left home and had left England, one for Saskatchewan and one for São Paulo, from where they communicated little, for they were occupied with children of their own. Dr Perholt's husband also, had left home, had left

Dr Perholt, had removed himself after two years of soul-
searching, two years of scurrying in and out of his/their home,
self-accusation, irritability, involuntary impotence, rejection
of lovingly cooked food, ostentatious display of concealed mes-
sages, breathed phone-calls when Dr Perholt appeared to be
sleeping, missed dinner engagements, mysterious dips in the
balance at the bank, bouts of evil-smelling breath full of
brandy and stale smoke, also of odd-smelling skin, with
touches of alien sweat, hyacinths and stephanotis. He had
gone to Majorca with Emmeline Porter and from there had
sent a fax message to Gillian Perholt, saying he was a coward
for doing it this way, but it was also done to save her, and
that he was never coming home.

Gillian Perholt happened to be in her study when the fax
began to manifest itself, announced by a twangling bell and
a whirring sound. It rose limp and white in the air and flopped
exhausted over the edge of the desk—it was long and self-
exculpatory, but there is no need for me to recount it to you,
you can imagine it very well for yourself. Equally, you can
imagine Emmeline Porter for yourself, she has no more to do
with this story. She was twenty-six, that is all you need to
know, and more or less what you supposed, probably, anyway.
Gillian watched the jerky progress and flopping of the fax
with admiration, not for Mr Perholt's fluency, but for the way
in which agitated black scribbling could be fed into a machine
slit in Majorca and appear simultaneously in Primrose Hill.
The fax had been bought for Mr Perholt, an editorial consultant, to work from home when he was let go or made redundant in the banal sense, but its main user was Gillian Perholt,
who received E-mail and story variants from narratologists in
Cairo and Auckland, Osaka and Port of Spain. Now the fax
was hers, since he was gone. And although she was now redundant as a woman, being neither wife, mother nor mistress,
she was by no means redundant as a narratologist but on the
contrary, in demand everywhere. For this was a time when
women were privileged, when female narratologists had skills
greatly revered, when there were pythonesses, abbesses and

sibyls in the world of narratology, who revealed mysteries and kept watch at the boundaries of correctness.

On receiving the fax, Gillian Perholt stood in the empty study and imagined herself grieving over betrayal, the loss of love, the loss of companionship perhaps, of respect in the world, maybe, as an aging woman rejected for one more youthful. It was a sunny day in Primrose Hill, and the walls of the study were a cheerful golden colour, and she saw the room fill up with golden light and felt full of lightness, happiness and purpose. She felt, she poetically put it to herself, like a prisoner bursting chains and coming blinking out of a dungeon. She felt like a bird confined in a box, like a gas confined in a bottle, that found an opening, and rushed out. She felt herself expand in the space of her own life. No more waiting for meals. No more grumbling and jousting, no more exhausted anticipation of alien feelings, no more snoring, no more farts, no more trace of stubble in the washbasin.

She considered her reply. She wrote:

OK. Agree. Clothes in bales in store. Books in chests ditto. Will change locks. Have a good time. G.

She knew she was lucky. Her ancestresses, about whom she thought increasingly often, would probably have been dead by the age she had reached. Dead in childbed, dead of influenza, or tuberculosis, or puerperal fever, or simple exhaustion, dead, as she travelled back in time, from worn-out unavailing teeth, from cracked kneecaps, from hunger, from lions, tigers, sabre-toothed tigers, invading aliens, floods, fires, religious persecution, human sacrifice, why not? Certain female narratologists talked with pleasurable awe about wise crones but she was no crone, she was an unprecedented being, a woman with porcelain-crowned teeth, laser-corrected vision, her own store of money, her own life and field of power, who flew, who slept in luxurious sheets around the world, who gazed out at the white fields under the sun by day and the brightly turning stars by night as she floated redundant.

The conference in Ankara was called 'Stories of Women's Lives'. This was a pantechnicon title to make space for everyone, from every country, from every genre, from every time. Dr Perholt was met at the airport by an imposing bearded Turkish professor, dark and smiling, into whose arms she rushed with decorous cries of joy, for he was an old friend, they had been students together amongst mediaeval towers and slow, willow-bordered rivers, they had a story of their own, a very minor sub-plot, a thread now tenuous, now stronger, but never broken, in the tapestry of both lives. Dr Perholt was angry at the blonde Lufthansa hostess who bowed gravely to the grey businessmen as they disembarked, Good-bye, sir and thank you, good-bye, sir and thank you, but gave Dr Perholt a condescending 'Bye-bye, dear.' But Orhan Rifat, beyond the airport threshold, was as always alive with projects, new ideas, new poems, new discoveries. They would visit Izmir with a group of Turkish friends. Gillian would then visit Istanbul, his city.

The conference, like most conferences, resembled a bazaar, where stories and ideas were exchanged and changed. It took place in a cavernous theatre with no windows on the outside world but well provided with screens where transparencies flickered fitfully in the dark. The best narratologists work by telling and retelling tales. This holds the hearer from sleep and allows the teller to insert him- or herself into the tale. Thus a fierce Swiss writer told the horrid story of Typhoid Mary, an innocent polluter, an unwitting killer. Thus the elegant Leyla Doruk added passion and flamboyance to her version of the story of the meek Fanny Price, trembling and sickly in the deepest English wooded countryside. Orhan Rifat was to speak last: his title was 'Powers and Powerlessness: Djinns and Women in *The Arabian Nights*'. Gillian Perholt spoke before him. She had chosen to analyse the 'Clerk's Tale' from *The Canterbury Tales*, which is the story of Patient Griselda.

No one has ever much liked this story, although it is told by one of Chaucer's most sympathetic pilgrims, the book-loving, unworldly Clerk of Oxford, who took it from Petrarch's Latin, which was a rendering of Boccaccio's Italian. Gillian Perholt did not like this story; that was why she had chosen to tell it, amongst the stories of women's lives. What do I think of, she had asked herself, on receiving the invitation, when I think of 'Stories of Women's Lives', and had answered herself with a thrill and a shudder, Patient Griselda.

So now she told it, in Ankara, to a mixed audience of scholars and students. Most of the Turkish students were like students everywhere, in jeans and T-shirts, but conspicuous in the front row were three young women with their heads wrapped in grey scarves, and dotted amongst the young men in jeans were soldiers—young officers—in uniform. In the secular Turkish republic the scarves were a sign of religious defiance, an act of independence with which liberal-minded Turkish professors felt they should feel sympathy, though in a Muslim state much of what they themselves taught and cared about would be as objectionable, as forbidden, as the covered heads were here. The young soldiers, Gillian Perholt observed, listened intently and took assiduous notes. The three scarved women, on the other hand, stared proudly ahead, never meeting the speakers' eyes, as though completely preoccupied with their own conspicuous self-assertion. They came to hear all the speakers. Orhan had asked one of them, he told Gillian, why she dressed as she did. 'My father and my fiancé say it is right,' she had said. 'And I agree.'

The story of Patient Griselda, as told by Gillian Perholt, is this:

There was once a young marquis, in Lombardy, whose name was Walter. He enjoyed his life, and his sports—hunting and hawking—as young men do, and had no desire to marry, perhaps because marriage appeared to him to be a form of confinement, or possibly because marriage is the end of youth, and its freedom from care, if youth is free from care. However his people came and urged him to take a wife, perhaps, as they told him, because he should think of begetting an heir, perhaps because they felt marriage would steady him. He professed himself moved by their arguments and invited them to his wedding, on a certain day he fixed on — with the condition that they swore to accept this bride, whoever she might be.

It was one of Walter's peculiarities that he liked to make people swear in advance to accept unconditionally and without repining whatever he himself might choose to do.

So the people agreed and made ready for the wedding on the chosen day. They made a feast and prepared rich clothes, jewels and bedlinen for the unknown bride. And on the chosen day the priest was waiting, and the bridal procession mounted, and still no one knew who the bride was to be.

Now Griseldis or Grisilde or Grisildis or Grissel or Griselda was the daughter of a poor peasant. She was both beautiful and virtuous. On the day fixed for the wedding she set out to fetch water from the well; she had all the domestic virtues and meant to finish her housework before standing in the lane with the other peasants to cheer as the bridal procession wound past. Weddings make spectators — participating spectators — of us all. Griselda wanted to be part of the wedding, and to look at the bride, as we all do. We all like to look at brides. Brides and princesses, those inside the story, imagined from the outside. Who knows but Griselda was looking forward to imagining the feelings of this unknown woman as she rode past.

Only the young lord rode up, and did not ride past, but stopped, and made her put down her pitcher, and wait. And he spoke to her father, and said that it was his intention to make Griselda his wife, if her father would give his consent to her will. So the young lord spoke to the young woman and said he wanted to make her his bride, and that his only requirement was that she should promise to obey him in everything, to do whatever he desired, without hesitating or repining, at every moment of the day or night. And Griselda, 'quakynge for drede' as Chaucer tells us, swore that never willingly, in act or thought, would she disobey him, on pain of death — though she would fear to die, she told the young lord.

And then young Walter commanded immediately that her clothes should be taken off and that she should be clothed in the rich new garments he had prepared, with her hair dressed and her head crowned with a jewelled coronet. And so she went away to be married, and to live in the castle, and Chaucer tells us, he takes care to tell us, that she showed great qualities of judgment, reconciliation of disputes, bounty and courtesy in her new position, and was much loved by the people.

But the story goes inexorably on, past the wedding, into the ominous future foreshadowed by the pledge exacted and vouchsafed. And consider this, said Gillian Perholt at this point in the story: in almost all stories of promises and prohibitions, the promises and prohibitions carry with them the inevitability of failure, of their own breaking. Orhan Rifat smiled into his beard, and the soldiers wrote rapidly, presumably about promises and prohibitions, and the grey-scarved women stared fixedly ahead.

After a time, Chaucer says, Griselda gave birth to a daughter, although she would rather have borne a son; but everyone rejoiced, for once it is seen that a woman is not barren, a son may well come next. And at this point it came into Walter's head that he must test his wife. It is interesting, said Gillian, that here the Clerk of Oxford dissociates himself as narrator from his protagonist, and says he cannot see why this testing seemed to be necessary. But he goes on to tell how Walter informed his wife gravely that the people grumbled at having a peasant's daughter set over them, and did not want such a person's child to be set above them. He therefore proposed, he said, to put her daughter to death. And Griselda answered that she and her child were his to do with as he thought best.

So Walter sent a rough sergeant to take the child, from the breast. And Griselda kissed it good-bye, asking only that the baby should be buried where wild creatures could not tear it.

And after a further time, Griselda gave birth to a son, and the husband, still intent on testing, had this child too taken from the breast and carried away to be killed. And Griselda kept steadily to her pact, assuring him that she was not grieved or hurt; that her two children had brought her only sickness at first 'and after, woe and pain'.

And then there was a lull in the narrative, said Gillian, a lull long enough for the young children who were secretly being brought up in Bologna to reach puberty, adolescence, a marriageable age. A lull as long as the space between acts III and IV of *A Winter's Tale* during which Hermione the Queen is hidden away and thought to be dead, and her daughter, Perdita, abandoned and exposed, is brought up by shepherds, wooed by a Prince, and forced to flee to Sicily where she is happily reunited with her repentant father and her lost mother who appears on a pedestal as a statue and is miraculously given her life and happiness again by art. In the *Winter's Tale*, said Gillian, the lovely daughter is the renewal of the mother, as the restoration of Persephone was the renewal of the fields in Spring, laid waste by the rage of Demeter, the mother-goddess. Here Gillian's voice faltered. She looked out at the audience and told them how Paulina, Hermione's friend and servant, had taken on the powers of witch, artist, storyteller, and had restored the lost queen to life. Personally, said Gillian, I have never been able to stomach—to bear—that plotted dénouement, which is the opposite of the restoration of Persephone in Spring. For human beings do not die and spring up again like the grass and the corn, they live one life and get older. And from Hermione—and as you may know already, from Patient Griselda—most of that life has been taken by plotting, has been made into a grey void of forced inactivity.

What did Griselda do whilst her son, and more particularly her daughter were growing up? The story gallops. A woman's life runs from wedding to childbirth to nothing in a twinkling of an eye. Chaucer gives no hint of subsequent children, though he insists that Griselda remained true in love and patience and submission. But her husband had to excess Paulina's desire to narrate, to orchestrate, to direct. He busied himself, he gained a dispensation from the pope to put away his wife Griselda, and to marry a young bride. The people muttered about the murdered children. But Walter, if we are to believe the story, went to his patient wife and told her that he intended to replace her with a younger and more acceptable bride, and that she must return to her father, leaving behind the rich clothes and jewels and other things which had been his gift. And still Griselda was patient, though Chaucer here gives her words of power in her patience which keep the reader's sympathy, and fend off the reader's impatience which might sever that sympathy.

Naked, Griselda tells her husband, she came from her father, and naked she will return. But since he has taken all her old clothes she asks him for a smock to cover her nakedness, since 'the womb in which your children lay, should not, as I walk, be seen bare before the people. Let me not,' says Griselda, 'go by the way like a worm. In exchange for my maidenhead which I brought with me and cannot take away, give me a smock.' And Walter graciously allows her the shift she stands in, to cover her nakedness.

But Walter thought of other twists to the intrigue, since every twist made his plotted dénouement more splendid and satisfactory. No sooner, it seemed, was Griselda back at home, than her husband was there, asking her to return to the castle and prepare the rooms and the feast for his new young bride. No one could do it better, he told her. You might think that the pact was over on her return to her father's house, but this was not Griselda's idea: patiently she returned, patiently she cooked, cleaned, prepared, made up the marriage bed.

And the bridal procession arrived at the castle, with the beautiful girl in the midst, and Griselda worked away in the hall in her poor clothes, and the feast was set, and the lords

and ladies sat down to eat. Now indeed, apparently, Griselda
was a belated spectator at the wedding. Walter called Griselda
to him and asked her what she thought of his wife and her
beauty. And Griselda did not curse her, or indeed him, but
answered always patiently, that she had never seen a fairer
woman, and that she both beseeched and warned him 'never
to prick this tender maiden with tormenting' as he had done
her, for the young bride was softly brought up and would not
endure it.

And now Walter had his dénouement, the end of his story,
and revealed to Griselda that his bride was not his bride, but
her daughter, and the squire her son, and that all would now
be well and she would be happy, for he had done all this
neither in malice nor in cruelty, but to test her good faith,
which he had not found wanting. So now they could be recon-
ciled.

And what did Griselda do? asked Gillian Perholt. And what
did she say, and what did she do? repeated Dr Perholt. Her
audience was interested. It was not a story most of them knew
beyond the title and its idea, Patient Griselda. Would the
worm turn? one or two asked themselves, moved by Griselda's
image of her own naked flesh. They looked up to Dr Perholt
for an answer, and she was silent, as if frozen. She stood on
the stage, her mouth open to speak, and her hand out, in a
rhetorical gesture, with the lights glittering on her eyeballs.
She was an ample woman, a stout woman, with a soft clear
skin, clothed in the kind of draped linen dress and jacket that
is best for stout women, a stone-coloured dress and jacket,
enlivened by blue glass beads.

And Gillian Perholt stared out of glassy eyes and heard her
voice fail. She was far away and long ago — she was a pillar of
salt, her voice echoed inside a glass box, a sad piping like a
lost grasshopper in winter. She could move neither fingers nor
lips, and in the body of the hall, behind the grey-scarved
women, she saw a cavernous form, a huge, female form, with
a veiled head bowed above emptiness and long slack-sinewed
arms, hanging loosely around emptiness, and a draped, cowled

garment ruffling over the windy vacuum of nothing, a thing banal in its conventional awfulness, and for that very reason appalling because it was there, to be seen, her eyes could distinguish each fold, could measure the red rims of those swollen eyes, could see the cracks in the stretched lips of that toothless, mirthless mouth, could see that it was many colours, and all of them grey, grey. The creature was flat breasted and its withered skin was exposed above the emptiness, the windy hole that was its belly and womb.

This is what I am afraid of, thought Gillian Perholt, whose intelligence continued to work away, to think of ways to ascertain whether or not the thing was a product of hallucination or somehow out there on an unexpected wavelength.

And just as Orhan rose to come to her help, seeing her stare like Macbeth at the feast, she began to speak again, as though nothing had happened, and the audience sighed and sat back, ill at ease but courteous.

And what did Griselda do? asked Gillian Perholt. And what did Griselda say and what did she do? repeated Dr Perholt. First, all mazed, uncomprehending, she swooned. When she revived, she thanked her husband for having saved her children, and told her children that her father had cared for them tenderly — and she embraced both son and daughter, tightly, tightly, and still gripping them fell again into terrible unconsciousness, gripping so tightly that it was almost impossible for the bystanders to tear the children from her grasp. Chaucer does not say, the Clerk of Oxford does not say, that she was strangling them, but there is fear in his words, and in the power of her grip, all her stoppered and stunted energy forcing all three into unconsciousness, unknowing, absence from the finale so splendidly brought about by their lord and master.

But of course, she was revived, and again stripped of her old clothes, and dressed in cloth of gold and crowned with jewels and restored to her place at the feast. To begin again.

And I wish to say a few words, said Gillian Perholt, about the discomfort of this terrible tale. You might suppose it was one of that group of tales in which the father or king or lord tries to marry his daughter, after his wife's death, as the original Leontes tried to marry Perdita in the tale that precedes the *Winter's Tale*, the tale of a man seeking the return of spring and youth and fertility in ways inappropriate for human beings as opposed to grass and the flowers of the field. This pattern is painful but natural, this human error which tales hasten to punish and correct. But the peculiar horror of Patient Griselda does not lie in the psychological terror of incest or even of age. It lies in the narration of the story and Walter's relation to it. The story is terrible because Walter has assumed too many positions in the narration; he is hero, villain, destiny, God and narrator—there is no *play* in this tale, though the Clerk and Chaucer behind him try to vary its tone with reports of the people's contradictory feelings, and with the wry final comment on the happy marriage of Griselda's son, who

> fortunat was eek in mariage,
> Al putte he nat his wyf in greet assay.
> This world is nat so strong, it is no nay,
> As it hath been in olde tymes yoore.

And the commentator goes on to remark that the moral is *not* that wives should follow Griselda in humility, for this would be impossible, unattainable, even if desired. The moral is that of Job, says the Clerk, according to Petrarch, that human beings must patiently bear what comes to them. And yet our own response is surely outrage—at what was done to Griselda—at what was taken from her, the best part of her life, what could not be restored—at the energy stopped off. For the stories of women's lives in fiction are the stories of stopped energies—the stories of Fanny Price, Lucy Snowe, even Gwendolen Harleth, are the stories of Griselda, and all come to that moment of strangling, willed oblivion.

Gillian Perholt looked up. The creature, the ghoul, was gone. There was applause. She stepped down. Orhan, who was forthright and kind, asked if she felt unwell and she said that she had had a dizzy turn. She thought it was nothing to worry about. A momentary mild seizure. She would have liked to tell him about the apparition too, but was prevented. Her tongue lay like lead in her mouth, and the thing would not be spoken. What cannot be spoken continues its vigorous life in the veins, in the brain-cells, in the nerves. As a child she had known that if she could describe the grey men on the stairs, or the hag in the lavatory, they would vanish. But she could not. She imagined them lusciously and in terror and occasionally saw them, which was different.

Orhan's paper was the last in the conference. He was a born performer, and always had been, at least in Gillian's experience. She remembered a student production of *Hamlet* in which they had both taken part. Orhan had been Hamlet's father's ghost and had curdled everyone's blood with his deep-voiced rhetoric. His beard was now, as it had not been then, 'a sable silvered', and had now, as it had had then, an Elizabethan cut — though his face had sharpened from its youthful thoughtfulness and he now bore a resemblance, Gillian thought, to Bellini's portrait of Mehmet the Conqueror. She herself had been Gertrude, although she had wanted to be Ophelia, she had wanted to be beautiful and go passionately mad. She had been the Queen who could not see the spirit stalking her bedchamber; this came into her mind, with a renewed, now purely imaginary vision of the Hermione-Griselda ghoul, as she saw Orhan, tall, imposing, smiling in his beard, begin to speak of Scheherazade and the djinniyah.

'It has to be admitted,' said Orhan, 'that misogyny is a driving force of pre-modern story collections — perhaps especially of the frame stories — from *Katha Sarit Sagara, The Ocean of Story*, to the *Thousand and One Nights, Alf Layla wa-Layla*. Why this should be so has not, as far as I know, been fully explained, though there are reasons that could be put forward from social structures to depth psychology — the

sad fact remains that women in these stories for the most part
are portrayed as deceitful, unreliable, greedy, inordinate in
their desires, unprincipled and simply dangerous, operating
powerfully (apart from sorceresses and female ghouls and
ogres) through the structures of powerlessness. What is
peculiarly interesting about the *Thousand and One Nights* in
terms of the subject of our conference, is the frame story,
which begins with two kings driven to murderous despair by
the treachery of women, yet has a powerful heroine-narrator,
Scheherazade, who must daily save her own life from a blanket
vicarious vengeance on all women by telling tales in the night,
tales in the bed, in the bedchamber, to her innocent little
sister — Scheherazade whose art is an endless beginning and
delaying and ending and beginning and delaying and
endng — a woman of infinite resource and sagacity,' said Orhan
smiling, 'who is nevertheless using cunning and manipulation
from a position of total powerlessness with the sword of her
fate more or less in her bedchamber hanging like the sword
of Damocles by a metaphorical thread, the thread of her narrative, with her shroud daily prepared for her the next morning.
For King Shahriyar, like Count Walter, has taken upon himself
to be husband and destiny, leaving only the storytelling element, the plotting, to his wife, which is enough. Enough to
save her, enough to provide space for the engendering and
birth of her children, whom she hides from her husband as
Walter hid his from Griselda, enough to spin out her life until
it becomes love and happy-ever-after, so to speak, as Griselda's
does. For these tales are not psychological novels, are not concerned with states of mind or development of character, but
bluntly with Fate, with Destiny, with what is prepared for
human beings. And it has been excellently said by Pasolini
the filmmaker that the tales in the *Thousand and One Nights*
all end with the disappearance of destiny which 'sinks back
into the somnolence of daily life.' But Scheherazade's own
life could not sink back into somnolence until all the tales
were told. So the dailiness of daily life is her end as it is
Cinderella's and Snow-White's but not Mme Bovary's or Julien

Sorel's who die but do not vanish into the afterlife of stories. But I am anticipating my argument, which, like my friend and colleague Dr Perholt's argument, is about character and destiny and sex in the folk-tale, where character is *not* destiny as Novalis said it was, but something else is.

And first I shall speak of the lives of women in the frame story, and then I shall briefly discuss the story of Camaralzaman and Princess Budoor, which is only half-told in the manuscripts of the *Nights* . . .

Gillian Perholt sat behind the grey-scarved women and watched Orhan's dark hooked face as he told of the two kings and brothers Shahriyar and Shahzaman, and of how Shahzaman, setting out on a journey to his brother, went back home to bid his wife farewell, found her in the arms of a kitchen boy, slew them both immediately, and set out on his journey consumed by despair and disgust. These emotions were only relieved when he saw from his brother's palace window the arrival in a secret garden of his brother's wife and twenty slave girls. Of these ten were white and ten black, and the black cast off their robes revealing themselves to be young males, who busily tupped the white females, whilst the queen's black lover Mas'ud came out of a tree and did the same for her. This amused and relieved Shahzaman, who saw that his own fate was the universal fate, and was able to demonstrate to his brother, at first incredulous and then desperate with shame and wrath, that this was so. So the two kings, in disgust and despondency, left the court and their life at the same moment and set out on a pilgrimage in search of someone more unfortunate than themselves, poor cuckolds as they were.

Note, said Orhan, that at this time no one had attempted the lives of the queen and her black lover and the twenty lascivious slaves.

And what the two kings met was a djinn, who burst out of the sea like a swaying black pillar that touched the clouds, carrying on his head a great glass chest with four steel locks. And the two kings (like Mas'ud before them) took refuge in a tree. And the djinn laid himself down to sleep, as luck, or chance, or fate would have it, under that very tree, and opened the chest to release a beautiful woman — one he had carried away on her wedding night — on whose lap he laid his head and immediately began to snore. Whereupon the woman indicated to the two kings that she knew where they were, and would scream and reveal their presence to the djinn unless they immediately came down and satisfied her burning sexual need. The two kings found this difficult, in the circumstances, but were persuaded by threats of immediate betrayal and death to do their best. And when they had both made love to the djinn's stolen wife, as she lay with opened legs on the desert sand under the tree, she took from both of them their rings, which she put away in a small purse on her person, which already contained ninety-eight rings of varying fashions and materials. And she told the two kings with some complacency that they were all the rings of men with whom she had been able to deceive the djinn, despite being locked in a glass case with four steel locks, kept in the depths of the raging roaring sea. And the djinn, she explained, had tried in vain to keep her pure and chaste, not realising that nothing can prevent or alter what is predestined, and that when a woman desires something, nothing can stop her.

And the two kings concluded, after they were well escaped, that the djinn was more unfortunate than they were, so they returned to the palace, put Shahriyar's wife and the twenty slaves to the sword, replaced the female slaves in the harem, and instituted the search for virgin brides who should all be put to death after one night 'to save King Shahriyar from the wickedness and cunning of women'. And this led to Scheherazade's resourceful plan to save countless other girls by substituting narrative attractions for those of inexperienced virginity, said Orhan, smiling in his beard, which took her a thousand and one nights. And in these frame stories, said Orhan, destiny for men is to lose dignity because of female rapacity and duplicity, and destiny for women is to be put to the sword on that account.

What interests me about the story of Prince Camaralzaman, said Orhan, is the activity of the djinn in bringing about a satisfactory adjustment to the normal human destiny in the recalcitrant prince. Camaralzaman was the beloved only son of Sultan Shahriman of Khalidan. He was the child of his father's old age, born of a virgin concubine with ample proportions, and he was very beautiful, like the moon, like new anemones in spring, like the children of angels. He was amiable but full of himself, and when his father urged him to marry to perpetuate his line, he cited the books of the wise, and their accounts of the wickedness and perfidy of women, as a reason for refraining, 'I would rather die than allow a woman to come near me,' said Prince Camaralzaman, 'Indeed,' he said grandly, 'I would not hesitate to kill myself if you wished to force me into marriage.' So his father left the topic for a year, during which Camaralzaman grew even more beautiful, and then asked again, and was told that the boy had done even more reading, which had simply convinced him that women were immoral, foolish and disgusting, and that death was preferable to dealing with them. And after another year, on the advice of his vizir, the king approached the prince formally in front of his court and was answered with insolence. So, on the advice of the vizir, the king confined his son to a ruined Roman tower, where he left him to fend for himself until he became more amenable.

Now, in the water-tank of the tower lived a djinniyah, a female djinn, who was a Believer, a servant of Suleyman, and full of energy. Djinns, as you may or may not know, are one of the three orders of created intelligences under Allah — the angels, formed of light, the djinns, formed of subtle fire, and man, created from the dust of the earth. There are three orders of djinns — flyers, walkers and divers; they are shape-shifters, and like human beings, divided into servants of God and servants of Iblis, the demon lord. The Koran often exhorts the djinns and men equally to repentance and belief, and there do exist legal structures governing the marriage and sexual relations of humans and djinns. They are creatures of this world, sometimes visible, sometimes invisible; they haunt bathrooms and lavatories, and they fly through the heavens. They have their own complex social system and hierarchies, into which I will not divagate. The djinniyah in question, Maimunah, was a flyer, and flew past the window of Camaralzaman's tower, where she saw the young man, beautiful as ever in his sleep, flew in and spent some time admiring him. Out again in the night sky she met another flying afrit, a lewd unbeliever called Dahnash who told her excitedly of a beautiful Chinese Princess, the lady Budoor, confined to her quarters by her old women, for fear she should stab herself, as she had sworn to do when threatened with a husband, asking, 'How shall my body, which can hardly bear the touch of silks, tolerate the rough approaches of a man?' And the two djinns began to dispute, circling on leathery wings in the middle air, as to which human creature, the male or the female, was the most beautiful. And the djinniyah commanded Dahnash to fetch the sleeping princess from China and lay her beside Prince Camaralzaman for comparison, which was performed, within an hour. The two genies, male and female, disputed hotly — and in formal verse — without coming to any conclusions as to the prize for beauty. So they summoned up a third being — a huge earth-spirit, with six horns, three forked tails, a hump, a limp, one immense and one pygmy arm, with claws and hooves, and monstrously lengthy masculinity. And this being performed a triumphal dance about the bed, and announced that the only way to test the relative power of these perfect beauties was to wake each in turn and see which showed the greater passion for the other, and the one who aroused the greater lust would be the winner. So this was done; the prince was woken, swooning with desire and respect, and put to sleep with his desire uncomsummated, and the princess was then woken, whose consuming need aroused power and reciprocating desire in the sleeping prince, and 'that happened which did happen'. And before I go on to recount and analyse the separation and madness of Camaralzaman and Budoor, the prince's long search, disguised as a geo-

mancer, for his lost love, their marriage, their subsequent
separation, owing to the theft of a talisman from the princess's
drawers by a hawk, Princess Budoor's resourceful disguise as
her husband, her wooing of a princess, her wooing of her own
husband to what he thought were unnatural acts — before I
tell all this I would like to comment on the presence of the
djinns at this defloration of Budoor by Camaralzaman, their
unseen delight in the human bodies, the strangeness of the
apprehension of the secret consummation of first love as in
fact the narrative contrivance of a group of bizarre and deeply
involved onlookers, somewhere between gentlemen betting at
a horse-race, *entremetteurs, metteurs-en-scène* or storytellers
and gentlemen and ladies of the bedchamber. This moment
of narrative,' said Orhan, 'has always puzzled and pleased me
because it is told from the point of view of these three magical
beings, the prime instigator female, the subordinate ones
male. What is the most private moment of choice in a human
life — the loss of virginity, the mutual loss of virginity indeed,
in total mutual satisfaction and bliss — takes place as a function
of the desire and curiosity and competitive urgings of fire-
creatures from sky and earth and cistern. Camaralzaman and
Budoor — here also like Count Walter — have tried to preserve
their freedom and their will, have rejected the opposite sex
as ugly and disgusting and oppressive — and there in deepest
dream they give way to their destiny which is conducted somewhere between comedy and sentimentality by this bizarre unseen trio — of whom the most redundant, from the point of
view of the narrative, is also the largest, the most obtrusive,
the most memorable, the horned, fork-tailed appallingly dis-
proportioned solid earth-troll who capers in glee over the perfectly proportioned shapes of the two sleeping beauties. It is
as though our dreams were watching us and directing our lives
with external vigour whilst we simply enact their pleasures
passively, in a swoon. Except that the djinns are more solid
than dreams and have all sorts of other interests and preoccupa-
tions besides the young prince and princess . . .'

The soldiers were writing busily; the scarved women stared
ahead motionlessly, holding their heads high and proud. Gil-

lian Perholt listened with pleasure to Orhan Rifat, who had
gone on to talk more technically about the narrative imagination and its construction of reality in tales within tales within
tales. She was tired; she had a slight temperature; the air of
Ankara was full of fumes from brown coal, calling up her
childhood days in a Yorkshire industrial city, where sulphur
took her breath from her and kept her in bed with asthma,
day after long day, reading fairy-tales and seeing the stories
pass before her eyes. And they had gone to see *The Thief of
Baghdad* when she was little; they had snuffed the sulphur
as the enchanted horse swooped across the screen and the genie
swelled from a speck to a cloud filling the whole sea-shore.
There had been an air-raid whilst they were in the cinema:
the screen had flickered and jumped, and electric flashes had
disturbed the magician's dark glare; small distant explosions
had accompanied the princess's wanderings in the garden;
they had all had to file out and hide in the cellars, she remembered, and she had wheezed, and imagined wings and fire in
the evening air. What did I think my life was to be, then?
Gillian Perholt asked herself, no longer listening to Orhan
Rifat as he tried to define some boundary of credulity between
fictive persons in the fictions of fictive persons in the fiction
of real persons, in the reader and the writer. I had this idea
of a woman I was going to be, and I think it was before I
knew what sex was (she had been thinking with her body
about the swooning delight of Camaralzaman and Princess
Budoor) but I imagined I would be married, a married woman,
I would have a veil and a wedding and a house and someone —
someone devoted, like the thief of Baghdad, and a dog. I
wanted — but not by any stretch of the imagination to be a
narratologist in Ankara, which is so much more interesting
and surprising, she told herself, trying to listen to what Orhan
Rifat was saying about thresholds and veils.

The next day she had half a day to herself and went to
the Museum of Anatolian Civilisations, which all her Turkish

friends assured her she should not miss, and met an Ancient
Mariner. The British Council car left her at the entrance to
the museum, which is a modern building, cut into the hillside,
made unobtrusively of wood and glass, a quiet, reflective,
thoughtful, elegant place, in which she had looked forward
to being alone for an hour or two, and savouring her delightful
redundancy. The ancient person in question emerged sound-
lessly from behind a pillar or statue and took her by the elbow.
American? he said, and she replied indignantly, No, English,
thus embarking willy-nilly on a conversation. I am the official
guide, this person claimed. I fought with the English soldiers
in Korea, good soldiers, the Turks and the English are both
good soldiers. He was a heavy, squat, hairless man, with rolling
folds between his cranium and his shoulders, and a polished
gleam to his broad naked head, like marble. He wore a sheepskin jacket, a military medal, and a homemade-looking badge
that said GUIDE. His forehead was low over his eye-sockets—
he had neither brows nor lashes and his wide mouth opened
on a whitely gleaming row of large false teeth. I can show you
everything, he said to Gillian Perholt, gripping her elbow, I
know things you will never find out for yourself. She said
neither yes nor no, but went down into the hall of the museum,
with the muscular body of the ex-soldier shambling after her.
Look, he said, as she stared into a reconstructed earth-
dwelling, look how they lived in those days, the first people,
they dug holes like the animals, but they made them comfortable for themselves. Look here at the goddess. One day, think,
they found themselves turning the bits of clay in their hands,
and they saw a head and a body, see, in the clay, they saw a
leg and an arm, they pushed a bit and pinched bit here and
there, and there She was, look at her, the little fat woman.
They loved fat, it meant strength and good prospects of children and living through the winter, to those naked people,
they were probably thin and half starved with hunting and
hiding in holes, so they made her fat, fat, fat was life to them.
And who knows why they made the first little woman, a doll,
an image, a little offering to the goddess, to propitiate her—

what came first, the doll or the goddess we cannot know—
but we *think* they worshipped her, the fat woman, we think
they thought everything came out of her hole, as they came
out of their underground houses, as the plants and trees come
out in the spring after the dark. Look at her here, here she
is very old, eight thousand years, nine thousand years before
your Christian time-counting, here she is only the essential,
a head and arms, and legs and lovely fat belly, breasts to feed,
no need even for hands or feet, here, see no face. Look at
her, made out of the dust of the earth by human fingers so
old, so old you can't really imagine.

And Gillian Perholt looked at the little fat dolls with their
bellies and breasts, and pulled in her stomach muscles, and
felt the fear of death in the muscles of her heart, thinking of
these centuries-old fingers fashioning flesh of clay.

And later, he said, guiding her from figure to figure, she
became powerful, she became the goddess in the lion throne,
see here she sits, she is the ruler of the world now, she sits
in her throne with her arms on the lion-heads, and see there,
the head of the child coming out between her legs, see how
well those old people knew how to show the little skull of the
baby as it turns to be born.

There were rows of the little baked figurines; all generically
related, all different also. The woman in rolls of fat on the
squat throne, crowned with a circlet of clay, and the arms of
the throne were standing lions and her buttocks protruded
behind her, and her breasts fell heavy and splayed, and her
emptying belly sagged realistically between her huge fat knees.
She was one with her throne, the power of the flesh. Her
hands were lion-heads, her head bald as the ancient soldier's
and square down the back of the fat neck as his was.

We don't like our girls fat now, said the ancient one, regret-
fully. We like them to look like young boys, the boys out of
the Greek gymnasium round the corner. Look at her, though,
you can see how powerful she was, how they touched her
power, scratching the shape into her breasts there, full of
goodness they thought and hoped.

Gillian Perholt did not look at the old soldier whose voice was full of passion; she had not exactly consented to his accompanying narrative, and the upper layer of her consciousness was full of embarrassed calculations about how much Turkish cash she was carrying and how that would convert into pounds sterling, and how much such a guide might require at the end of this tale, if she could not shed him. So they trod on, one behind the other, she never turning her head or meeting his eye, and he never ceasing to speak into her ear, into the back of her studious head, as he darted from glass case to glass case, maneuvering his bulk lightly and silently, as though shod with felt. And in the cases the clay women were replaced by metal stags and sun-discs, and the tales behind her were tales of kings and armies, of sacrifice and slaughter, of bride-sacrifice and sun-offerings, and she was helplessly complicit, for here was the best, the most assured raconteur she could hope to meet. She knew nothing of the Hittites or the Mesopotamians or the Babylonians or the Sumerians, and not much of the Egyptians and the Romans in this context, but the soldier did, and made a whole wedding from a two-spouted wine-jar in the form of ducks, or from a necklace of silver and turquoise, and a centuries-old pot of kohl he made a nervous bride, looking in a bronze mirror—his whisper called up her black hair, her huge eyes, her hand steadying the brush, her maid, her dress of pleated linen. He talked too, between centuries and between cases, of the efficiency of the British and Turkish soldiers fighting side by side on the Korean hillsides, and Gillian remembered her husband saying that the Turks' punishments for pilfering and desertion had been so dreadful that they were bothered by neither. And she thought of Orhan, saying, 'People who think of Turks think of killing and lasciviousness, which is sad, for we are complicated and have many natures. Including a certain ferocity. And a certain pleasure in good living.'

The lions of the desert were death to the peoples of Anatolia, said the old guide, as they neared the end of their journey, which had begun with the earth-dwellers and moved through

the civilisations that built the sun-baked ziggurats, towards
the lion-gates of Nineveh and Assyria. That old goddess, she
sat on the lion-throne, the lions were a part of her power, she
was the earth and the lions. And later the kings and the warriors tamed the lions and took on their strength, wore their
skins and made statues of them as guardians against the wild.
Here are the Persian lions, the word is Aslan, they are strength
and death, you can walk through that carved lion-gate into
the world of the dead, as Gilgamesh did in search of Enkidu
his friend who was dead. Do you know the story of Gilgamesh,
the old man asked the woman, as they went through the
lion-gates together, she always in front and with averted eyes.
The museum had arranged various real carved walls and gates
into imaginary passages and courtyards, like a minor maze in
a cool light. They were now, in the late afternoon, the only
two people in the museum, and the old soldier's voice was
hushed, out of awe perhaps, of the works of the dead, out
of respect perhaps, for the silence of the place, where the glass
cases gleamed in the shadows.

See here, he said, with momentary excitement, see here is
the story of Gilgamesh carved in stone if you know how to
read it. See here is the hero clothed in skins and here is his
friend the wild man with his club—here is their meeting, here
they wrestle and make friends on the threshold of the king's
palace. Do you know Enkidu? He was huge and hairy, he
lived with the beasts in the woods and fields, he helped them
escape the trappers and hunters. But the trappers asked Gilgamesh the king to send a woman, a whore, who tempted
Enkidu to leave the world of the gazelles and the herds and
come to the king, who fought him and loved him. And they
were inseparable, and together they killed the giant Hum-
baba—tricked and killed him in the forest. They trick and
kill him, they are young and strong, there is nothing they
cannot do. But then Gilgamesh's youth and strength attract
the attention of the goddess Ishtar—she was the goddess of
Love, and also of War—she is the same goddess you know,
ma'am, as Cybele and Astarte—and when the Romans came

with their Diana she was the same goddess — terrible and beautiful — whose temples were surrounded by whores — holy whores — whose desires could not be denied. And Ishtar wanted to marry Gilgamesh but he repelled her — he thought she would trick him and destroy him, and he made the mistake of telling her so, telling her he didn't want her, he wanted to remain free — for she had destroyed Tammuz, he said, whom the women wailed for, and she had turned shepherds into wolves and rejected lovers into blind moles, and she had destroyed the lions in pits and the horses in battle, although she loved their fierceness. And this made Ishtar angry — and she sent a great bull from heaven to destroy the kingdom, but the heroes killed the bull — see here in the stone they drive their sword behind his horns — and Enkidu ripped off the bull's thigh and threw it in the face of Ishtar. And she called the temple whores to weep for the bull and decided Enkidu must die. See here, he lies sick on his bed and dreams of death. For young men, you know, they do not know death, or they think of it as a lion or a bull to be wrestled and conquered. But sick men know death, and Enkidu dreamed of His coming — a birdman with a ghoul-face and claws and feathers — for the loathsome picture of death, you see, is from the vulture — and Enkidu dreamed that this Death was smothering him and turning him into the bird-man and that he was going to the Palace of the gods of the underworld — and there, Enkidu saw in this dream, there was no light at all and no joy and the people ate dust and fed on clay. There is a goddess down there too — here she is — Ereshkigal the Queen of the underworld. And both Gilgamesh and Enkdiu wept at this dream — it terrified them — it took away all their strength — and then Enkidu died, in terrible pain, and Gilgamesh could not be comforted. He would not accept that his friend was gone and would never come back. He was young and strong, he would not accept that there was death walking in the world. Young men are like that, you know, it's a truth — they think they can defy what's coming because their blood is hot and their bodies are strong.

And Gilgamesh remembered his ancestor, Uta-Napishtim who was the only man who had survived when the earth was flooded; they said he lived in the underworld and had the secret of living forever. So Gilgamesh travelled on and travelled on, and came to a mountain called Mashu, and at the mountain's gate were the man-scorpions, demons you know, like dragons. We can pretend that this gate is the gate of the underworld — the Sumerian people, the Babylonian people, they made great solid gates to their buildings and built guardians into the gates. See here are lions, and here, at this gate, are genies — you say genies? — yes, genies, — there were good genies and bad genies in Babylon, they were called *utukku* and some were good and some were evil — the good ones were like these guardians here who are bulls with wings and wise faces of men — they are called *shedu* or *lamassu* — they stand here as guardians, but they could take other shapes, they walked invisibly behind men in the streets; every one had his genie, some people say, and they protected them — there is an old saying, 'he who has no genie when he walks in the streets wears a headache like a garment'. That's interesting, don't you think?

Gillian Perholt nodded. She had a headache herself — she had had a kind of penumbral headache, accompanied by occasional stabs from invisible stilettos or ice-splinters since she had seen the Griselda-ghoul, and everything shimmered a little, with a grey shimmer, in the space between the gate and the narratives carved in relief on the stone tablets. The old soldier had become more and more animated, and now began to act out Gilgamesh's arrival at the gates of Mount Meshu, almost dancing like a bear, approaching, stepping back, staring up, skipping briskly from the courtyard to the space between the gateposts, raising his fingers to his bald skull for horns and answering himself in the person of the scorpion-men. (These are *good* genies, ma'am, said the old soldier parenthetically. The scorpion-men might have been dangerous ones, *edimmu* or worse, *arallu*, who came out of the underworld and caused pestilence, they sprang from the goddess's bile, you must imagine terrifying scorpion-men in the place of these bulls with wings.) They say, Why have you come? And Gilgamesh says, For Enkidu my friend. And to see my father Uta-Napishtim among the gods. And they say, No man born of woman has gone into the mountain; it is very deep; there is no light and the heart is oppressed with darkness. Oppressed with darkness. He skipped out again and strode resolutely in, as Gilgamesh. She thought, he is a descendant of the ashiks of whom I have read, who dressed in a uniform of skins, and wore a skin hat and carried a club or a sword as a professional prop. They made shadows with their clubs on café walls and in market squares. The old soldier's shadow mopped and mowed amongst the carved *utukku*: he was Gilgamesh annihilated in the dark; he came out into the light and became Siduri, the woman of the vine, in the garden at the edge of the sea with golden bowl and golden vats of wind; he became Urshanabi the ferryman of the Ocean, disturbed at the presence of one who wore skins and ate flesh, in the other world. He was, Gillian Perholt thought suddenly, related to Karagöz and Hacivat, the comic heroes and animators of the Turkish shadow-puppets, who fought both demons from the underworld and fat capitalists. Orhan Rifat was a skilled puppeteer: he had a leather case full of the little figures whom he could bring to life against a sheet hung on a frame, against a white wall.

'And Uta-Napishtim,' said the Ancient Mariner, sitting down suddenly on a stone lion, and fixing Gillian Perholt with his eye, 'Uta-Napishtim told Gilgamesh that there was a plant, a flower, that grew under the water. It was a flower with a sharp thorn that would wound his hands—but if he could win it he would have his lost youth again. So Gilgamesh tied heavy stones to his feet and sank into the deep water and walked in the seabed, and came to the plant which did prick him, but he grasped it and brought it up again into the light. And Gilgamesh set out again with Urshanabi the ferryman to take the flower back to the old men of his city, Uruk, to bring back their lost youths. And when they had travelled on and on, said the Ancient Mariner, weaving his way between the ancient monuments in his shuffling dance, he came to a deep well of cool water, and he bathed in it, and refreshed himself. But deep in the pool there was a snake, and this snake sensed the sweetness of the flower. So it rose up through the water, and snatched the flower, and ate it. And then it cast off its skin, in the water, and swam down again, out of sight. And Gilgamesh sat down and wept, his tears ran down his face, and he said to Urshanabi the ferryman, "Was it for this that I worked so hard, is it for this that I forced out my heart's blood? For myself I have gained nothing—I don't have it, a beast out of the earth has it now. I found a sign and I have lost it."'

The heavy bald head turned towards Gillian Perholt and the lashless eyelids slid blindly down over the eyeballs for a moment in what seemed to be exhaustion. The thick hands fumbled at the pockets of the fleece-lined jacket for a moment, as though the fingers were those of Gilgamesh, searching for what he had lost. And Gillian's inner eye was full of the empty snakeskin, a papery shadowy form of a snake which she saw floating at the rim of the well into which the muscular snake had vigorously vanished.

'What does it mean, my lady?' asked the old man. 'It means that Gilgamesh must die now—he has seen that he could grasp the thorn and the flower and live forever—but the snake took it just by chance, not to hurt him, but because it liked the sweetness. It is so sad to hold the sign and lose it, it is a sad story—because in most stories where you go to find something you bring it back after your struggles, I think, but here the beast, the creature, just took it, just by chance, after all the effort. They were a sad people, ma'am, very sad. Death hung over them.'

When they came out into the light of day she gave him what Turkish money she had, which he looked over, counted, and put in his pocket. She could not tell if he thought it too little or too much: the folds of his bald head wrinkled as he considered it. The British Council driver was waiting with the car; she walked towards him. When she turned to say good-bye to the Mariner, he was no longer to be seen.

Turks are good at parties. The party in Izmir was made up of Orhan's friends—scholars and writers, journalists and students. 'Smyrna,' said Orhan, as they drove into the town, holding their noses as they went along the harbour-front with its stench of excrement, 'Smyrna of the merchants,' as they looked up at the quiet town on its conical hill. 'Smyrna where we like to think Homer was born, the place most people agree he was probably born.'

It was spring, the air was light and full of new sunshine. They ate stuffed peppers and vineleaves, kebabs and smoky aubergines in little restaurants; they made excursions and ate roasted fishes at a trestle table set by a tiny harbour, looking at fishing boats that seemed timeless, named for the stars and the moon. They told each other stories. Orhan told of his tragi-comic battle with the official powers over his beard, which he had been required to shave before he was allowed to teach. A beard in modern Turkey is symbolic of religion or Marxism, neither acceptable. He had shaved his beard temporarily but now it flourished anew, like mown grass, Orhan said, even thicker and more luxuriant. The conversation moved to poets and politics: the exile of Halicarnassus, the imprisonment of the great Nazim Hikmet. Orhan recited Hikmet's poem, 'Weeping willow', with its fallen rider and the drumming beat of the hooves of the red horsemen, vanishing at the gallop. And Leyla Serin recited Faruk Nafiz Çamlibel's *Göksu*, with its own weeping willow.

Whenever my heart would wander in Göksu
The garden in my dreams falls on the wood.
At dusk the roses seem a distant veil
The phantom willow boughs a cloak and hood.

Bulbuls and hoopoes of a bygone age
Retell their time-old ballads in the dark

The blue reflecting waters hear and show
The passing of Nedim with six-oared barque . . .

And Gillian told the story of her encounter with the old
soldier in the Anatolian museum. 'Maybe he was a djinn,'
said Orhan. 'A djinn in Turkish is spelled C-I-N and you can
tell one, if you meet it, in its human form, because it is naked
and hairless. They can take many forms but their human form
is hairless.'

'He had a hairy coat,' said Gillian, 'but he was hairless. His
skin was ivory-yellow, beeswax colour, and he had no hair
anywhere,'

'Certainly a djinn,' said Orhan.

'In that case,' said the young Attila, who had spoken on
'Bajazet in the Harem', 'how do you explain the Queen of
Sheba?'

'What should I explain about her?' said Orhan.

'Well,' said Attila, 'in Islamic tradition, Solomon travelled
from Mecca to Sheba to see this queen, who was said to have
hairy legs like a donkey because she was the daughter of a
djinn. So Solomon asked her to marry him, and to please him
she used various unguents and herbs to render the legs as
smooth as a baby's skin . . .'

'*Autres pays, autres moeurs*,' said Leyla Doruk. 'You can't
pin down djinns. As for Dr Perholt's *naqqual*, he seems to
be related to the earth-spirit in the story of Camaralzaman,
don't you think so?'

They went also on an excursion to Ephesus. This is a white
city risen, in part, from the dead: you can walk along a marble
street where St Paul must have walked; columns and porticoes,
the shell of an elegant library, temples and caryatids are again
upright in the spring sun. The young Attila frowned as they
paced past the temple façades and said they made him shiver:
Gillian thought he was thinking of the death of nations, but
it turned out that he was thinking of something more primitive

and more immediate, of earthquakes. And when he said that, Gillian looked at the broken stones with fear too.

In the museum are two statues of the Artemis of Ephesus, whose temple, the Artemision, was one of the Seven Wonders of the Ancient World, rediscovered in the nineteenth century by a dogged and inspired English engineer, John Turtle Wood. The colossal Artemis is more austere, and like Cybele, the Magna Mater, turret-crowned, with a temple on her head, under whose arches sit winged sphinxes. Her body is a rising pillar: her haunches can be seen within its form but she wears like a skirt the beasts of the field, the wood, the heavens, all geometrically arranged in quadrangles between carved stone ropes, in twos and threes: bulls, rams, antelopes, winged bulls, flying sphinxes with women's breasts and lion-heads, winged men and huge hieratic bees, for the bee is her symbol, and the symbol of Ephesus. She is garlanded with flowers and fruit, all part of the stone of which she is made: lions crouch in the crook of her arm (her hands are lost) and her headdress or veil is made of ranks of winged bulls, like the genies at the gates in the Ankara museum. And before her she carries, as a date-palm carries dates, her triple row of full breasts, seven, eight, eight, fecundity in stone. The lesser Artemis, whom the Turks call Güzel Artemis and the French La Belle Artémis, stands in front of a brick wall and has a less Egyptian, more oriental, faintly smiling face. She too wears the beasts of earth and air like a garment, bulls and antelopes, winged bulls and sphinxes, with the lions couched below the rows of pendent breasts in their shadow. Her headdress too is woven of winged bulls, though her temple crown is lost. But she has her feet, which are side by side inside a reptilian frill or scallop or serpent-tail, and at these feet are honey-combed beehives. Her eyes are wide, and heavy lidded: she looks out of the stone.

The party admired the goddess. Orhan bowed to her, and Leyla Doruk and Leyla Serin explained her cult to Gillian Perholt, how she was certainly really a much older goddess than the Greek Artemis or the Roman Diana, an Asian earth-goddess, Cybele, Astarte, Ishtar, whose temple was served by virgins and temple prostitutes, who combined extremes of abundant life and fierce slaughter, whose male priests castrated themselves in a frenzy of devotion, like those dying gods, Tammuz, Attis, Adonis, with whose blood the rivers ran red to the sea. The women wept for these dying divinities, said Leyla Serin. It was believed that Coleridge found his wonderful phrase, 'woman wailing for her demon lover', in descriptions of these ritual mournings.

There was a priest, said Leyla Doruk, the Megabyxus; that is a Persian word, and it means set free by God. He was probably a foreign eunuch. There were three priestesses — the Virgin Priestess, the Novice, the Future Priestess and the Old Priestess who taught the young ones. The priestesses were called Melissae, which is bees. And there were priests called the Acrobatae who walked on tiptoe, and priests called the Essenes, another non-Greek word, *essen* means king bee — the Greeks didn't know that the queen bee is a queen, but we know now. . . .

'Her breasts are frightening,' said Gillian Perholt. 'Like Medusa's snakes, too much, but an orderly too much.'

'Some people now say the breasts are not breasts but eggs,' said Attila. 'Symbols of rebirth.'

'They *have* to be breasts,' said Gillian Perholt. 'You cannot see this figure and not read those forms as breasts.'

'Some say,' said Leyla Doruk, smiling, 'that they were bulls' testicles, sacrificed to her, you know, hung round her in her honour, as the — the castrated priests' — parts — once were.'

They were ripe and full and stony.

'They are metaphors,' said Orhan. 'They are many things at once, as the sphinxes and winged bulls are many things at once.'

'You admire her, our goddess,' said Leyla Doruk.

She is not yours, thought Gillian. You are latecomers. She is older and stronger. Then she thought: but she is more yours than mine, all the same. The brick wall behind the Güzel Artemis, the beautiful Artemis, was hung with plastic ivy, fading creamy in the sunlight.

The two Leylas stood with Gillian Perholt in front of the Güzel Artemis and each took her by one arm, laughing.

'Now, Dr Perholt,' said Leyla Osman, 'you must make a wish. For here, if you stand between two people with the same name, and wish, it will come true.'

Leyla Doruk was large and flowing; Leyla Serin was small and bird-like. Both had large dark eyes and lovely skins. They made Gillian Perholt feel hot, Anglo-Saxon, padded and clumsy. She was used to ignoring these feelings. She said, laughing, 'I am enough to a narratologist to know that no good ever comes of making wishes. They have a habit of twisting the wishers to their own ends.'

'Only foolish wishes,' said Leyla Serin. 'Only the unin-structed, who don't think.'

'Like the peasant who saved a magic bird which gave him three wishes, and he wished for a string of sausages in his pan, and they were there, and his wife said that that was a foolish wish, a stupid wish, a string of sausages with the whole world to wish for, and he was so mad at her, he wished the sausages would stick to her nose, and they did, and that was two wishes, and he had to use the third on detaching them.'

For a moment this fictive Nordic peasant's wife, decorated with sausage strings, was imaginatively present also before the goddess with her rows of dangling breasts. Everyone laughed. Wish, Gillian, said Orhan. You are quite intelligent enough not to wish for anything silly.

'In England,' said Gillian, 'when we wish, when we cut our birthday-cakes, we scream out loud, to turn away the knife, I suppose.'

'You may scream if you want to,' said Leyla Serin.

'I am not in England,' said Gillian Perholt. 'And it is not my birthday. So I shall not scream, I shall concentrate on being intelligent, as Orhan has commanded.'

She closed her eyes, and concentrated, and wished, seeing the red light inside her eyelids, as so often before, hearing a faint drumming of blood in her ears. She made a precise and careful wish to be asked to give the keynote address at the Toronto Conference of Narratologists in the fall and added a wish for a first-class air-fare and a hotel with a swimming pool, as a kind of wishing-package, she explained to the blood thrumming in her eyes and ears, and opened the eyes again, and shook her head before the smiling Artemis. Everyone laughed. You looked so serious, they said, squeezing her arms before they let go, and laughing.

They walked through old-new Ephesus and came to the theatre. Orhan stood against the ruined stage and said something incantatory in Turkish which he then explained to Gillian was Dionysus' first speech, his terrible, smiling, threatening speech at the beginning of *The Bacchae*. He then threw one arm over his shoulder and became cloaked and tall and stiffly striding where he had been supple and smiling and eastern. 'Listen, Gillian,' he said:

> I could a tale unfold whose lightest word
> Would harrow up thy soul, freeze thy young blood
> Make thy two eyes like stars, start from their spheres,
> Thy knotted and combined locks to part.
> And each particular hair to stand on end
> Like quills upon the fretful porpentine.
> But this eternal blazon must not be
> To ears of flesh and blood.

'Angels and ministers of grace defend us,' said Gillian, laughing, remembering the young Orhan stalking the English student stage; thinking too of Mehmet the Conqueror, as Bellini saw him, eloquent, watchful and dangerous.

'I was good,' said Orhan, 'in those days. It was his part. Shakespeare himself played the Ghost. Did you know that, Attila? When you speak these words you speak the words he spoke.'

'Not on this stage,' said Attila.

'Now,' said Orhan, 'Now it is here.'

Angels had made Gillian think of St Paul. Angels had sprung open St Paul's prison in Ephesus. She had sat in Sunday school, hearing a fly buzzing against a smeared high window in the vestry and had hated the stories of St Paul and the other apostles because they were true, they were told to her as true stories, and this somehow stopped off some essential imaginative involvement with them, probably because she didn't believe them, if required to believe they were true. She was Hamlet and his father and Shakespeare: she saw Milton's snake and the miraculous flying horse of the Thief of Baghdad, but St Paul's angels rested under suspicion of being made-up because she had been told they were special because *true*. St Paul had come here to Ephesus to tell the people here that Artemis was not true, was not real, because she was a god made with hands. He had stood here, precisely here, in this theatre, she understood slowly; this real man, a provincial interloper with a message, had stood here, where she now stood. She found this hard to believe because St Paul had always seemed to her so cardboard, compared, when she met them later, to Dionysus, to Achilles, to Priam. But he had come here with his wrath against hand-made gods. He had changed the world. He had been a persecutor and had been blinded by light on the road to Damascus (for that moment he was not cardboard, he was consumed by light) and had set out to preach the new god, whom he had not, in his human form, known. In Ephesus he had caused 'no small stir'. His preaching had angered Demetrius, a silversmith, who made silver shrines for the goddess. And Demetrius stirred up the people of Ephesus against the saint, who claimed 'they be no gods which are made with hands' and told them that the foreign preacher would not only set their craft at naught but also 'the temple of the great goddess Diana should be despised, and her magnificence should be destroyed, whom all Asia and the world worshippeth.'

'And when they heard these sayings, they were full of wrath, and cried out, saying, Great is Diana of the Ephesians.'

'And the whole city was filled with confusion: and having caught Gaius and Artistarchus, men of Macedonia, Paul's companions in travel, they rushed with one accord into the theatre.'

'And there for two hours they continued to cry, "Great is Diana of the Ephesians."'

And because of the uproar, which was calmed by the town clerk, Paul left the city of Ephesus and set off for Macedonia.

So the bristling apostle was beaten by commerce and the power of the goddess.

'You know,' said Leyla Doruk, 'that your Virgin Mary came and died here. It is not certain, as it is not certain that Homer was born in Izmir, but it is said to be so, and her house was discovered because of a sick German lady in the nineteenth century who saw it in visions, the house and the hills, and when they came to look it was there, or so they say. We call it Panaya Kapulu, there is a Christian church too. She came with John, they say, and died here.'

At a nightclub in Istanbul once, Gillian had been shocked, without quite knowing why, to find one of those vacant, sweetly pink and blue church Virgins, life-size, standing as part of the decorations, part hat-stand, part dumb-waitress, as you might find a many-handed Hindu deity or a plaster Venus in an equivalent occidental club. Now suddenly, she saw a real bewildered old woman, a woman with a shriveled womb and empty eyes, a woman whose son had been cruelly and very slowly slaughtered before her eyes, shuffling through the streets of Ephesus, waiting quietly for death until it came. And then, afterwards, this old woman, this real dead old woman had in part become the mother goddess, the Syria Dea, the crowned Queen. She was suddenly aware of every inch of her own slack and dying skin. She thought of the stone eyes of the goddess, of her dangerous dignity, of her ambiguous plump breasts, dead balls, intact eggs, wreathed round her in triumph and understood that real-unreal was not the point, that the goddess was still, and always had been, and in the foreseeable future would be more alive, more energetic, infinitely more powerful than she herself, Gillian Perholt, that she would stand here before her children, and Orhan's children, and their children's children and smile, when they themselves were scattered atomies.

And when she thought this, standing amongst a group of smiling friends in the centre of the theatre at Ephesus, she experienced again the strange stoppage of her own life that had come with the vision of Patient Griselda. She put out a hand to Orhan and could move no more; and it seemed that she was in a huge buzzing dark cloud, sparking with flashes of fire, and she could smell flowers, and her own blood, and she could hear rushing and humming in her veins, but she could not move a nerve or a muscle. And after a moment, a kind of liquid sob rose in her throat, and Orhan saw the state she was in, and put an arm round her shoulder, and steadied her, until she came to herself.

In the aeroplane on the way back to Istanbul, Orhan said to Gillian:

'Forgive me, are you quite well?'

'Never better,' said Gillian, which was in many senses true. But she knew she must answer him. 'I do truly mean, I feel more alive now than ever before. But lately I've had a sense of my fate—my death, that is—waiting for me, manifesting itself from time to time, to remind me it's there. It isn't a battle. I don't fight it off. It takes charge for a moment or two, and then lets go again, and steps back. The more alive I am, the more suddenly it comes.'

'Should you see a doctor?'

'When I am so *well*, Orhan?'

'I am delighted to see you so well,' said Orhan. The plane came down into Istanbul and the passengers began a decorous and delightful clapping, applause perhaps for the pilot's skill, applause perhaps for another successful evasion of fate.

In Istanbul Orhan Rifat, a very happily married man, returned to his family, and Gillian Perholt settled in for a few days in the Peri Palas Hotel, which was not the famous Pera Palas, in the old European city across the Golden Horn, but

a new hotel, of the kind Gillian liked best, combining large
hard beds, elegant mirrored bathrooms, lifts and a swimming
pool with local forms and patterns—tiled fountains, Turkish
tiles with pinks and cornflowers in the bathrooms, carpets
woven with abundant silky flowers in the small sitting rooms
and writing rooms. It was constructed around a beehive of
inner courtyards, with balconies rising one above the other,
and silky translucent white-gold curtains behind functional
double-glazed balcony doors. Gillian had developed a late
passion for swimming. Flying distorts the human body—the
middle-aged female body perhaps particularly—the belly bal-
loons, the ankles become cushions of flesh and air, the knees
round into puffballs, toes and fingers are swollen and shiny.
Gillian had learned never to look in the mirror on arrival, for
what stared out at her was a fleshy monster. She had learned
to hurry to the pool, however little she felt inclined to exert
herself, for what air pressure inflates, water pressure delicately
makes weightless and vanishing. The pool at the Peri Palas
was empty on the day of Gillian's arrival, and very satisfactory,
if small. It was underground, a large tank, tiled in a dark
emerald green, lit from within by gold-rimmed lamps, and
the walls of its cavern were tiled with blue and green tiles
covered with chrysanthemums and carnations, edged with
gold mosaic, glinting and gleaming in the golden light. Oh
the bliss, said Gillian to herself as she extended her sad body
along the green rolls of swaying liquid and felt it vanish, felt
her blood and nerves become pure energy, moved forward
with a ripple like a swimming serpent. Little waves of her own
making lapped her chin in this secret cistern; her ears were
full of the soft whisper and plash of water, her eyes were wide
upon green and green, woven with networks of swaying golden
light. She basked, she rolled, she flickered ankles and wrists,
she turned on her back and let her hair fan on the glassy
curves. The nerves unknotted, the heart and lungs settled and
pumped, the body was alive and joyful.

When Orhan took her to Topkapi her body was still comfortable from the swimming, which her skin remembered as the

two of them looked down from the Sultan's upper window
on the great dark tank under cedars where once the women
of the harem swam together in the sun. In the harem too,
was the Sultan's bath, a quite different affair, a central box
inside a series of carved boxes and cupboards inside the quarters of the Valide Sultan, his mother, where his nakedness
could be guarded by many watchful eyes from assassin's knives.
Here too, as in Ephesus, Gillian Perholt struggled with the
passions of real stories. Here in the cages the sons of the sultans
had waited for the eunuchs with the silken cords that would
end their lives and make the throne safe for the chosen one.
Here intriguing or unsatisfactory women had been caught and
tied in sacks and drowned; here captives, or unsatisfactory
servants, had been beheaded for a whim of an absolute ruler.
How did they live with such fear? She said to Orhan:

'It is as you said of Shahriyar and I said of Walter — there
must be a wonderful pleasure for some people in being other
people's fates and destinies. Perhaps it gave them the illusion
that their own fates too were in their own hands —'

'Perhaps,' said Orhan. 'Perhaps life mattered less to them,
their own or anyone else's.'

'Do you really think they thought that?'

'No,' said Orhan, looking around the empty maze of hidden
rooms and secret places. 'No, not really. We like to say that.
They believed in a future life. We can't imagine that.'

Showing her round Istanbul, nevertheless, Orhan became
more Turkish. Before the great gold throne of Murat III stud-
ded with emeralds, and cushioned in gold and white silk, he
said, 'We were a nomadic people. We came over the steppes
from Mongolia, from China. Our thrones are portable trea-
sures, our throne-rooms resemble tents, we put our skill into
small things, daggers and bowls and cups.' She remembered
the rhythms of his recitation of the poem of the red horsemen.

In the Haghia Sophia she had her third encounter with
Fate, or with something. Haghia Sophia is a confusing place,

echoing and empty, hugely domed and architecturally uncertain, despite its vast and imposing space: it has been church and mosque and modern museum; it has minarets and patches, ghosts, of ruined gold mosaics of Byzantine emperors and the Christian mother and child. The emperor Justinian built it from eclectic materials, collecting pillars and ornaments from temples in Greece and Egypt, including pillars from the temple of the Goddess in Ephesus. It could feel — Gillian had expected it to feel — like a meeting-place of cultures, of East and West, the Christian Church and Islam, but it did not. It felt like an empty exhausted barn, exhausted by battle and pillage and religious rage. Whatever had been there had gone, had fled long ago, Gillian felt, and Orhan too showed no emotion, but returned to his European academic self, pointing out the meanings of the mosaics and talking of his own new thoughts about the absurdities of the theories of Marcuse which had been all the rage in the sixties, when they began to teach. 'There is a curious pillar here,' he said vaguely, 'somewhere or other, with a hole of some sort, where people wish; you might like to see that, if I can find it. The stone is worn away by people touching it, I forget what it does, but you might like to see it.'

'It doesn't matter,' said Gillian.

'They put a brass casing round the magic stone to preserve it,' said Orhan. 'But the pilgrims have worn it away, they have eaten into the pillar just with touching, through the brass and the stone. Now where is it, I should be able to find it. It is like wearing away with waterdrops, wearing away with faith, I find that quite interesting, I wish I could remember what it *does*.'

When they came to it, there was a family already clustered round it, a Pakistani father and his wife and two daughters, richly beautiful in saris, one pink and gold, one peacock and flame, one blue and silver. They had found the pillar with the hole and its brass casing, and the three women were clustered round it, stroking, putting their hands in and out, chattering like subdued birds. The father, dignified in his black coat, approached Orhan, and asked if he spoke English. Orhan said yes, and was asked to help translate an account of the pillar from a French-Turkish guidebook.

Whilst he did this, the three women, in their fluttering silk, turned laughing to Gillian Perholt, and stretched out three soft hands with gold bangles on their wrists, pulling her by her sleeve, by her hand, towards the pillar, laughing softly. They patted Dr Perholt's shoulders, they put arms around her and pushed and pulled, smiling and laughing, they took her hand in theirs with strong, wiry grips and inserted it into the hole, showing her in mime what she must do, turn her hand in the hole, touching the inside rim, round, round, round, three times. She pulled back instinctively, out of an English hygienic horror of something so much touched by so many, and out of a more primitive fear, of something clammy and moist and nasty in the dark inside. But the women insisted; they were surprisingly forceful. There was liquid of some kind in there, some pool of something in the stem of the pillar. Dr Perholt's skin crawled and the women laughed, and Orhan recited the story of the pillar in English to the other man. Apparently, he said, it had been touched by St Gregory Thaumaturge, the Miracle-Worker, he had put his power into it. The water inside the pillar was efficacious for diseases of vision and for fertility. The women laughed more loudly, clustering round Dr Perholt. The father told Orhan how he had made pilgrimage to all the holy shrines of Islam; he had travelled far and seen much. He supposed Orhan too, had made pilgrimages. Orhan nodded, grave and non-committal; he was interested. The West was evil, said the respectable black-coated pilgrim. Evil, decadent, and sliding into darkness. But power was arising. There would be a jihad. True religion would bring the cleansing sword and destroy the filth and greed and corruption of the dying West, and a religious world would be established in its ashes; these things were not only possible, they were already happening. The seeds were sown, the sparks were set, the field of spears would spring up, the fire would

consume. This was what he said, this paterfamilias, standing
in Haghia Sophia whose stones had run with blood, whose
cavernous spaces had been piled high with corpses, whose
spirit had died, Gillian Perholt felt, but maybe felt because
she could not feel the new spirit, which spoke to this family,
and in them filled her with fear. Orhan, she saw, was in some
way enjoying himself. He prolonged the conversation, nod-
ding gravely, inserting mild questions—'you have seen signs,
mn?'—making no move to change his interlocutor's impression that he was a good Muslim, in a mosque.

His family came everywhere with him, said the pilgrim.
They like to see new places. And she, does she speak English?

It was clear that Gillian had been taken for a quiet Muslim
wife. She had been standing two paces behind Orhan as he
cast about for the magic pillar. Orhan replied gravely:

'She *is* English. She is a visiting professor. An eminent visiting professor.'

Orhan, a child of Atatürk's new world, was enjoying himself. Atatürk had emancipated women. Leyla Serin and Leyla
Doruk were also his children, powerful people, thinking teach-
ers. Orhan liked drama, and he had made a nice little revela-
tory clash. The Pakistani gentleman was not happy. He and
Gillian looked at each other, both, she thought, remembering
things he had said a moment ago about London being a sewer
of decay and the Commonwealth a dead body, putrefying
and shriveling away to nothing. She could not meet the Pakistani's eye; she was English and embarrassed for him. He could
not meet her eye. She was a woman, and should not have
been there, with a man who was not her husband, in a museum
that was also a mosque. He gathered his flock—who still smiled
at Gillian, fluttering their elegant fingers in farewell. 'Hrmph,'
said Orhan. 'Istanbul is a meeting-place for many cultures.
You didn't like the pillar, Gillian? Your face was very funny,
very ladylike.'

'I don't like Haghia Sophia,' said Gillian. 'I expected to. I
like the idea of Sophia, of Wisdom, I like it that she is wise
and female, I expected to feel—something—in her church.

And there is a wet hole for fertility wishes. In a pillar that might have come from the Temple of Artemis.'

'Not that pillar, I think,' said Orhan.

'If I was a postmodernist punster,' said Gillian, 'I would make something of Haghia Sophia. She has got old, she has turned into a Hag. But I can't, because I respect etymologies, it means holy. *Hag* is my word, a northern word, nothing to do with here.'

'You have said it now,' said Orhan. 'Even if you repudiate it. Lots of American students here do think *hag* is *hag*. They get excited about crones.'

'I don't,' said Gillian.

'No,' said Orhan, not revealing what he himself thought about hags and crones. 'We shall go to the Bazaar. Shopping is good for the souls of western women. And eastern. And men like it too.'

It was true that the Grand Bazaar was livelier and brighter than the vast cavern of Haghia Sophia. Here was a warren of arcades, of Aladdin's caves full of lamps and magical carpets, of silver and brass and gold and pottery and tiles. Here and there behind a shop-front, seated in an armchair at a bench surrounded by dangling lamps and watershakers from the baths, or sitting cross-legged on a bale of carpets amongst a tent of carpets, Orhan had ex-students who brought cups of Turkish coffee, tulip-shaped glasses of rose tea to Gillian, and displayed their wares. The carpet-seller had written a Ph.D. on *Tristram Shandy*, and now travelled into Iraq, Iran, Afghanistan, bringing back carpets on journeys made by camel, by jeep, into the mountains. He showed Gillian pallid kilims in that year's timid Habitat colours, pale 1930s eau-de-nil and bois-de-rose with a sad null grey. No, said Gillian, no, she wanted richness, the dark bright blues, the crimsons and scarlets, the golds and rusts of the old carpets with their creamy blossoms, their trees full of strange birds and flowers. The West is fickle, said Bulent the carpet-seller, they say they want these insipid colours this year, and the women in India and

Iran buy the wool and the silk, and the next year, when the carpets are made, they want something else, black and purple and orange, and the women are ruined, their profit is lost, heaps of carpets lie round and rot. I think you will like this carpet, said Bulent, pouring coffee; it is a wedding carpet, a dowry carpet, to hang on the wall of a nomad's tent. Here is the tree of life, crimson and black on midnight blue. This you like. Oh yes, said Gillian, seeing the dark woven tree against the yellows and whites of her Primrose Hill room, now hers alone. The woman, whoever she was, had made it strong and complex, flaunting and subtle. I can't haggle, said Gillian to Orhan, I'm English. You would be surprised, said Orhan, at some English people's skill in that art. But Bulent is my student, and he will give you a fair price, for love of *Tristram Shandy*. And suddenly Gillian felt well again, full of life and singing with joy, away from the puddle in the pillar and the brooding Hag, hidden away in an Aladdin's cave made of magic carpets with small delightful human artefacts, an unknown woman's wedding carpet, sentimental Sterne's monumental fantasia on life before birth, black-brown coffee poured from a bright copper pan, tasting rich and almost, but not quite, unbearably strong and sweet.

Another of Orhan's students had a little shop in the central square of the market-maze, Iç Bedesten, a shop whose narrow walls were entirely hung with pots, pans, lamps, bottles, leather objects, old tools whose purpose was unguessable, chased daggers and hunting knives, shadow-puppets made of camel skin, perfume flasks, curling tongs.

'I will give you a present,' said Orhan. 'A present to say good-bye.'

(He was leaving the next day for Texas where a colloquium of narratologists was studying family sagas in Dallas. Gillian had a talk to give at the British Council and three more days in Istanbul.)

'I will give you the shadow puppets, Karagöz and Hacivat, and here is the magic bird, the Simurgh, and here is a woman involved with a dragon, I think she may be a djinee, with a little winged demon on her shoulders, you might like her.'

The small figures were wrapped carefully in scarlet tissue. Whilst this was happening Gillian poked about on a bench and found a bottle, a very dusty bottle amongst an apparently unsorted pile of new/old things. It was a flask with a high neck, that fitted comfortably into the palms of her hands, and had a glass stopper like a miniature dome. The whole was dark, with a regular whirling pattern of white stripes moving around it. Gillian collected glass paperweights: she liked glass in general, for its paradoxical nature, translucent as water, heavy as stone, invisible as air, solid as earth. Blown with human breath in a furnace of fire. As a child she had loved to read of glass balls containing castles and snowstorms, though in reality she had always found these disappointing and had transferred her magical attachment to the weights in which coloured forms and carpets of geometric flowers shone perpetually and could be made to expand and contract as the sphere of glass turned in her fingers in the light. She liked to take a weight back from every journey, if one could be found, and had already bought a Turkish weight, a cone of glass like a witch's hat, rough to touch, greenish-transparent like ice, with the concentric circles, blue, yellow, white, blue, of the eye which repels the evil eye, at the base.

'What is this?' she asked Orhan's student, Feyyaz.

He took the flask from her, and rubbed at the dust with a finger.

'I'm not an expert in glass,' he said, 'It could be çesm-i bülbül. Or it could be fairly recent Venetian glass. Çesm-i bülbül means nightingale's eye. There was a famous Turkish glass workshop at Incirköy—round about 1845 I think—made this famous Turkish glass, with this spiral pattern of opaque blue and white stripes, or red sometimes, I think. I don't know why it is called eye of the nightingale. Perhaps nightingales have eyes that are transparent and opaque. In this country we were obsessed with nightingales. Our poetry is full of nightingales.'

'Before pollution,' said Orhan, 'before television, everyone
came out and walked along the Bosphorus and in all the gar-
dens, to hear the first nightingales of the year. It was very
beautiful. Like the Japanese and the cherry blossom. A whole
people, walking quietly in the spring weather, listening."
Feyyaz recited a verse in Turkish and Orhan translated.

In the woods full of evening the nightingales are silent
The river absorbs the sky and its fountains
Birds return to the indigo shores from the shadows
A scarlet bead of sunshine in their beaks.

Gillian said, 'I must have this. Because the word and the
thing don't quite match, and I love both of them. But if it
is çesm-i bülbül it will be valuable . . .'
'It probably isn't,' said Feyyaz. 'It's probably recent Venetian. Our glassmakers went to Venice in the eighteenth century
to learn, and the Venetians helped us to develop the tech-
niques of the nineteenth century. I will sell it to you as if it
were Venetian, because you like it, and you may imagine it
is çesm-i bülbül and perhaps it will be, is, that is.'

'Feyyaz wrote his doctoral thesis on Yeats and Byzantium,'
said Orhan.
Gillian gave the stopper an experimental twist, but it would
not come away, and she was afraid of breaking it. So the
nightingale's-eye bottle too was wrapped in scarlet tissue, and
more rose tea was sipped, and Gillian returned to her hotel.
That evening there was a farewell dinner in Orhan's house,
with music and raki and generous beautiful food. And the
next day, Gillian was alone in her hotel room.

Time passes differently in the solitude of hotel rooms. The
mind expands, but lazily, and the body contracts in its bright
box of space. Because one may think of anything at all, one
thinks for a long time of nothing. Gillian in hotel rooms was
always initially tempted by channel-surfing on the television;

she lay amongst crimson and creamy roses on her great bed
and pointed the black lozenge with its bright buttons imperiously at the screen. Transparent life flickered and danced across
it: Gillian could make it boom with sound, the rush of traffic
and violins, voices prophesying war and voices dripping with
the promise of delectable yogurt / Orangina / tutti-frutti / Mars
Bars frozen stiff. Or she could leave it, which she preferred,
a capering shadow-theater. Ronald Reagan, smiling and
mouthing, glassy in the glass box between the glassy wings
of his speech, or an aeroplane falling in flames on a mountain,
fact or stunt? a priest driving a racing-car round a corniche,
narrative or advertisement? Turks discussing the fullness and
fatness of tomatoes in a field, more new cars, in cornfields,
up mountains, falling from skyscrapers, a houri applying a
tongue tip to raspberry fudge and sighing, an enormous tsetse
fly expending enormous energy in puncturing a whole screen-
ful of cowflesh, jeeps full of dirty soldiers in helmets brandishing machine-guns, trundling through dusty streets, fact
or drama, which? tennis.

Tennis in French, from courts like red deserts, tennis from
Monte Carlo where it was high noon, under the sun past which
Istanbul had begun to roll two hours ago, tennis male and it
appeared, live, on a channel where nothing ever happened
but the human body (and mind, indeed, also) stretched, extended, driven, triumphant, defeated, in one endless, beautifully designed narrative. Dr Perholt was accustomed to say,
in her introductory talks on narratology, that whoever designed the rules and the scoring-system of tennis was a narrative
genius of the first order, comparable to those ancient storytellers who arranged animal-helpers in threes and thought up
punishments for disregarded prohibitions. For the more even
the combat, said Dr Perholt, the more difficult the scoring
makes it for one combatant to succeed. At deuce, at six-all,
the stakes are raised, not one but two points are needed to
assure victory, not one but two games, thus ensuring the maximum tension and the maximum pleasure to the watchers.
Tennis in the glass box she loved as she had loved bedtime

stories as a child. She loved the skill of the cameramen — the quick shot of a sweating face in a rictus of strain, the balletic shot of the impossibly precise turning feet, the slow lazy repeat of the lung-bursting leap, taken at the speed with which a leaf falls slowly through the air, slowly, slowly, resting on air, as the camera can make these heavy muscled men hang at rest in their billowing shirts. She had only come to love tennis so much when she was beyond being expected to take part in it; when her proper function was only as audience. Now she delighted in its geometry, the white lines of increasing difficulty, of hope and despair, the acid gold sphere of the ball, the red dust flying, the woven chequered barrier of the net. She had her narrative snobbisms. A live match was always more enticing than a recorded one, even if it was impossible for her to find out first the score of the latter, for someone, somewhere, *knew* who had won, the tense was past, and thus the wonderful open-endedness of a story which is most beautifully designed towards satisfactory closure but is still undecided, would be lost, would be a cheat. For darkness might descend on a live match, or the earth open. A live match was live, was a story in progress towards an end which had not yet come but which must, *almost certainly* come. And in the fact of the *almost* was the delight.

A live match (Becker-Leconte) was promised within an hour. She had time for a shower, she judged, a good hot shower, and then she could sit and dry slowly and watch the two men run. So she turned on the shower, which was large and brassy, behind a glass screen at one end of the bath, an enclosing screen of pleasing engraved climbing roses with little birds sitting amongst their thorny stems. It had a pleasant brass frame, the glass box. The water was a little cloudy, and a little brassy itself in colour, but it was hot, and Gillian disported herself in its jets, soaped her breasts, shampooed her hair, looked ruefully down at what it was better not to look at, the rolls of her midriff, the sagging muscles of her stomach. She remembered, as she reached for her towel, how perhaps ten

NEW SUBSCRIBERS' DISCOUNT

SAVE $12 off the cover price and $6 off the regular subscription rates with this coupon.

THE PARIS REVIEW

Enclosed is my check for:

☐ $28 for 1 year (new subscriptions and gifts only)
☐ $34 for 1 year (4 issues)
☐ $1,000 for a lifetime subscription
(All payment must be in U.S. funds. Postal surcharge of $7 per 4 issues outside USA)

☐ Send me information on becoming a *Paris Review* Associate.
Bill this to my Visa/MasterCard:

_____
Card number   Exp. date

☐ New subscription   ☐ Renewal subscription
☐ New address

Name _____

Address _____

City _____ State _____ Zip code _____

Please send gift subscription to:

Name _____

Address _____

City _____ State _____ Zip code _____

Gift announcement signature _____

Please send me the following:

☐ The Paris Review T-Shirt ($15.00)
   Color _____ Size _____ Quantity _____
☐ The following back issues: Nos. _____
   See listing at back of book for availability.

☐ The Paris Review Print Series catalogue ($1.00)

Name _____

Address _____

City _____ State _____ Zip code _____

☐ Enclosed is my check for $ _____
☐ Bill this to my Visa/MasterCard:

_____
Card number   Exp. date

Impress someone, and save.

Give *The Paris Review* for only $28 a year when you renew your subscription at the regular rate. You save $12 off the newsstand price!

years ago she had looked complacently at her skin on her throat, at her solid enough breasts and had thought herself well-preserved, unexceptionable. She had tried to imagine how this nice, taut, flexible skin would crimp and wrinkle and fall and had not been able to. It was her skin, it was herself, and there was no visible reason why it should not persist. She had known intellectually that it must, it must give way, but its liveliness then had given her the lie. And now it was all going, the eyelids had soft little folds, the edges of the lips were fuzzed, if she put on lipstick it ran in little threads into the surrounding skin.

She advanced naked towards the bathroom mirror in room 49 in the Peri Palas Hotel. The mirror was covered with shifting veils of steam, amongst which, vaguely, Gillian saw her death advancing towards her, its hair streaming dark and liquid, its eyeholes dark smudges, its mouth open in its liquescent face in fear of their convergence. She dropped her head sadly, turned aside from the encounter, and took out the hanging towelling robe from its transparent sheath of plastic. There were white towelling slippers in the cupboard with Peri Palas written on them in gold letters. She made herself a loose turban of a towel and thus solidly enveloped she remembered the çesm-i bülbül bottle and decided to run it under the tap, to bring the glass to life. She took it out of its wrappings — it was really *very* dusty, almost clay-encrusted — and carried it into the bathroom where she turned on the mixer-tap in the basin, made the water warm, blood-heat, and held the bottle under the jet, turning it round and round. The glass became blue, threaded with opaque white canes, cobalt-blue, darkly bright, gleaming and wonderful. She turned it and turned it, rubbing the tenacious dust-spots with thumbs and fingers, and suddenly it gave a kind of warm leap in her hand, like a frog, like a still-beating heart in the hands of a surgeon. She gripped and clasped and steadied, and her own heart took a fierce, fast beat of apprehension, imagining blue glass splinters everywhere. But all that happened was that the stopper, with a faint glassy grinding, suddenly flew out of the neck of the flask and fell tinkling but unbroken, into the basin. And out of the bottle in her hands came a swarming, an exhalation, a fast-moving dark stain which made a high-pitched buzzing sound and smelled of woodsmoke, of cinnamon, of sulphur, of something that might have been incense, of something that was not leather, but was? The dark cloud gathered and turned and flew in a great paisley or comma out of the bathroom. I am seeing things, thought Dr Perholt, following, and found she could not follow, for the bathroom door was blocked by what she slowly made out to be an enormous foot, a foot with five toes as high as she was, surmounted by yellow horny toenails, a foot encased in skin that was olive-coloured, laced with gold, like snakeskin, not scaly but somehow mailed. It was between transparent and solid. Gillian put out a hand. It was palpable, and very hot to the touch, not hot as a coal but considerably hotter than the water in which she had been washing the bottle. It was dry and slightly electric. A vein beat inside the ankle, a green-gold tube encasing an almost emerald liquid.

Gillian stood and considered the foot. Anything with a foot that size, if at all proportionate, could not be contained in one hotel room. Where was the rest? As she thought this, she heard sounds, which seemed to be speech of some kind, deep, harsh, but musical, expletives perhaps, in a language she couldn't identify. She put the stopper back in the bottle, clutching it firmly, and waited.

The foot began to change shape. At first it swelled and then it diminished a little, so that Gillian could have squeezed round it, but thought it more prudent not to try. It was now the size of a large armchair, and was drawn back, still diminishing, so that Gillian felt able to follow. The strange voice was still muttering, in its incomprehensible speech. Gillian came out and saw the djinn, who now took up half her large room, curled round on himself like a snake, with his huge head and shoulders pushing against the ceiling, his arms stretched round inside two walls, and his feet and body wound over her bed and trailing into the room. He seemed to be wearing a green silk tunic, not too clean, and not long enough, for she could see the complex heap of his private parts in the very centre of her rosy bed. Behind him was a great expanse of shimmering many-coloured feathers, peacock feathers, parrot feathers, feathers from birds of Paradise, which appeared to be part of a cloak that appeared to be part of him, but was not wings that sprouted in any conventional way from shoulder-blade or spine. Gillian identified the last ingredient of his smell, as he moved his cramped members to look down on her. It was a male smell, a strong horripilant male smell.

His face was huge, oval, and completely hairless. He had huge bruised-green oval eyelids over eyes sea-green flecked with malachite. He had high cheekbones and an imperious hooked nose, and his mouth was wide and sculpted like Egyptian pharaohs'.

In one of his huge hands was the television, on whose pearly screen, on the red dust, Boris Becker and Henri Leconte rushed forward, jumped back, danced, plunged. The smack of the tennis ball could be heard, and the djinn had turned one of his large, elegantly carved ears, to listen.

He spoke to Gillian.

She said, 'I don't suppose you speak English.'

He repeated his original remark. Gillian said,

'Français? Deutsch? Español? Português?' She hesitated. She could not remember the Latin for Latin, and was not at all sure she could converse in that language. 'Latin,' she said finally.

'*Je sais le Français*,' said the djinn. '*Italiano anche. Era in Venezia.*'

'*Je préfère le français*,' said Gillian. 'I am more fluent in that language.'

'Good,' said the djinn in French. He said, 'I can learn quickly, what is your language?'

'*Anglais.*'

'Smaller would be better,' he said, changing tack. 'It was agreeable to expand. I have been inside that bottle since 1850 by your reckoning.'

'You look cramped,' said Gillian, reaching for the French words, 'in here.'

The djinn considered the tennis players.

'Everything is relative. These people are extremely small. I shall diminish somewhat.'

He did so, not all at once, so that for a moment the now only slightly larger-than-life being was almost hidden behind the mound of his private parts, which he than shrank and tucked away. It was almost a form of boasting. He was now curled on Gillian's bed, only one and a half times as large as she was.

'I am beholden to you,' said the djinn, 'for this release. I am empowered, indeed required, to grant you three wishes on that account. If there is anything you desire.'

'Are there limits,' asked the narratologist, 'to what I may wish for?'

'An unusual question,' said the djinn. He was still somewhat distracted by the insect-like drama of Boris Becker and Henri Leconte. 'In fact different djinns have different powers. Some can only grant small things—'

'Like sausages—'

'A believer—a believing djinn—would find it repugnant to grant anyone of your religion pork sausages. But they are possible. There are laws of the praeternatural within which we work, all of us, which cannot be broken. You may not, for instance, wish to have all your wishes granted in perpetuity. Three is three, a number of power. You may not wish for eternal life, for it is your nature to be mortal, as it is mine to be immortal. I cannot by magic hold together your atomies, which will dissolve—'

He said, 'It is good to speak again, even in this unaccustomed tongue. Can you tell me what these small men are made of, and what they are at? It resembles royal tennis as it was played in the days of Suleiman the Magnificent—'

'It is called "lawn tennis" in my language. *Tennis sur gazon*. As you can see, this is being played on clay. I like to watch it. The men,' she found herself saying, 'are very beautiful.'

'Indeed,' agreed the djinn. 'How have you enclosed them? The atmosphere here is full of presences I do not understand — it is all bustling and crowded with — I cannot find a word in my language or your own, that is, your second tongue, — electrical emanations of living beings, and not only living beings but fruits and flowers and distant places — and some high mathematical game with travelling figures I can barely seize, like motes in the invisible air — something terrible has been done to my space — to exterior space since my incarceration — I have trouble in holding this exterior body together, for all the currents of power are so picked at and intruded upon . . . Are these men magicians, or are you a witch, that you have them in a box?'

'No, it is science. It is natural science. It is television. It is done with light waves and sound waves and cathode rays — I don't know *how* it is done, I am only a literary scholar, we don't know much, I'm afraid — we use it for information and amusement. Most people in the world now see these boxes, I suppose.'

'*Six-all, première manche,*' said the television. '*Jeu décisif. Service Becker.*'

The djinn frowned.

'I am a djinn of some power,' he said. 'I begin to find out how these emanations travel. Would you like a homunculus of your own?'

'I have three wishes,' said Dr Perholt cautiously. 'I do not want to expend one of them on the possession of a tennis-player.'

'*Entendu,*' said the djinn. 'You are an intelligent and cautious woman. You may wish when you will and the praeternatural laws require me to remain at your service until all three wishes have been made. Lesser djinns would tempt you into making your wishes rapidly and foolishly, for their own ends, but I am God-fearing and honourable (despite which I have spent much of my long life shut up in bottles), and I will not do that. All the same, I shall attempt to catch one of these travelling butterflies. They are spread along the waves of the

atmosphere—not as we are when we travel—*in* the waves—
I should be able to *concentrate* one—to move the matter as
well as the emanation—the pleasure is to use the laws of its
appearance here and intensify—I could easily *wish* him here—
but I will, I will have him along his own trajectory—so—and
so—'

A small Boris Becker, sandy-browed, every gold hair on his
golden body gleaming sweat, was standing on the chest of
drawers, perhaps twice the size of his television image, which
was frozen in mid-stroke on the screen. He blinked his sandy
lashes over his blue eyes and looked around, obviously unable
to see more than a blur around him.

'*Scheiße*,' said the tiny Becker. '*Scheiße und scheiße. Was
ist mit mir?*'

'I could manifest us to him,' said the djinn. 'He would be
afeard.'

'Put him back. He will lose the set.'

'I could expand him. Life-size. We could speak to him.'

'Put him back. It isn't *fair*.'

'You don't want him?'

'*Scheiße. Warum kann ich nicht . . .*'

'No. I don't.'

The Becker on the screen was frozen into an attitude, his
racket raised, his head back, one foot lifting. Henri Leconte
advanced towards the net. The commentator announced that
Becker had had a seizure, which delighted the djinn, who
had indeed seized him. '*Scheiße*,' said the forlorn small Becker
in the bedroom. 'Return him,' said Dr Perholt imperiously,
adding quickly, 'That is not one of my three wishes, you must
do what seems to you best, but you must understand that you
are disappointing millions of people, all round the world,
interrupting this story—I'm sorry, *déformation professionelle*,
I should say, this game—'

'Why are your homunculi not three-dimensional?' asked
the djinn.

'I don't know. We can't do that. We may learn. You seem
to understand it better than I do, however long you have been
in that bottle. Please put him back.'

'To please you,' said the djinn with grave gallantry. He picked up the mannikin-Becker, twisted him rapidly like a top, murmured something, and the Becker on the screen collapsed on the court in a heap.

'You have hurt him.' said Gillian accusingly.

'It is to be hoped not,' said the djinn with an uncertain note. Becker in Monte Carlo got up unsteadily and was escorted off the court, his hands to his head.

'They will not be able to continue,' said Gillian crossly, and then put her hand to her mouth in amazement, that a woman with a live djinn on her bed should still be interested in the outcome of a tennis match, only part of which she had seen.

'You could wish him well,' said the djinn, 'but he will probably be well anyway. More than probably, almost certainly. You must wish for your heart's desire.'

'I wish,' said Gillian, 'for my body to be as it was when I last really *liked* it, if you can do that.'

The great green eyes settled on her stout figure in its white robe and turban.

'I can do that,' he said, 'I can do that. If you are quite sure that that is what you most desire. I can make your cells as they were, but I cannot delay your Fate.'

'It is courteous of you to tell me that. And yes, it is what I desire. It is what I have desired hopelessly every day these last ten years, whatever else I may have desired.'

'And yet,' said the djinn, 'you are well enough as you are, in my opinion. Amplitude, madame, is desirable.'

'Not in my culture. And moreover, there is the question of temporal decay.'

'That I suppose, but do not wholly understand sympathetically. We are made of fire, and do not decay. You are made of dust, and return to it.'

He raised his hand and pointed at her, one finger lazily extended, a little like Michelangelo's Adam.

She felt a fierce contraction in the walls of her belly, in her loose womb.

'I am glad to see you prefer ripe women to green girls,' said

the djinn. 'I too am of that opinion. But your ideal is a little
meager. Would you not care to be rounder?'

'Excuse me,' said Gillian, suddenly modest, and retreated
into the bathroom, where she opened her robe and saw in
the demisted mirror a solid and unexceptionable thirty-five-
year-old woman, whose breasts were full but not softened,
whose stomach was taut, whose thighs were smooth, whose
nipples were round and rosy. Indeed the whole of this service-
able and agreeable body was flushed deep rose, as though she
had been through a fire, or a steam bath. Her appendix scar
was still there, and the mark on her knee where she had fallen
on a broken bottle hiding under the stairs from an air raid
in 1944. She studied her face in the mirror; it was not beautiful
but it was healthy and lively and unexceptionable; her neck
was a clean column and her teeth, she was happy to see and
feel, more numerous, more securely planted. She undid the
coiled towel and her hair sprang out, damp, floppy, long and
unfaded. I can go in the streets, she said to herself, and still
be recognisably who I am, in my free and happy life; only I
shall *feel* better, I shall like myself more. That was an *intelligent* wish, I shall not regret it. She brushed out her hair, and
went back to the djinn, who was lolling on the bedspread,
watching Boris Becker, who had lost the first set, and was
ranging the court like a tiger in the beginning of the second.
The djinn had also helped himself to the glossy shopping
magazines which lay in the drawer of the bedside table, and
to the Gideon Bible which, with the Koran, was also there.
From these he appeared to have absorbed the English language
by some kind of cerebral osmosis.

'Hmn,' he said in that language, 'Who is she that looketh
forth as the morning, fair as the moon, clear as the sun, and
terrible as an army with banners? This is your language, I can
learn its rules quickly, I find. Are you pleased, madame, with
the outcome of your wish? We have a little sister and she hath
no breasts: what shall we do for our sister in the day when
she shall be spoken for? I see from these images that in this
time you prefer your ladies without breasts, like boys. A curi-

ous form of asceticism, if that is what is, or perversity possibly, it may be. I am not a djinn who ever needed to lurk in bath-houses to catch young boys from behind. I have consorted with ladies of all kinds, with the Queen of Sheba herself, with the Shulamite whose breasts were like clusters of grapes and ripe pomegranates, whose neck was a tower of ivory and the smell of whose nose was like apples. A boy is a boy and a woman is a woman, my lady. But these images have lovely eyes, they are skillful with the kohl.'

'If you consorted with the Queen of Sheba,' said the scholar, 'how did you come to be shut in what I believe is at the earliest a *nineteenth-century* bottle, çesm-i bülbül, if not Venetian?'

'Certainly çesm-i bülbül,' said the djinn. 'Freshly made and much prized by its owner, the beautiful Zefir, wife of Mustafa Emin Bey, in Smyrna. I came into that bottle through a foolish accident and a too-great fondness for the conversation of women. That was my third incarceration: I shall be more care-ful in the future. I am happy to tell you my history, whilst you decide upon your two remaining wishes, but I am also curious to know your own—are you wife, or widow, and how do you come to be inhabiting this splendid apartment with flowing waters in the Peri Palas as your shining books tell me this place is called? What I know of England is little and unfriendly. I know the tale of the pale slaves from the island in the north of whom a Roman bishop said "*Non Angli sed angeli.*" And I know about Bisnismen, from the conversation in the caravanserai in Smyrna. You are rumoured to be thick red people who cannot bend or smile, but I have learned never to trust rumours and I find you graceful.'

'My name is Gillian Perholt,' said Dr Perholt. 'I am an independent woman, a scholar, I study tale-telling and narra-tology.' (She thought he could learn this useful word; his green eyes glittered.) 'I am in Turkey for a conference, and return to my island in a week's time. I do not think my history will interest you, much.'

'On the contrary. I am temporarily in your power, and it is always wise to understand the history of those who hold power over you. I have lived much of my life in harems, and in harems the study of apparently uneventful personal histories is a matter of extreme personal importance. The only truly independent woman I have known was the Queen of Sheba, my half-cousin, but I see that things have changed since her day. What does an independent woman wish for, Djil-yan Peri-han?'

'Not much,' said Gillian, 'that I haven't got. I need to think. I need to be intelligent. Tell me the story of your three incarcerations. If that would not bore you.'

She was later to wonder how she could be so matter-of-fact about the presence of the gracefully lounging Oriental daimon in a hotel room. At the time, she unquestioningly accepted his reality and his remarks as she would have done if she had met him in a dream—that is to say, with a certain difference, a certain knowledge that the reality in which she was was not everyday, was not the reality in which Dr Johnson refuted Bishop Berkeley's solipsism with a robust kick at a trundling stone. She was accustomed also to say in lectures, that it was possible that the human need to tell tales about things that were unreal originated in dreams, and that memory had certain things also in common with dreams; it re-arranged, it made clear, simple narratives, certainly it invented as well as recalling. Hobbes, she told her students, had described imagination as decayed memory. She had at no point the idea that she might 'wake up' from the presence of the djinn and find him gone as though he had never been; but she did feel she might move suddenly—or he might—into some world where they no longer shared a mutual existence. But he persisted, his finger-nails and toe-nails solid and glistening, his flesh with its slightly simmering quality, his huge considering eyes, his cloak of wings, his scent, with its perfumes and smokiness, its pheromones, if djinns have pheromones, a question she was not ready to put to him. She suggested ordering a meal from room service, and together they chose charred vegetable salad, smoked turkey, melons and passion fruit sorbet; the djinn made himself scarce whilst this repast was wheeled in, and added to it, upon his reappearance, a bowl of fresh figs and pomegranates and some intensely rose-perfumed lou-koum. Gillian said that she need not have ordered anything if he could do that, and he said that she did not allow for the effects of curiosity on one who had been cramped in a bottle since 1850 (your reckoning, he said in French)—he desired greatly to see the people and way of life of this late time.

'Your slaves,' he said, 'are healthy and smiling. That is good.'

'There are no slaves, we no longer have slaves—at least not in the West and not in Turkey—we are all free,' said Gillian, regretting this simplification as soon as it was uttered.

'No slaves,' said the djinn thoughtfully. 'No sultans, maybe, either?'

'No sultans, A republic. Here. In my country we have a Queen. She has no power. She is—a representative figure.'

'The Queen of Sheba had power,' said the djinn, folding his brow in thought, and adding dates, sherbet, quails, *marrons glacés* and two slices of *tarte aux pommes* to the feast spread before them. 'She would say to me, as her spies brought her news of his triumphal progress across the desert, the great Suleiman, blessed be his memory, she would say, 'How can I, a great Queen, submit to the prison house of marriage, to the invisible chains which bind me to the bed of a man?' I advised her against it. I told her her wisdom was hers and she was free as an eagle floating on the waves of the air and seeing the cities and palaces and mountains below her with an even eye. I told her her body was rich and lovely but her mind was richer and lovelier and more durable—for although she was partly of our kind, she was a mortal being, like you—djinns and mortals cannot produce an immortal scion, you know, as donkeys and horses can only produce a seedless mule. And she said she knew I was in the right: she sat amongst the cushions in her inner room, where no one came, and twisted her dark hair in her hand, and knit her brow in thought, and

I looked at the great globes of her breasts and the narrowness
of her waist and her huge soft fundament like two great heaps
of silky sand, and was sick with desire for her, though I said
nothing of that, for she liked to play with me a little, she had
known me since she was born, I had come visibly in and out
of her sleeping-chamber and kissed her soft mouth and stroked
her back as she grew, and I knew as well as any of her female
slaves the little touches that made her shiver with bliss, but
all was in play only, and she liked to consult me on serious
matters, on the intentions of the kings of Persia and Bessarabia,
on the structure of a ghazal, on medicines for choler and
despair, on the disposition of the stars. And she said she knew
I was right, and that her freedom was her true good, not to
be surrendered, and that only I—an immortal djinn—and a
few women, advised her so, but that most of her court, men
and women, and her human family were in favour of marriage
with this Suleiman (blessed be his memory), who advanced
across the desert day by day, growing in her mind as I could
grow and shrink before her eyes. And when he came, I saw
that I was lost, for she desired him. It is true to say that he
was desirable, his loins and his buttocks in his silk trousers were
of a perfect beauty, and his fingers were long and wonderfully
quick—he could play a woman as well as he could play a lute
or a flute—but at first she did not know that she desired him,
and I, like a fool, went on telling her to think of her proud
autonomy, of her power to go in and out as she pleased.
And she agreed with all I said, she nodded gravely and once
dropped a hot tear, which I licked up—never have I desired any
creature so, woman or djinn or peri or boy like a fresh-peeled
chestnut. And then she began to set him tasks which seemed
impossible—to find a particular thread of red silk in the whole
palace, to guess the secret Name of the djinn her mother, to
tell her what women most desire—and I knew even more surely
that I was lost, for he could speak to the beasts of the earth
and the birds of the air, and djinns from the kingdom of fire,
and he found ants to discover the thread, and an Ifrit from
the kingdom of fire to tell him the name, and he looked into

her eyes and told her what women most desire, and she lowered her eyes and said he was right, and granted him what *he* desired, which was to wed her and take her to his bed, with her lovely curtain of flesh still unparted and her breath coming in little pants of desire that I had never heard, never, and never should again. And when I saw him tear her maidenhead and the ribbon of red blood flow on to the silk sheets, I gave a kind of groan, and he became aware of my presence. He was a great magician, blessed be his name, and could see me well enough, though I was invisible. And he lay there, bathed in her sweat and his, and took account of certain little love-bites — most artistically placed, and unfortunately not invisible — in the soft hollows of her collar-bone, and — elsewhere, you may imagine. And he could see the virgin blood well enough, or I imagine my fate might have been worse, but he imprisoned me with a word of power in a great metal flask there was in the room, and sealed me in with his own seal, and she said nothing, she made no plea for me — though I am a believer, and not a follower of Iblis — only lay back and sighed, and I saw her tongue caress her pearly teeth, and her soft hand reach out to touch those parts of him which had given her such pleasure, and I was nothing to her, a breath in a bottle. And so I was cast into the Red Sea, with many others of my kind, and languished there for two and a half thousand years until a fisherman drew me up in his net and sold the bottle to a travelling pedlar, who took me to the bazaar in Istanbul where I was bought by a handmaid of Princess Mihrimah, daughter of Suleiman the Magnificent, and taken to the Abode of Bliss, the Eski Saray, the harem in the palace.'

'Tell me,' said Gillian Perholt, interrupting his story, 'What do women most desire?'

'Do you not know?' said the djinn. 'If you do not know already, I cannot tell you.'

'Maybe they do not all desire the same thing.'

'Maybe you do not. Your own desires, Djil-yan Peri-han, are not clear to me. I cannot read your thoughts, and that intrigues me. Will you not tell me your life?'

'It is of no interest. Tell me what happened when you were bought by Princess Mihrimah.'

'This lady was the daughter of the Sultan, Suleiman the Magnificent and his concubine Roxelana la Rossa, the woman out of Galicia, daughter of a Ukrainian priest and known in Turkish as Hurrem, the laughing one. She was terrible as an army with the banners, Roxelana. She defeated the Sultan's early love, Gülbahar, the Rose of Spring, whom he adored, and when she bore him a son, she laughed him fiercely into marrying her, which no concubine, no Christian, had ever achieved. And when the kitchens burned—in your year 1540 it must be—she marched her household into the Seraglio—a hundred ladies-in-waiting and the eunuchs, all quaking in their shoes for fear of being disembowelled on the spot—but they were more afraid of her laughter—and so she settled in the palace itself. And Mihrimah's husband, Rüstem Pasha, was the grand vizir after Ibrahim was strangled. I remember Suleiman the Magnificent—his face was round with blue eyes, the nose of a ram, the body of a lion, a full beard, a long neck—he was a big man, a king of men, a man without fear or compromise, a glorious man. . . . Those who came after were fools and boys. That was her fault, Roxelana's fault. She intrigued against his son Mustafa, Gülbahar's son, who was like his father and would have been a wise ruler—she persuaded Suleiman he was treacherous, and so when he came boldly into his father's presence they were waiting for him, the mutes with the silk strangling cords, and he tried to cry to the janissaries who loved him, but the stranglers beat him down and stopped his breath. I saw it all, for I had been sent to see it by my new young mistress, a slave girl who belonged to Mihrimah and opened my bottle, believing it contained perfume for her mistress's bath. She was a Christian and a Circassian, Gülten, pale for my tastes, and tremulous and given to weeping and wringing her hands. And when I appeared to her in that secret bathroom she could only faint and I had great trouble in rousing her and explaining to her that she had three wishes, because she had released me, and that I meant her no harm and could do her no harm, for I was the slave of the bottle until the wishes were performed. And the poor silly thing was distractedly in love with Prince Mustafa and wished immediately that she could find favour in his eyes. Which came about—he sent for her—I spoke to him—I escorted her to his bedchamber, I told her how to please him—he was very much like his father and loved poems, and singing, and good manners. And then the silly girl wished she could become pregnant—'

'That was only natural.'

'Natural but very stupid. Better to use the wish *against* pregnancy, my lady, and also foolish to waste the wish in such a hurry, for they were both young and lusty and hot-blooded, and what did happen would have happened without my interference, and I could have helped her in more important ways. For of course when Roxelana heard that Gülten was to bear Mustafa's child, she ordered her eunuchs to sew her up in a sack and throw her from the Seraglio Point into the Bosphorus. And I thought to myself, having flown back from Mustafa's execution, that at any moment she would bethink herself of me, and wish—I don't know exactly what—but wish to be far away—or out of the sack—or back in Circassia—I waited for her to formulate the wish, because once she had made it we would both be free, I to fly where I pleased and she to live, and bear her child. But her limbs were frozen cold, and her lips were blue as lapis with terror, and her great blue eyes were staring out of her head—and the gardeners—the executioners were also the gardeners, you know—bundled her into the sack like a dead rosebush—and carried her away to the cliff over the Bosphorus. And I thought of rescuing her at every moment—but I calculated that she *must*, even involuntarily, wish for her life, and that if I delayed, and went invisibly through the garden in the evening—the roses were in full bloom, the perfume was intense to swooning—and over she went, and drowned, before I could quite make up my mind to the fact that she was in no state to make any wish.

So there was I, said the djinn, half-emancipated, you could say, but still tied to the bottle by the third unperformed task. I found I was free to wander during the day within a certain range of the enchanted flask, but I was compelled to return at night and shrink myself to its compass and sleep there. I was a prisoner of the harem, and likely to remain so, for my bottle was securely hidden under a tile in the floor of a bathroom, a secretly loosened tile, known only to the drowned Circassian. For women closed into those places find many secret places to hide things, for they like to have one or two possessions of their own—or a place to hide letters—that no one else, they fondly think, knows of. And I found I was unable to attract anyone's attention to the tile and the bottle; these things were out of my power.

And so I haunted the Topkapı Sarayı for just under a hundred years, attached by a silken cord you might say poetically, to the flask hidden in the bathroom floor, I saw Roxelana persuade Suleiman the Magnificent to write to the Shah Tahmasp of Persia, with whom their youngest son, Bayezid, had taken refuge, and command the Shah to execute the young Prince—which he would not do for hospitality's sake, but allowed it to be done by Turkish mutes, as was customary, and Bayezid was put to death, with his four sons and a fifth, three years of age, hidden in Bursa. He would have made an excellent ruler, too, I think—and so it was generally thought.'

'*Why?*' asked Gillian Perholt.

'It was customary, my lady, and Roxelana wished to assure a safe succession for her eldest son Selim, Selim the Sot, Selim the drunkard, Selim the poet, who died in a bathhouse after too many flasks of wine. Roxelana was long dead, buried beside the Süleymaniye, and Mihrimah her daughter built a new mosque to commemorate Suleiman, with the help of the great arthitect, Sinan, who made the Süleymaniye in holy rivalry with Haghia Sophia. And I watched sultans come and go—Murad III who was ruled by women, and strangled five of his brothers, Mehmed III who strangled nineteen of his, and then gave them sumptuous burials—he died when a dervish predicted he would live another fifty-five days—on the fifty-fifth, in fear and trembling. I watched Mustafa, the holy madman, who was brought from the cages of the princes, deposed, brought back after the slaughter of the boy Osman, and deposed by Murad IV who was the most cruel. Can you imagine a man, my lady, who could see a circle of lovely girls dancing in a meadow, and order them all to be drowned because they sang too loudly? No one spoke in those days, in the palace, for fear of attracting his attention. He could have a man killed because his teeth chattered involuntarily for fear of being put to death. And when he was dying he ordered the death of his only surviving brother, Ibrahim. But his mother, Kösem, the Greek, the Valide Sultan, lied to him and said it was done, when it was not. I saw him smile and try to get up to see the corpse, and fall back in his death-throes.

As for Ibrahim. He was a fool, a cruel fool, who loved things of the harem where he had grown up. He listened to an old storyteller in the harem—a woman from north of the Ukraine, who told him of northern kings who made love to their concubines in rooms entirely lined with sables, and with sables on their couches and sables on their bodies. So he made himself a great robe, sable without, sable within, with great jewels for buttons, which he wore whilst he satisfied his lust—the smell was not good, after a time. And he believed that the pleasures of the flesh would be more intense the larger the expanse of flesh with which he coped, so he sent out janissaries over all his lands to seek out the fleshiest, the hugest women, and bring them to his couch, where he scrambled all over them dragging the edges of his dark furs like a beast. And that is how I came to return to my bottle, for the fattest of all, the most voluptuous, the most like a sweet-breathed cow, whose anklets were twice your present waist, madame—she was an Armenian Christian, she was docile and short of breath—it was she who was so heavy that she dislodged the tile under which my bottle lay concealed—and so I stood before her in the bathroom and she wheezed with anxiety. I told her that the Valide Sultan planned to have her strangled that night at the banquet she was dressing for, and I thought she would utter a wish—wish herself a thousand miles away, or wish that someone would strangle the Valide Sultan—or even wish a small wish, such as 'I wish I knew what to do', and I would have told her what to do, and rushed on wide wings to the ends of the earth afterwards.

But this globular lady was self-satisfied and slow-witted, and all she could think of to say was 'I wish you were sealed up in your bottle again, infidel Ifrit, for I want nothing to do with dirty djinns. You smell bad,' she added, as I coiled myself back into atomies of smoke and sighed myself into the flask and replaced the stopper. And she carried my flask through the rose-garden where my white Circassian had been carried, and threw me over the Seraglio Point into the Bosphorus. She undertook this herself; I could feel the voluptuous rippling and juddering of her flesh as she progressed along the paths. I was about to say she had not taken so much exercise in years, but that would be unjust—she had to use her musculature very vigorously in certain ways to cope with the more extreme projects of Sultan Ibrahim. And Kösem did have her strangled that night, just as I had told her. It would have been more interesting to have been released by those doughty Sultanas, by Roxelana or Kösem, but my luck was femininity.

And so I tossed about in the Bosphorus for another two hundred and fifty years and was then fished up by another fisherman and sold as an antique to a merchant of Smyrna, who gave me—or my flask—as a love-token to his young wife Zefir, who had a collection of curious-shaped bottles and jars in her quarters in the harem. And Zefir saw the seal on the bottle and knew what it was, for she was a great reader of tales and histories. She told me later she spent all night in fear, wondering whether to open the flask in case I might be angry, like the djinn who threatened to kill his rescuer because he had become enraged over the centuries, that the poor man had taken so long to come to his aid. But she was a brave creature, Zefir, and ardent for knowledge, and mortally bored, so one day, alone in her chamber she pushed away the seal. . . .'

'What was she like?' said Gillian, since the djinn appeared to have floated off into a reminiscent reverie.

His eyelids were half-closed and the edges of his huge nostrils fluttered.

'Ah,' he said, 'Zefir. She had been married at fourteen to the merchant, who was older than she was, and was kind enough to her, kind enough, if you call treating someone like a toy dog or a spoiled baby or a fluffy fat bird in a cage being kind. She was good-looking enough, a sharp, dark person, with secret black-brown eyes and an angry line of a mouth that pulled in at the corners. She was wayward and angry, Zefir, and she had nothing at all to do. There was an older wife who didn't like her and didn't talk to her, and servants, who seemed to her to be mocking her. She spent her time sewing huge pictures in silk—pictures of stories—the stories from the Shahnama, of Rüstem and the Shah Kaykavus who tried to emulate the djinns and fly, and devised a method of some ingenuity—he tied four strong yet hungry eagles to a throne, and four juicy legs of mutton to the rising posts of the canopy of the throne—and then he seated himself, and the eagles strove to reach the meat, and lifted the throne— and the shah—towards the heavens. But the eagles tired, and the throne and its occupant fell to earth—she had embroidered him coming down headlong and head first, and she had sewed him a rich carpet of flowers to fall on, for she thought him aspiring, and not a fool. You should have seen the beauty of her silk legs of muttons, like the life—or rather, death. She was a great artist, Zefir, but no one saw her art. And she was angry because she knew she was capable of many things she couldn't even define to herself, so they seemed like bad dreams—that is what she told me. She told me she was eaten up with unused power and thought she might be a witch— except, she said, if she were a man, these things she thought about would be ordinarily acceptable. If she had been a man, and a westerner, she would have rivalled the great Leonardo whose flying machines were the talk of the court of Suleiman one summer—

'So I taught her mathematics, which was bliss to her, and astronomy, and many languages, she studied secretly with me, and poetry—we wrote an epic poem about the travels of the Queen of Sheba—and history, I taught her the history of Turkey and the history of the Roman Empire, and the history of the Holy Roman Empire—I bought her novels in many languages, and philosophical treatises, Kant and Descartes and Leibnitz—'

'Wait,' said Gillian. 'Was this her wish, that you should teach her these things?'

'Not exactly,' said the djinn. 'She wished to be wise and learned, and I had known the Queen of Sheba, and what it was to be a wise woman . . ."

'Why did she not wish to *get out of there?*' asked Gillian.

'I advised against it. I said the wish was bound to go wrong, unless she was better-informed about the possible places or times she might wish herself into—I said there was no hurry'

'You enjoyed teaching her.'

'Rarely among humankind can there have been a more intelligent being.' said he djinn. 'And not only intelligent.' He brooded.

'I taught her other things also,' he said. 'Not at first. At first I flew in and out with bags of books and papers and writing things that I then hid by temporarily vanishing them into her bottle collection—so she could always call on Aristotle from the red glass perfume-bottle, or Euclid from the green tear-bottle, without needing me to re-embody them—'

'And did that count as a wish?' asked Gillian severely.

'Not really,' The djinn was evasive. 'I taught her a few magical skills—to help her—because I loved her—'

'You loved her—'

'I loved her anger. I loved my own power to change her frowns to smiles. I taught her what her husband had not taught her, to enjoy her own body, without all the gestures of submission and non-disturbance of his own activities the silly man seemed to require.'

'You were in no hurry for her to escape—to exercise her new powers somewhere else—'

'No. We were happy. I like being a teacher. It is unusual in djinns—we have a natural propensity to trick and mislead your kind. But your kind is rarely as greedy for knowledge as Zefir. I had all the time in the world—'

'*She* didn't,' said Gillian who was trying to feel her way into this story, occluded by the djinn's own feelings, it appeared. She felt a certain automatic resentment of this long-dead Turkish prodigy, the thought of whom produced the dreaming smile on the lips of what she had come to think of—so quickly—as *her* djinn. But she also felt troubled on Zefir's behalf, by the djinn's desire to be both liberator and imprisoner in one.

'I know,' said the djinn. 'She was mortal, I know. What year is it now?'

'It is 1991.'

'She would be one hundred and sixty-four years old, if she lived. And our child would be one hundred and forty, which is not possible for such a being.'

'A child?'

'Of fire and dust. I planned to fly with him round the earth, and show him the cities and the forests and the shores. He would have been a great genius—maybe. I don't know if he was ever born.'

'Or she.'

'Or she. Indeed.'

'What happened? Did she wish for *anything at all*? Or did you prevent her to keep her prisoner? How did you come to be in my çesm-i bülbül bottle? I do not understand.'

'She was a very clever woman, like you, Djil-yan, and she knew it was wise to wait. And then—I think—I know—she began to wish—to desire—that I should stay with her. We had a whole world in her little room. I brought things from all over the world—silks and satins, sugar-cane and paw-paw, sheets of green ice, Donatello's *Perseus*, aviaries full of parrots, waterfalls, rivers. One day, unguardedly, she wished she could fly with me when I went to the Americas, and then she could have bitten off her tongue, and almost wasted a second wish undoing the first, but I put a finger on her lip—she was so quick, she understood in a flash—and I kissed her, and we flew to Brazil, and to Paraguay, and saw the Amazon river which is as great as a sea, and the beasts in the forests there, where no man treads, and she was blissfully warm against my heart inside the feathered cloak—there are spirits with feathered cloaks out there, we found, whom we met in the air above the forest canopy—and then I brought her back to her room, and she fainted with joy and disappointment.'

He came to another halt, and Dr Perholt, savouring loukoum, had to encourage him.

'So she had two wishes. And became pregnant. Was she happy to be pregnant?'

'Naturally, in a way, she was happy, to be carrying a magic child. And naturally, in another, she was afraid: she said perhaps she should ask for a magic palace where she could bring up the child in safety in a hidden place—but that was not what she wanted—she said also she was not sure she wanted a child at all, and came near wishing him out of existence—'

'But you saved him.'

'I loved her. He was mine. He was a small seed, like a curved comma of smoke in a bottle; he grew and I watched him. She loved me, I think, she could not wish him undone.'

'Or her. Or perhaps you could see which it was?'

He considered.

'No. I did not see. I supposed, a son.'

'But you never saw him born.'

'We quarreled. Often. I told you she was angry. By nature. She was like a squall of sudden shower, thunder and lightning. She berated me. She said I had ruined her life. Often. And then we played again. I would make myself small, and hide. One day, to amuse her, I hid in the new çesm-i bülbül bottle that her husband had given her: I flowed in gracefully and curled myself; and she began suddenly to weep and rail and said 'I wish I could forget I had ever seen you.' And so she did. On the instant.'

'But—' said Dr. Perholt.

'But?' said the genie.

'But why did you not just flow out of the bottle again? Solomon had not sealed that bottle—'

'I had taught her a few sealing-spells, for pleasure. For my pleasure, in being in her power, and hers, in having power. There are humans who play such games of power with manacles and ropes. Being inside a bottle has certain things—a *few* things—in common with being inside a woman—a certain pain that at times is indistinguishable from pleasure. We cannot die, but at the moment of becoming infinitesimal inside the neck of a flask, or a jar, or a bottle—we can shiver with the apprehension of extinction—as humans speak of dying when they reach the height of bliss, in love. To be nothing, in the bottle—to pour my seed into her—it was a little the same. And I taught her the words of power as a kind of wager— a form of gambling. Russian roulette,' said the djinn, appearing to pluck these unlikely words from the air.

'So I was in, and she was out, and had forgotten me,' he concluded.

'And now,' said the djinn, 'I have told you the history of my incarcerations, and you must tell me your history.'

'I am a teacher. In a university. I was married and now I am free. I travel the world in aeroplanes and talk about storytelling.'

'Tell me your story.'

A kind of panic overcame Dr Perholt. It seemed to her that she had no story, none that would interest this hot person with his searching look and his restless intelligence. She could not tell him the history of the western world since Zefir had mistakenly wished him forgotten in a bottle of çesm-i bülbül glass, and without that string of wonders, how could he understand her?

He put a great hand on her towelled shoulder. Through the towel, even, his hand was hot and dry.

'Tell me anything,' said the djinn.

She found herself telling him how she had been a girl at a boarding-school in Cumberland, a school full of girls, a school with nowhere to hide from gaggles and klatsches of girls. It may be she told him this because of her imagined vision of Zefir, in the women's quarters in Smyrna in 1850. She told him about the horror of dormitories full of other people's sleeping breath. I am a naturally *solitary* creature, the doctor told the djinn. She had written a secret book, her first book, she told him, during this imprisonment, a book about a young man called Julian who was in hiding, disguised as a girl called Julienne, in a similar place. In hiding from an assassin or a kidnapper, she could barely remember, at this distance, she told the djinn. Her voice faded. The djinn was impatient. Was she a lover of women in those days? No, said Dr Perholt, she believed she had written the story out of an emptiness, a need to imagine a boy, a man, the Other. And how did the story progress, asked the djinn, and could you not find a real boy or man, how did you resolve it? I could not, said Dr Perholt. It seemed silly, in writing, I could see it was silly. I filled it with details, realistic details, his under-wear, his problems with gymnastics, and the more realism I tried to insert into what was really a cry of desire—desire for nothing specific—the more silly my story. It should have been farce or fable, I see that now, and I was writing passion and tragedy and buttons done with verisimilitude. I burned it in the school furnace. My imagination failed. I got all enmeshed in what was realism and what was reality and what was true— my need not to be in that place—and my imagination failed. Indeed it may be because Julian/Julienne was such a ludicrous figure that I am a narratologist and not a maker of fictions. I tried to conjure him up—he had long black hair in the days when all Englishmen had short back-and-sides—but he remained resolutely absent, or almost absent. Not quite. From time to time, he had a sort of being, he was a sort of wraith. Do you understand this?'

'Not entirely,' said the djinn. 'He was an emanation, like this Becker you would not let me give you.'

'Only the emanation of an absence.' She paused. 'When I
was younger there was a boy who was real.'

'Your first lover.'

'No. No. Not flesh and blood. A golden boy who walked
beside me wherever I went. Who sat beside me at table, who
lay beside me at night, who sang with me, who walked in my
dreams. Who disappeared when I had a headache or was sick,
but was always there when I couldn't move for asthma. His
name was Tadzio, I don't know where I got that from, he
came with it, one day, I just looked up and I saw him. He
told me stories. In a language only we two spoke. One day I
found a poem which said how it was, to live in his company.
I did not know anyone else knew, until I read that poem.'

'I know those beings—' said the djinn. 'Zefir had known
one. She said he was always a little transparent but moved
with his own will, not hers. Tell me your poem.'

> When I was but thirteen or so
> I went into a golden land,
> Chimborazo, Cotopaxi
> Took me by the hand.
>
> My father died, my brother too,
> They passed like fleeting dreams,
> I stood where Popocatapetl
> In the sunlight gleams.
>
> I dimly heard the Master's voice,
> And boys' far-off at play,
> Chimborazo, Cotopaxi
> Had stolen me away.
>
> I walked in a great golden dream
> To and fro from school—
> Shining Popocatapetl
> The dusty streets did rule.

I walked home with a gold dark boy
And never a word I'd say
Chimborazo, Cotopaxi
Had taken my speech away:

I gazed entranced upon his face
Fairer than any flower —
O shining Popocatapetl
It was thy magic hour:

The houses, people, traffic seemed
Thin fading dreams by day,
Chimborazo, Cotopaxi
They had stolen my soul away.

'I love that poem,' said Dr Perholt. 'It has two things: names and the golden boy. The names are not the names of the boy, they are the romance of language, and *he* is the romance of language—he is more real than—reality—as the goddess of Ephesus is more real than I am—'

'And I am here,' said the djinn.

'Indeed,' said Dr Perholt. 'Incontrovertibly.'

There was a silence. The djinn returned to the topic of Dr Perholt's husband, her children, her house, her parents, all of which she answered without—in her mind or his—investing any of these now truly insignificant people with any life or colour. My husband went to Majorca with Emmeline Porter, she said to the djinn, and decided not to come back, and I was glad. The djinn asked about the complexion of Mr Perholt and the nature of the beauty of Emmeline Porter and received null and unsatisfactory answers. They are wax images, your people, said the djinn indignantly.

'I do not want to think about them.'

'That is apparent. Tell me something about yourself—something you have never told anyone—something you have never trusted to any lover in the depth of any night, to any friend, in the warmth of a long evening. Something you have kept for me.'

And the image sprang in her mind, and she rejected it as insignificant.

'Tell me,' said the djinn.

'It is insignificant.'

'Tell me.'

'Once, I was a bridesmaid. To a good friend from my college who wanted a white wedding, with veils and flowers and organ music, though she was happily settled with her man already, they slept together, she said she was blissfully happy, and I believe she was. At college, she seemed very poised and formidable — a woman of power, a woman of sexual experience, which was unusual in my day —'

'Women have always found ways —'

'Don't sound like the *Arabian Nights*. I am telling you something. She was full of bodily grace, and capable of being happy, which most of us were not, it was fashionable to be disturbed and anguished, for young women in those days — probably young men too. We were a generation when there was something shameful about being an unmarried woman, a spinster — though we were all clever, like Zefir, my friends and I, we all had this greed for knowledge — we were scholars —'

'Zefir would have been happy as a teacher of philosophy, it is true,' said the djinn. 'Neither of us could quite think what she could be — in those days —'

'And my friend — whom I shall call Susannah, it wasn't her name, but I can't go on without one — my friend had always seemed to me to come from somewhere rather grand, a beautiful house with beautiful things. But when I arrived for the wedding her house was much like mine, small, like a box, in a row of similar houses, and there was a settee, there was a three-piece suite in moquette —'

'A three-piece suite in moquette?' enquired the djinn. 'What horrid thing is this to make you frown so?'

'I knew it was no good telling you anything out of my world. It is too big for those rooms, it is too heavy, it *weighs everything down*, it is chairs and a sofa that sat on a beige carpet with splashy flowers on—'

'A sofa—' said the djinn, recognising a word. 'A carpet.'

'You don't' know what I'm talking about. I should never have started on this. All English stories get bogged down in whether or not the furniture is socially and aesthetically acceptable. This wasn't. That is, I thought so then. Now I find everything interesting, because I live my own life.'

'Do not heat yourself. You did not like the house. The house was small and the three-piece suite in moquette was big, I comprehend. Tell me about the marriage. The story is presumably about the marriage and not about the chairs and sofa.'

'Not really. The marriage went off beautifully. She had a lovely dress, like a princess out of a story—those were the days of the princess-line in dresses—I had a princess-line dress too, in shot taffeta, turquoise and silver, with a heart-shaped neck, and she was wearing several net skirts, and over those silk, and over that white lace—and a *mass* of veiling—and real flowers in her hair—little rosebuds—there wasn't room for all those billows of wonderful stuff in her tiny bedroom. She had a bedside lamp with Peter Rabbit eating a carrot. And all this shimmering silk and stuff. On the day, she looked so lovely, out of another world. I had a big hat with a brim, it suited me. You can imagine the dresses, I expect, but you can't imagine the house, the place."

'If you say I cannot,' replied the djinn, obligingly. 'Why do you tell me this tale? I cannot believe this is what you have not told.'

'The night before the wedding,' said Gillian Perholt, 'we bathed together, in her parents' little bathroom. It had tiles with fishes with trailing fins and big soulful cartoon eyes—'

'Cartoon?'

'Disney. It doesn't matter. *Comic* eyes.'

'Comic tiles?'

'It doesn't matter. We didn't share the bath, but we washed together.'

'And—' said the djinn. 'She made love to you.'

'No,' said Dr Perholt. 'She didn't. I saw myself. First in the mirror, and then I looked down at myself. And then I looked across at her—she was pearly-white and I was more golden. And she was soft and sweet—'

'And you were not?'

'I was perfect. Just at that moment, just at the very end of being a girl, and before I was a woman, really, I was perfect.'

She remembered seeing her own small, beautifully rising breasts, her warm, flat, tight belly, her long slender legs and ankles, her waist—her waist—

'She said, "Some man is going to go mad with desire for you",' said Gillian Perholt. 'And I was all proud inside my skin, as never before or since. All golden.' She thought. 'Two girls in a suburban bathroom,' she said, in an English deprecating voice.

The djinn said, 'But when I changed you, that was not what you became. You are very nice now, very acceptable, very desirable now, but not perfect.'

'It was terrifying. I was terrified. It was like—' she found a completely unexpected phrase—'like having a weapon, a sharp sword, I couldn't handle.'

'Ah yes,' said the djinn. 'Terrible as an army with banners.'

'But it didn't belong to me. I was tempted to—to love it—myself. It was lovely. But unreal. I mean, it was *there*, it was real enough, but I knew in my head it wouldn't stay—something would happen to it. I owed it—' she went on, searching for feelings she had never interrogated—'I owed it—some sort of adequate act. And I wasn't going to live up to it.' She caught her breath on a sigh. 'I am a creature of the mind, not the body, Djinn. I can look after my mind. I took care of that, despite everything.'

'Is that the end of the story?' said the djinn after another silence. 'Your stories are strange, glancing things. They peter out, they have no shape.'

'It is what my culture likes, or liked. But no, it is not the end. There is a little bit more. In the morning Susannah's father brought my breakfast in bed. A boiled egg in a woolly cosy, a little silver-plated pot of tea, in a cosy knitted to look like a cottage, toast in a toast-rack, butter in a butter-dish, all on a little tray with unfolding legs, like the trays old ladies have in homes.'

'You didn't like the — the whatever was on the teapot? Your aesthetic sense, which is so violent, was in revolt again?'

'He suddenly leaned forwards and pulled my nightdress off my shoulders. He put his hands round my perfect breasts,' said Dr Perholt who was fifty-five and now looked thirty-two, 'and he put his sad face down between them — he had glasses, they were all steamed up and knocked sideways, he had a little bristly moustache that crept over my flesh like a centipede, he *snuffled* amongst my breasts, and all he said was "I can't bear it" and he rubbed his body against my counterpane — I only half-understood, the counterpane was artificial silk, eau-de-nil colour — he snuffled and jerked and twisted my breasts in his hands — and then he unfolded the little legs of the tray and put it over my legs and went away — to give away his daughter, which he did with great dignity and charm. And I felt sick, and felt my body was to blame. As though out of *that*,' she said lucidly, 'was spun snuffling and sweat and three-piece suites and artificial silk and tea-cosies —'

'And that is the end of the story?' said the djinn.

'That is where a storyteller would end it, in my country.'

'Odd. And you met *me* and asked for the body of a thirty-two-year-old woman.'

'I didn't. I asked for it to be as it was when I last *liked* it. I didn't like it then. I half-worshipped it, but it scared me — This is *my* body, I find it pleasant, I don't mind looking at it —'

'Like the potter who puts a deliberate flaw in the perfect pot.'

'Maybe. If having lived a little is a flaw. Which it is. That girl's ignorance was a burden to her.'

'Do you know now what other things you will wish for?'

'Ah, you are anxious to be free.'

'On the contrary, I am comfortable, I am curious, I have all the time in the world.'

'And I have everything I wish for, at present. I have been thinking about the story of the Queen of Sheba and what the answer might be to the question of what all women desire. I shall tell you the story of the Ethiopian woman whom I saw on the television box.'

'I am all ears,' said the djinn, extending himself on the bedspread and shrinking himself a little, in order to be able to accommodate himself at full length. 'Tell me, this box, you can turn it to spy anywhere you desire in the world, you can see Manaus or Khartoum as you please?'

'Not exactly, though partly. For instance the tennis was coming live—we call it "live" when we see it simultaneously with its happening—from Monte Carlo. But also we can make images—stories—which we can replay to ourselves. The Ethiopian woman was part of a story—a film—made for the Save the Children Fund—which is a charitable body—which had given some food to a village in Ethiopia where there had been drought and famine, food specifically to give to the children, to keep them alive through the winter. And when they brought the food, they filmed the people of the village, the head men and the elders, the children playing, and then they came back, the research workers came back, half a year later, to see the children and weigh them, to see how the food they had given had helped them.'

'Ethiopia is a fierce country of fierce people,' said the djinn. 'Beautiful and terrible. What did you see in your box?'

'The aid workers were very angry—distressed and angry. The head man had promised to give the food only to the families with the small children the project was helping and studying—"project" is—'

'I know. I have known projectors in my time.'

'But the head man had not done as he was asked. It was against his beliefs to feed some families and not others, and it was against everyone's beliefs to feed small children and not grown men, who could work in the fields, if anything could be grown there. So the food had been shared out too sparsely—and everyone was thinner—and some of the children were dead—many, I think—and others were very ill because the food had not been given to them.

'And the workers—the relief workers—the charitable people from America and Europe—were angry and upset—and the cameramen (the people who make the films) went out into the fields with the men who had had the food, and had sowed their crops in hope of rain—and had even had a little rain—and the men lifted the seedlings and showed the cameramen and the officials that the roots had been eaten away by a plague of sawfly, and there would be no harvest. And those men, standing in those fields, holding those dying, stunted seedlings, were in complete despair. They had no hope and no idea what to do. We had seen the starving in great gatherings on our boxes, you must understand—we knew where they were heading, and had sent the food because we were moved because of what we had seen.

'And then, the cameras went into a little hut, and there in the dark were four generations of women, the grandmother, the mother and the young girl with her baby. The mother was stirring something in a pot over a fire—it looked like a watery soup—with a wooden stick—and the grandmother was sitting on a kind of bed against the wall, where the hut roof—which seemed conical—met it. They were terribly thin, but they weren't dying—they hadn't given up yet, they hadn't got those eyes looking out at nothing, or those slack muscles just waiting. They were beautiful people still, people with long faces and extraordinary cheek-bones, and a kind of dignity in their movement—or what westerners like me read as dignity, they are upright, they carry their heads up—

'And they interviewed the old woman. I remember it partly because of her beauty, and partly because of the skill of the cameraman—or woman—she was angular but not awkward, and she had one long arm at an angle over her head, and her legs extended on this bench—and the photographer had made them squared, as it were *framed* in her own limbs—she spoke out of an enclosure made by her own body, and her eyes were dark holes and her face was long, long. She made the edges of the box out of her body. They wrote in English letters across the screen a translation of what she was saying. She said there was no food, no food any more and the little girl would starve, and there would be no milk, there would be no more food. And then she said "It is because I am a woman, I cannot get out of here, I must sit here and wait for my fate, if only I were not a woman I could go out and do something—" all in a monotone. With the men stomping about in the furrows outside kicking up dry dust and stunted seedlings in perfect despair.

'I don't know why I tell you this. I will tell you something else. I was told to wish on a pillar in Haghia Sophia—and before I could stop myself—it was—not a good pillar—I wished what I used to wish as a child.'

'You wished you were not a woman.'

'There were three veiled women laughing at me, pushing my hand into that hole.'

'I thought, perhaps, that was what the Queen of Sheba told Solomon that all women desired.'

The genie smiled.

'It was not. That was not what she told him. Not exactly.'

'Will you tell me what she told him?'

'If you wish me to.'

'I wish—Oh, no. No, that isn't what I wish.'

Gillian Perholt looked at the djinn on her bed. The evening had come, whilst they sat there, telling each other stories. A kind of light played over his green-gold skin, and a kind of glitter, like the glitter from the Byzantine mosaics, where a stone here or there will be set at a slight angle to catch the light. His plumes rose and fell as though they were breathing, silver and crimson, chrysanthemum-bronze and lemon, sapphire-blue and emerald. There was an edge of sulphur to his scent, and sandalwood, she thought, and something bitter—myrrh, she wondered, having never smelt myrrh, but remembering the king in the Christmas carol

Myrrh is mine, its bitter perfume
Breathes a life of gathering gloom,
Sorrowing, sighing, bleeding, dying
Sealed in a stone-cold tomb.

The outsides of his thighs were greener and the insides softer
and more golden. He had pulled down his tunic, not entirely
adequately: she could see his sex coiled like a folded snake
and stirring.

'I wish,' said Dr Perholt to the djinn, "I wish you would
love me."

'You honour me,' said the djinn, 'and maybe you have
wasted your wish, for it may well be that love would have
happened anyway, since we are together, and sharing our life
stories, as lovers do.'

'Love,' said Gillian Perholt, 'requires generosity. I found I
was jealous of Zefir and I have never been jealous of anyone.
I wanted—it was more that I wanted to give *you* something—
to give you my wish—" she said, incoherently. The great eyes,
stones of many greens, considered her and the carved mouth
lifted in a smile.

'You give and you bind,' said the djinn, 'like all lovers.
You give yourself, which is brave, and which I think you have
never done before—and I find you eminently lovable. Come.'

And without moving a muscle Dr Perholt found herself
naked on the bed, in the arms of the djinn.

Of their love-making she retained a memory at once precise,
mapped on to every nerve-ending, and indescribable. There
was, in any case, no one to whom she could have wished
to describe the love-making of a djinn. All love-making is
shape-shifting—the male expands like a tree, like a pillar, the
female has intimations of infinity in the spaces which narrow
inside her. But the djinn could prolong everything, both in
space and in time, so that Gillian seemed to swim across his
body forever like a dolphin in an endless green sea, so that
she became arching tunnels under mountains through which
he pierced and rushed, or caverns in which he lay curled like

dragons. He could become a concentrated point of delight at the pleasure-points of her arched and delighted body; he could travel her like some wonderful butterfly, brushing her here and there with a hot, dry, almost burning kiss, and then become again a folding landscape in which she rested and was lost, lost herself for him to find her again, holding her in the palm of his great hand, contracting himself with a sigh and holding her breast to breast, belly to belly, male to female. His sweat was like a smoke and he murmured like a cloud of bees in many languages — she felt her skin was on fire and was not consumed, and tried once to tell him about Marvell's lovers who had not 'world enough and time' but could only murmur one couplet in the green cave of his ear. 'My vegetable love should grow/Vaster than empires and more slow.' Which the djinn smilingly repeated, using the rhythm for a particularly delectable movement of his body.

And afterwards she slept. And woke alone in her pretty nightdress, amongst her pillows. And rose sadly and went to the bathroom, where the çesm-i bülbül bottle still stood, with her own finger-traces on its moist sides. She touched it sadly, running her fingers down the spirals of white — I have had a dream, she thought — and there was the djinn, bent into the bathroom like the Ethiopian woman in the television box, making an effort to adjust his size.

'I thought—'

'I know. But as you see, I am here.'

'Will you come to England with me?'

'I must, if you ask me. But also I should like to do that, I should like to see how things are now, in the world, I should like to see where you live, though you cannot describe it as interesting.'

'It will be, if you are there.'

But she was afraid.

And they went back to England, the narratologist, the glass bottle, and the djinn; they went back by British Airways, with

the bottle cushioned in bubble plastic in a bag at Gillian
Perholt's feet.

And when they got back, Dr Perholt found that the wish
she had made before Artemis between the two Leylas was also
granted: here was a letter asking her to give the keynote paper
in Toronto in the fall, and offering her a Club-class fare and
a stay in the Xanadu Hotel, which did indeed have a swim-
ming-pool, a blue pool under a glass dome, sixty-four floors
above Lake Superior's shores. And it was cold and clear in
Toronto, and Dr Perholt settled herself into the hotel room,
which was tastefully done in warm colours for cold winters,
in chestnuts, browns and ambers, with touches of flame. Hotel rooms have often the illusory presence of a magician's
stage set — their walls are bare concrete boxes, covered with
whipped-up white plaster, like icing on a cake, and then the
soft things are hung from screwed-in poles and hooks, damask
and voile, gilt-edged mirror and branching candelabra, to
give the illusion of richness. But all could be swept away in
a twinkling and replaced by quite other colours and textures —
chrome for brass, purple for amber, white-spotted muslin for
gold damask, and this spick-and-span temporariness is part
of the charm. Dr Perholt unpacked the nightingale's-eye bottle
and opened the stopper, and the djinn came out, human-size,
and waved his wing-cloak to uncramp it. He then shot out
of the window to look at the lake and the city, and returned,
saying that she must come with him over the water, which
was huge and cold, and that the sky, the atmosphere, was so
full of rushing faces and figures that he had had to thread
his way between them. The filling of the air-waves with politi-
cians and pop-stars, TV evangelists and vacuum cleaners, moving forests and travelling deserts, pornographic bottoms and
mouths and navels, purple felt dinosaurs and insane white
puppies — all this had deeply saddened the djinn, almost to
the point of depression. He was like someone who had had
the habit of riding alone across deserts on a camel, or rushing
off across savannah on an Arab horse, and now found himself

negotiating an endless traffic-jam of film-stars, tennis-players
and comedians, amongst the Boeings circling to find landing-
slots. The Koran and the Old Testament, he told Dr Perholt,
forbade the making of graven images, and whilst these were
not graven, they were images, and he felt they were infesta-
tions. The atmosphere, he told her, had always been full of
unseen beings — unseen by her kind — and still was. But it now
needed to be negotiated. It is as bad, said the djinn, in the
upper air as in bottles. I cannot spread my wings.

'And if you were entirely free,' said Dr Perholt, 'where would
you go?'

'There is a land of fire — where my kind play in the flames —'

They looked at each other.

'But I do not want to go,' said the djinn gently. 'I love you,
and I have all the time in the world. And all this chatter and
all these flying faces, they are also interesting. I learn many
languages. I speak many tongues. Listen.'

And he made a perfect imitation of Donald Duck, followed
by a perfect imitation of Chancellor Kohl's rotund German,
followed by the voices of the Muppets, followed by a surprising
rendition of Kiri Te Kanawa which had Dr Perholt's neighbours
banging on the partition wall.

The conference was in Toronto University, ivy-hung in Vic-
torian Gothic. It was a prestigious conference, to use an adjec-
tive that at this precise moment is shifting its meaning from
magical, from conjuring-tricks, to 'full of renown', 'respectable
in the highest', 'most honourable'. The French narratologists
were there, Todorov and Genette, and there were various ori-
entalists too, on the watch for western sentiment and distortion. Gillian Perholt's title was 'Wish-fulfillment and Narrative Fate: Some Aspects of Wish-fulfillment as a Narrative
Device'. She had sat up late writing it. She had never learned
not to put her lectures together under pressure and at the last
minute. It was not that she had not thought the subject-matter
out in advance. She had. She had thought long and carefully,

with the çesm-i bülbül bottle set before her like a holy image, with its blue and white stripes enfolding each other and circling and diminishing to its mouth. She had looked at her own strong pretty newish fingers travelling across the page, and flexed the comfortable stomach-muscles. She had tried to be precise. Yet she felt, as she stood up to speak, that her subject had taken a great twist in her hands, like a magic flounder trying to return to the sea, like a divining-rod pointing with its own energy into the earth, like a conducting-rod shivering with the electrical forces in the air.

As usual, she had tried to incorporate the telling of a story, and it was this story that had somehow twisted the paper away from its subject. It would be tedious to recount all her arguments. Their tenor can be guessed from their beginning.

'Characters in fairy-tales,' said Gillian, 'are subject to Fate and enact their fates. Characteristically they attempt to change this fate by magical intervention in its workings, and characteristically too, such magical intervention only reinforces the control of the Fate which waited for them, which is perhaps simply the fact that they are mortal and return to dust. The most clear and absolute version of this narrative form is the story of the appointment in Samarra — of the man who meets Death, who tells him that he is coming for him that evening, and flees to Samarra to avoid him. And Death remarks to an acquaintance that their first meeting was odd "since I was to meet him in Samarra tonight."

'Novels in recent time, have been about choice and motivation. Something of the ineluctable consequentiality of Samarra still clings to Raskolnikov's "free" act of murder, for it calls down a wholly predictable and conventional vengeance. In the case of George Eliot's Lydgate, on the other hand, we do not feel that the "spots of commonness" in his nature are instruments of inevitable fate in the same way: it was possible for him *not* to choose to marry Rosamund and destroy his fortune and his ambition. We feel that when Proust decides to diagnose sexual inversion in *all* his characters he is substituting the novelist's desires for the Fate of the real world; and yet that when Swann wastes years of his life for a woman who was not even his type, he made a choice, in time, that was possible but not inevitable.

'The emotion we feel in fairy-tales when the characters are granted their wishes is a strange one. We feel the possible leap of freedom — I can have what I want — and the perverse certainty that this will change nothing; that Fate is fixed.

'I should like to tell you a story told to me by a friend I met in Turkey — where stories are introduced *bir var mis, bir yok mis*, perhaps it happened, perhaps it didn't, and have paradox as their inception.'

She looked up, and there, sitting next to the handsome figure of Todorov, was a heavy-headed person in a sheepskin jacket, with a huge head of white hair. This person had not been there before, and the white mane had the look of an extravagant toupée, which, with blue-tinted glasses, gave the newcomer a look of being cruelly in disguise. Gillian thought she recognized the lift of his upper lip, which immediately changed shape under her eyes as soon as she had this thought, becoming defiantly thin and pursed. She could not see in the eyes: when she tried, the glasses became almost sapphire in their rebarbative glitter.

'In the days when camels flew from roof to roof,' she began, 'and fish roosted in cherry trees, and peacocks were as huge as haystacks, there was a fisherman who had nothing, and who moreover had no luck fishing, for he caught nothing, though he cast his net over and over in a great lake full of weeds and good water. And he said, one more cast, and if that brings up nothing, I shall give up this métier, which is starving me, and take to begging at the roadside. So he cast, and his net was heavy, and he pulled in something wet and rolling and malodorous, which turned out to be a dead ape. So he said to himself, that is not nothing, nevertheless, and he dug a hole in the sand and buried the ape, and cast his net again, for a second last time. And this time too, it was full, and this time it struggled under the water, with a life of its own. So he pulled it up, full of hope, and what he had caught was a second ape, a moribund toothless ape, with great sores and scabs on its body, and a smell almost as disagreeable as its predecessor. Well, said the fisherman, I could tidy up this beast, and sell him to some street musician. He did not like the prospect. The ape then said to him—If you let me go, and cast again, you will catch my brother. And if you do not listen to his pleas, or make any more casts, he will stay with you and grant you anything you may wish for. There is a snag, of course, there is always a snag, but I am not about to tell you what it is.

'This limited honesty appealed to the fisherman, who disentangled the thin ape without much more ado, and cast again, and the net struggled away with satisfactory violence and it took all his force to bring it to shore. And indeed it contained an ape, a very large, glossy, *gleaming* ape, with, so my friend particularly told me, a most beautiful bottom, a mixture of very bright subtle blue, and a hot rose-colour, suffused with poppy-coloured veins.'

She looked at the sapphire-coloured dark glasses to see if she had done well and their owner nodded tersely.

'So the new ape said that if the fisherman would release him, and cast again, he would draw up a huge treasure, and a palace, and a company of slaves, and never want again. But the fisherman remembered the saying of the thin ape, and said to the new one "I wish for a new house, on the shore of this lake, and I wish for a camel, and I wish for a feast—of moderate proportions—to be ready-cooked in this house."

'And immediately all these things appeared, and the fisherman offered a share of the delicious feast to the two apes, and they accepted.'

'And he was a fisherman who had heard a great many tales in his time, and had an analytic bent, and he thought he understood that the danger of wishes lay in being overweening or hasty. He had no wish to find himself in a world where everything was made of gold and was quite inedible, and he had a strong intuition that the perpetual company of houris or the perpetual imbibing of sherbet and sparkling wine would be curiously wearisome. So he wished quietly for this and that: a shop full of tiles to sell and an assistant who understood them and was honest, a garden full of cedars and fountains, a little house with a servant-girl for his old mother, and finally a little wife, such as his mother would have chosen for him, who was not to be beautiful as the sun and moon but kind and comfortable and loving. And so he went on, very peacefully, creating a world much more like the peaceful world of "happy-ever-after" outside tales than the hectic one of the wishes granted by Grimm's flounder, or even Aladdin's djinn. And no one noticed his good fortune, much, and no one envied him or tried to steal it, since he was so discreet. And if he fell ill, or his little wife fell ill, he wished the illness away, and if someone spoke harshly to him he wished to forget it, and forgot.

'And the snag, you ask?'

'This was the snag. He began to notice, slowly at first, and then quicker and quicker, that every time he made a wish, the great gleaming ape became a little smaller. At first just a centimeter there, and a centimeter here, and then more and more, so that he had to be raised on many cushions to eat his meals, and finally became so small that he sat on a little stool on top of the dining-table and toyed with a tiny junket in a salt-cellar. The thin ape had long gone his way, and returned again from time to time, now looking quite restored, in an ordinary sort of hairy way, with an ordinary blue bottom, nothing to be excited about. And the fisherman said to the thin ape.

'"What will happen if I wish him larger again?"

'"I cannot say," said the ape. "That is to say, I won't say."

'And at night the fisherman heard the two apes talking. The thin one held the shining one in his hand and said sadly.'

'"It goes ill with you, my poor brother. You will vanish away soon; there will be nothing left of you. It is sad to see you in this state."

'"It is my Fate," said the once-larger ape. "It is my Fate to lose power and to diminish. One day I shall be so small, I shall be invisible, and the man will not be able to see me any more to make any more wishes, and there I shall be, a slave-ape the size of a pepper-grain or a grain of sand."

'"We all come to dust," said the thin ape sententiously.

'"But not with this terrible speed," said the wishing-ape. "I do my best, but still I am used and used. It is hard. I wish I were dead but none of my own wishes may be granted. Oh, it is hard, it is hard, it is hard."

'And at this, the fisherman, who was a good man, rose out of his bed and went into the room where the two apes were talking, and said,

'"I could not help hearing you and my heart is wrung for you. What can I do, O apes, to help you?"

'And they looked at him sullenly and would not answer.

'"I wish," said the fisherman then, "that you would take the next wish, if that is possible, and wish for your heart's desire."

'And then he waited to see what would happen.

'And both apes vanished as if they had never been.

'But the house, the wife, and the prosperous business did not vanish. And the fisherman continued to live as well as he could—though subject now to ordinary human ailments with the rest of us—until the day he died.'

'In fairy-tales,' said Gillian, 'those wishes that are granted and are not malign, or twisted towards destruction, tend to lead to a condition of beautiful stasis, more like a work of art than the drama of Fate. It is as though the fortunate had stepped off the hard road into an unchanging landscape where it is always spring and no winds blow. Aladdin's genie gives him a beautiful palace, and as long as this palace is subject to Fate, various magicians move it violently around the landscape, build it up and cause it to vanish. But at the end, it goes into stasis: into the pseudo-eternity of happy-ever-after. When we imagine happy-ever-after we imagine works of art:

a family photograph on a sunny day, a Gainsborough lady and her children in an English meadow under a tree, an enchanted castle in a snowstorm of feathers in a glass dome. It was Oscar Wilde's genius to make the human being and the work of art change places. Dorian Gray smiles unchangingly in his eternal youth and his portrait undergoes his Fate, which is a terrible one, a fate of accelerating deterioration. The tale of Dorian Gray and also Balzac's tale of *La Peau de Chagrin*, the diminishing piece of wild-ass's skin that for a time keeps Fate at bay, are related to other tales of the desire for eternal youth. Indeed we have methods now of granting a kind of false stasis, we have prostheses and growth hormone, we have plastic surgery and implanted hair, we can make humans into works of some kind of art or artifice. The grim and gallant fixed stares of Joan Collins and Barbara Cartland are icons of our wish for this kind of eternity.

'The tale of the apes, I think, relates to the observations of Sigmund Freud on the goal of all life. Freud was, whatever else he was, the great student of our desire, our will to live happily ever after. He studied our wishes, our fulfillment of our wishes, in the narrative of our dreams. He believed we rearranged our stories in our dream-life to give ourselves happy endings, each according to his or her secret needs. (He claimed not to know what women really wanted, and this ignorance colours and changes his stories). Then, in the repeated death-dreams of the soldiers of the First World War he discovered a narrative that contradicted this desire for happiness, for wish-fulfillment. He discovered, he thought, a desire for annihilation. He rethought the whole history of organic life under the sun, and came to the conclusion that what he called the 'organic instincts' were essentially *conservative* — that they reacted to stimuli by adapting in order to preserve, as far as possible, their original state. "It would be in contradiction to the conservative nature of the instincts," said Freud, "if the goal of life were a state of things which had never been attained." No, he said, what we desire must necessarily be an *old* state of things. Organisms strive, circuitously, to return to the inorganic — the dust, the stone, the earth — from which they came. *"The aim of all life is death,"* said Freud, telling his creation story in which the creation strives to return to the state before life was breathed into it, in which the shrinking of the peau de chagrin, the diminishing of the ape, is not the terrible concomitant of the life-force, but its secret desire.'

This was not all she said, but this was the second point at which she caught a flash of the sapphire glasses.

There were many questions, and Gillian's paper was judged a success, if somewhat confused.

Back in her hotel bedroom that night she confronted the djinn.

'You made my paper incoherent,' she said. 'It was a paper about fate and death and desire, and you introduced the freedom of wishing-apes.'

'I do not see what is incoherent.' said the djinn. 'Entropy rules us all. Power gets less, whether it derives from the magic arts or is made by nerves and muscle.'

Gillian said, 'I am ready now to make my third wish.'

'I am all ears,' said the djinn, momentarily expanding those organs to the size of elephants' ears. 'Do not look doleful, Djil-yan, it may not happen.'

'And where did you learn that catch-phrase? Never mind. I shall almost believe you are trying to prevent my wish.'

'No, no. I am your slave.'

'I wish,' said Gillian, 'I wish you could have whatever you wish for — that this last wish may be your wish.'

And she waited for the sound of thunder, or worse, the silence of absence. But what she heard was the sound of breaking glass. And she saw her bottle, the nightingale's-eye bottle, which stood on a glass sheet on the dressing-table, dissolve like tears, not into sharp splinters, but into a conical heap of tiny cobalt blue glass marbles, each with a white spiral coiled inside it.

'Thank you,' said the djinn.

'Will you go?' asked the narratologist.

'Soon,' said the djinn. 'Not now, not immediately. You wished also, remember, that I would love you, and so I do. I shall give you something to remember me by — until I return — which, from time to time, I shall do —'

'If you remember to return in my life-time,' said Gillian Perholt.

'If I do,' said the djinn, whose body now seemed to be clothed in a garment of liquid blue flame.

That night he made love to her, so beautifully that she wondered simultaneously how she could ever have let him go, and how she could ever have dared to keep such a being in Primrose Hill or in hotel bedrooms in Istanbul or Toronto.

And the next morning he appeared in jeans and a sheepskin jacket, and said they were going out together, to find a gift. This time his hair — still fairly improbably — was a mass of dreadlocks, and his skin inclined to the Ethiopian.

In a small shop, in a side-street, he showed her the most beautiful collection of modern weights she had ever seen. It is a modern Canadian art; they have artists who can trap a meshed and rolling geometrical sea, only visible at certain angles, and when visible glitters transparently with a rainbow of particles dusted with gold; they have artists who can enclose a red and blue flame forever in a cool glass sphere, or a dizzy cone of cobalt and emerald, reaching to infinity and meeting its own reflection. Glass is made of dust, of silica, of the sand of the desert, melted in a fiery furnace and blown into its solid form by human breath. It is fire and ice, it is liquid and solid, it is there and not there.

The djinn put into Dr Perholt's hands a huge, slightly domed sphere inside which were suspended like commas, like fishing-hooks, like fireworks, like sleeping embryos, like spurts of coloured smoke, like uncurling serpents, a host of coloured ribbons of glass amongst a host of breathed bubbles. They were all colours — gold and yellow, bright blue and dark blue, a delectable clear pink, a crimson, a velvet green, a whole host of busy movement. 'Like rushing seed,' said the djinn poetically. 'Full of forever possibilities. And impossibilities, of course. It is a work of art, a great work of craft, it is a joyful thing, you like it?'

'Oh yes,' said Dr Perholt. 'I have never seen so many colours in one.'

'It is called "The Dance of the Elements",' said the djinn, 'I think that it is not your sort of title, but it suits it, I think. No?'

'Yes,' said Dr Perholt, who was sorrowful and yet full of a sense of things being as they should be.

The djinn watched the wrapping of the weight in shocking-pink tissue, and paid for it with a rainbow-coloured credit card with a hologram of the Venus de Milo, which caused an almost excessive fizzing amongst the terminals in the card machine. On the pavement he said,

'Good-bye. For the present.'

'"Now to the elements,"' said Dr Perholt, '"Be free and fare thou well."'

She had thought of saying that some day, ever since she had first seen his monstrous foot from her bathroom door. She stood here, holding her glass weight. And the djinn kissed her hand, and vanished towards Lake Superior like a huge cloud of bees, leaving behind on the pavement a sheepskin jacket that shrank slowly, to childsize, to doll size, to matchbox size, to a few fizzing atoms, and was gone. He left also a moving heap of dreadlocks, like some strange hedgehog, which stirred a little, ran along a few feet, and vanished down a drain.

And did she ever see him again, you may ask? Or that may not be the question uppermost in your mind, but it is the only one to which you get an answer.

Two years ago, still looking thirty-five and comfortable, she was walking along Madison Avenue in New York, during a stop on the way to a narratological gathering in British Columbia, when she saw a shop window full of paperweights. These were not the work of artists like the Toronto artists who play with pure colour and texture, ribbons and threads and veils, stains and illusory movement. These were pure, old-fashioned, skilful representations: millefiori, lattice work, crowns, canes, containing roses and violets, lizards and butterflies. Dr Perholt went in, her eyes gleaming like the glass, and there in the dark shop were two elderly and charming men, happy men in a cavern bright with jewels, who for half an hour and with exquisite patience fetched out for Dr Perholt sphere after sphere from the glass shelves in which they were reflected, and admired with her basket-work of fine white containing cornflower-blue posies, multi-coloured cushions of geometric flowers, lovely as Paradise must have been in its glistening newness, bright with a brightness that would never come out into the dull air from its brilliant element.

Oh *glass*, said Dr Perholt to the two gentlemen, it is not possible, it is only a solid metaphor, it is a medium for seeing and a thing seen at once. It is what art is, said Dr Perholt to the two men, as they moved the balls of light, red, blue, green, on the visible and the invisible shelves.

'I like the geometrically patterned flowers best,' said Dr Perholt. 'More than the ones that aim at realism, at looking real, don't you agree?'

'On the whole,' said one of the two. 'On the whole, the whole effect is better with the patterning, with the geometry of the glass and the geometry of the canes. But have you seen these? These are American.'

And he gave her a weight in which a small snake lay curled on a watery surface of floating duckweed — a snake with a glass thread of a flickering tongue and an almost microscopic red-brown eye in its watchful but relaxed olive head. And he gave her a weight in which, in the solidity of the glass as though it were the deep water of a well, floated a flower, a flower with a rosy lip and a white hood, a green stem, long leaves trailing in the water, and a root specked and stained with its brown juices and the earth it had come from, a root trailing fine hairroots and threads and tendrils into the glassy medium. It was perfect because the illusion was near-perfect, and the attention to the living original had been so perfect that the undying artificial flower also seemed perfect. And Gillian thought of Gilgamesh, and the lost flower, and the snake. Here they were side by side, held in suspension.

She turned the weight over, and put it down, for its price was prohibitive.

She noticed, almost abstractedly, that there was a new dark age-stain on the back of the hand that held the weight. It was a pretty soft dried-leaf colour.

'I wish—' she said to the man behind the glass cage of shelves.

'You would like the flower,' said a voice behind her. 'And the snake with it, why not? I will give them to you.'

And there he was behind her, this time in a dark overcoat and a white scarf, with a rather large wide-brimmed black velvet hat, and the sapphire glasses.

'What a nice surprise to see you again, sir,' said the shop-owner, holding out his hand for the rainbow credit card with the Venus de Milo. 'Always unexpected, always welcome, most welcome.'

And Dr Perholt walked out into Madison Avenue with a gold-dark man and two weights, a snake and a flower. There are things in the earth, things made with hands and beings not made with hands that live a life different from ours, that live longer than we do, and cross our lives in stories, in dreams, at certain times when we are floating redundant. And Gillian Perholt was happy, for she had moved back into their world, or at least had access to it, as she had had as a child. She said to the djinn,

'Will you stay?'

And he said, 'No. But I shall probably return again.'

And she said, 'If you remember to return in my life-time.'

'If I do,' said the djinn.

David Wagoner

Love Still Has Something of the Sea

> *A few months before the outbreak*
> *of the Second World War, I took*
> *a walk with Thomas Mann. . . .*
> — Aldous Huxley
> Tomorrow and Tomorrow and Tomorrow

Aldous Huxley and Thomas Mann by the light
Gold after-light of a California sunset,
Strolled with their wives on a deserted beach
And spoke of Shakespeare, music, and Modern Love:
Was the Bitter Barren Woman of today
Even less knowable than the Fertile Goddess?

They mused there on the edge of America
Till their wives, who had drifted off, called their attention
To the outgoing tide and a phenomenon
In the sandy shallows: something like gray seaworms
Afloat or stranded, hundreds of thousands struggling
To mate or migrate beyond the Western World.

On closer look, they saw those quondam creatures,
Who made their way by means of the mass transport
Provided with a flush of embarrassment
By the City of the Angels and its outfall,
Were condoms joining the old tolerant sea.
They turned aside and talked about something else.

Don Bogen

Among Appliances

They are so busy and self-involved as I hear them muttering
    in the distance
that they strike me sometimes as sheer marvels:
the dishwasher filling its huge blue gullet—a cluck from the
    timer,
and spindly wings spew out scalding water in the dark—
or its basement cousin chugging yet another load through the
    changes,
whirling, rocking, belching gray suds and lint into the concrete
    washtubs.

Though I can never keep track of them all, I'm charmed by
    the cycles:
their varied lengths, sudden shifts and rigorous sense of time,
the control knob simple as a windup clock, language of click
    and whir,
mysterious pauses while something is draining or filling,
or silence even while something is gathering strength.
There's a music in these risings and fallings—odd rest,
    crescendo, diminuendo—
the soothing predictable pattern of potential and release.

I am no technophile, not all machines give this comfort.
Our vacuum cleaner is a ball and chain that growls as you try
    to make it work,
I have never wanted a yard big enough to need a power mower,
and lamps I have always thought of as most useful when
    unnoticed
like a perfectly attendant butler wearing a small hat.

I like the ones that have their own intricate lives —
not too private or powerful, like the bank machine that calls
    you by name and suddenly gulps your card,
nothing fussy or intimidating, nothing imitating a person,
but the stolid non-interactive types that work for years,
    supporting the whole household:
the refrigerator shuddering to keep cold then deciding — who
    knows when? — to defrost itself,
the furnace drumming up flames, beating a hot breeze through
    the frilly cast-iron vents,
the dryer tumbling socks and lingerie in a blurred luxurious
    jumble.
All these big boxes with their timers and thermostats,
defining the stages of their tasks, devouring what I feed them,
pulling the current up through the basement meter.

It is shameful but sometimes I want them all on.
I set the controls and leave, like an absent deist god,
but am also content to work among them with a broom or
    sponge for a time,
a robot master tidying up around laborious metal lives.

Two Poems by Gardner McFall

The Encounter

The burnt-red fox darts in front
of the car's path late at night,
and I'd like to call this an encounter,

though all I really catch is its pointed
tail tip, white in the headlights.
The nearly full moon glows

like an unexpected touch,
or only the thought hovering
between what if and why not.

I'd like to say the fox came back
and danced its fox dance just for me,
and, after I stopped the car and got out,

it put its fox face in my hand, trusting
I would not startle or offend,
but understand the risk it had taken,

moving out of the shadows, crossing
the grass and gravel between us.
Not that I would become fox or it human.

It is never a question of that,
but I would honor the difference,
the strange gift abandon brings.

Lament for Vijećnica

When the National Library burned for three days in August, the town was choked with snow. Those days I could not find a single pencil in the house, and even when I grabbed one it had no lead. Even the erasers left a black trace. Sadly my homeland burned. Liberated from their bodies, heroes of novels wandered around town mixing with the passersby and with the souls of dead warriors. I saw Werther sitting on the collapsed graveyard wall, and Quasimodo on the minarets; for days Raskolnikov and Meursault were whispering something in the cellar, Gavroche walked by dressed in a camouflage uniform, and Yossarian was already trading with the enemy. Not to mention young Sawyer, who threw himself into the river from Prince's Bridge for pocket money.

For three days I lived in the spectral town with a terrible suspicion that there were fewer and fewer people alive, and that the shells were falling only on my account. I locked myself in the house and leafed through tourist guides. I went out on the very day the radio announced that people had removed ten tons of coal from the Library cellar. And my pencil got its lead back.

The Bridge

Just before the war, a foreign film crew burst into Ruža's village and turned the country idyll into chaos: prefabricated shacks appeared, houses were quickly painted and skilled foreigners built a bridge in half a day under the eyes of the shamefaced local craftsmen. Through camera lenses, greedy villagers became a part of the history of the village, throwing themselves into a Western screenplay as dead Indians. They fell out of trees pierced by arrows, rolled down the steep cliffs riddled by Winchester bullets, threw themselves into the shallow river trying to escape from the cowboy leader; and at night they would heal their bruises of inexperience with Bosnian brandy and herbs. One evening the skilled workers took apart the set and disappeared into the night, leaving the village with nothing but the bridge which nobody crossed for a long time.

I watch Ruža writing a letter to her brother across the river down which real corpses float like shadows. Leaning over the letter, she resembles the bridge and the collapsed wall of the painted house, a film set. And I see her concealing the scar on her neck, the scar left there long ago by an extra who had handled his bow and arrow carelessly.

— translated from the Bosnian
by Amela Simic

Nin Andrews

The Book of Lies

It's true. I lied. Isn't that how
we stay alive? Dr. Metz in Old Testament
101 said Moses parted the reeds on a lake,
not the Red Sea. The orgasm was a fake
like the waves of applause and the wingbeats
of one hundred birds lifting from our hearts.
Give me a break. You call this love?
Outside the sky is white, not blue, and the only
person who calls me is from Purple Heart.
Have you any spare parts to give away? I do,
I do. The sign says cook needed, not cock
wanted. And when I said I love you, I meant
get lost, Asshole. The man with red hair
and green eyes cleaned me out of orgasms long ago,
and silk underpants too. He left for Chattanooga
in a red Camaro with six boxes of All Bran
and a blond bimbo so gorgeous she made me cry.
The archangels never blew their trumpets.
Silence is the music of the spheres and
The messiah's dark scream. The witch ate Hansel
and Gretel too. I live in a chocolate house
in Berlin. The red-haired man was never here.
When they tore down the wall, he left
with a suitcase full of bricks and my twin.
Her name was Faith. I never knew his.

Terese Svoboda

A Cure for Hiccups

Every time the door opens,
the mother bird flies off. What's left
     slumps and pulses. I determine
          it will live,
"house finch" in the book,
practiced at distraction, the mother
     always laying on lintels,
          the others, unhatched,
          just bad luck. "Mrs. Micawber

was never seen without one or the other
taking nourishment" wrote Dickens. Twins, nursing.
     And if the bird can't deliver extra lunches?
          I have only one door.

     Perhaps the other eggs hold in
     the mother's heat. I turn off
     the porchlight each dawn
to watch the daylilies open to their one day,
     and the baby, ending sleep
     with hiccups.
          I try to stare him into being, just as,
     in Emergency, they gave me
          those small shoes
               to look at.

Three Poems by Lise Goett

1933

> Dying's the best
> Of all the arts men learn in a dead place.
> —James Wright

Sometimes, on evenings like this, my mother will speak of
    Tom Scott,
going down to a place inside her beyond the river's high reach,
to a place where grief has no pallbearer except the river;
and I know she is thinking of that threadbare year of Depres-
    sion, the year
my mother was released from the egregious care of the mother
superior, smiling for a portrait of the student body

in a coat purchased with the sale of a calf's stiffened body.
Or was it the color of her hair that pulled Tom Scott
toward her, the fox-collared coat being my grandmother's
idea of what a perfect lady of fashion should wear, past reach
of a farm girl's dreams—or anyone's—that year
in Kentucky? As she walked on the banks of the Ohio, I think
    the river

must have been my mother's only true friend, the river-
slow current, its tracery, feeding my mother's love-starved
    body
as she waited for something to comfort her face, and her
    freshman year
beau, a writer of talent, a man named Tom Scott,
cut rushes on prayerful diagonals along the river's high reach—
a bouquet for the girl who suggested that my mother

be segregated from those who did not work. My mother,
the poorest girl in her sorority, waitressed at the river
café, working more shifts as she struggled to reach
the nickel she needed for graph paper, the twenty for Kotex,
 her body
a calendar, bleeding her, despite her good Scot
thrift, into greater and greater debt. The year

was 1933, what was to be their bridal year,
the year Tom Scott killed himself, cradling a mother-
of-pearl revolver, with two shots to the left ventricle, after
 Scott
lost his life savings on a horse named River-
land Sally in the Derby; and men said, Please God, no more
 bodies
in Lexington, Kentucky, where the stable boys still reach

to receive the reins of lost gentry as if reaching could save them. In that damnable year,
who knows if she ever embraced Tom Scott's body
in the deep and silent green. My mother's
voice goes slack, the woof of her life shining up like a river
through that threadbare year and the death of Tom Scott.

And I wish I could reach into the past and hand my mother
that nickel for graph paper. Every year, the Ohio River
rises, claiming the life of another Tom Scott.

After Twenty Years of Marriage

I saw it in a book on diseases of the mouth,
the smile that is heaven, the smile I cannot reach:
the youth known only by some gesture in the street
but held and loved in memory like honeyed plums
dripping through the slats back home—
the way the body does not want to separate from coitus
even though the love has died and failed us.
And so taking for a season these summer rooms,
we couched ourselves in the satin sheen of marble walks,
the tristesse of linen trousers, of peacocks
garnishing the lawns, while our friend
to make us see and feel the world stripped of its skin
described the paddocks where he sodomized his father's grooms
among the smell of thoroughbreds and leather.
We drank and lay like corpses in our summer suits
and rationed love like gasoline in wartime
while we talked of the soporific ignorance of America.
And after dinner coffee, and after coffee chocolates,
the soul rapt in a soulless human argument
making the afternoon sway
like the slow turning of the world upon its axis
as we sat and watched the shadows lengthen
from our Adirondack chairs—
that marriage of bodily fluids, Europe, death
which sunset sometimes betokens.
The sun, descending upon its worried tether,
rendered up its climax; and the sky
seemed more poignant for being faint
(like attenuated cries from distant hotel rooms)
in the afterglow of dusk. So Goya said:
Let us make love then under the roiling stars
even as the acids fade this corroded city.
This star, long burnt out, in whose light we make our truce,
like some light coming from the dead,
touches—one might even say blesses—
our oceangoing scow as it makes its difficult passage,
violet bleeding into dusk.

Conversion

All day, we loitered at the throat of the penny arcade
to hear how the fisherman's cast had taken the eye of Vilas
Puchomsky, a pain radiating down to the sexual curve.
Girls who had been prom queens, corsages of gallica roses
with crowning pink buds pinned to our blouses, teetered
on lives of uncloistered desire to hear how the hook
entered the pulp, tearing the flesh like a lichee nut
with the force of a swift and ready conversion.

At dusk, the fly-speckled marquee flickered with inconstant
    love
and our boys suckled long-necked colas and pilsners,
and we asked them to hug us all the tighter while the nuns
    sang
from the hill, "Le Dieu Qui Nous Aime Bien," for it seemed
that the boy's name had called his fate into the world,
the line cutting through the air like the wings of a hawk,
his face buried in a shirt of bruised muslin.
And later, over the cracked and rutted road home, his story
came to us like a voice speaking from behind a steel grate,
a blue light hovering above the lake's teal horizon.

One day at school, he removed his eye and touched us,
tiered like the blessed and the damned in the bleachers
behind the parochial school, the glass eye sucking our arms
where lips might have gone, a touch like benediction —
a taste of terror with some pleasure in it, a pleasure
already sown with remorse and the seeds of turning away.

But at night, we prayed to a god with a foraging heart,
a god with a silvering face, rippling his luminous skin—
the line gilt along the line's trajectory, the plummet like shot—
thinking how grace must enter the body like this
as we slipped out under the nameless bowl of stars
to feel the hunger of our own darkness:
the sweep and whisper of the line,
the suck and gape of the eyeless socket,
the god who reels us in.

Marc Woodworth

Adrian Leverkühn's Song for the Clearwings

The Empire's train rolls west from Pressburg's heights;
I fall from sleep to sleep, dreaming of clearwings,
thousands, flying over father's meadows,

their movement legato — a shimmer over staffs
of sweet grass, sweeter than any music
I could make now, past what's pure, past all belief

in unadulterated signs of love,
those signs which father found in everything
God made — a butterfly, the linden grove,

pollen dust, pearling on a mussel-shell . . .
He tried too hard to read the world,
as if the Esmeralda's wing-spots could reveal

Nature's design. He had it wrong.
His brand of faith made him see no more
than beauty where all was deception.

I now know things to be more random and exact —
Last night, my Esmeralda, spoilt hot-house whore,
made me sick with joy between her legs. The act

wasn't for pleasure, or not for pleasure
of the kind I imagine most men go to women for.
Her sickroom had the odor of stale fear —

the unchanged sheets burned from her heat,
a half-dead bunch of feverfew sullied
the water in a blown-glass vase, the street

below her window teemed with Slavs
in a brute darkness cast there by the razed castle
high above the Danube's scrawled bass clef.

The brush of her brown arm a year ago
had sent me reeling from her madam's house.
Since then, I've craved that touch: a slow,

poisonous yearning for defilement.
She told me she was ill—a kind of camouflage
like insects use to put off prey. I spent

myself on her despite the warning—
and there was nothing there to call nature
in her fever-screams, those pitch-black songs

that haunt my dreams of the false order
where we still gather under the linden
singing in round, *Es tönen die Lieder,*

while clearwings, *Hetaera Esmeralda,*
weave pure notes above the chastened grasses
and I know already what I haven't words to say:

There's nothing to hold back the increments
of desire that turn the world to ash,
the world unmade by the one monstrous art,

the one true song I am meant to write
of the raw place where the spirit starves
and the train passes beyond any city's light.

Frederick Tibbetts

Dissonant Interval

For noble persons, madness seems to have been
A matter of custom—in the old romances.
Alas! I shall be mad, they say, and at once

They are: putting off sanity like a mantle,
To go naked into the hazards of winter.
When they lie on the ground, the beasts and fowls

Come by and are afraid. The reader, too:
Wondering if sense could be the subject
Of some more fearsome lord within the will.

Sir Orfeo consents to live in the wild,
Haunted near morning by the king and his rout
Who ride through with dim cry and blowing.

And the lay consoles us only with the device
Whereby someone may come to his senses
The way he comes upon a ring, a key, a favor—

Then, says the hymn, let the strings resound
In wonder at his doings. What is
Called a dissonance isn't always heard as such.

Take the *ut* and *fa* of a fourth: this was
Once a concord. When? —Pick out some fourths
In parallel, and you may hear a pardon

For having been so long detained at the contest.
Winter has crept away. The falconer
Has set his charges flying on their errands.

Portraits

Ken Lum

The catalyst for this work happened to have been a moment in Germany in 1993 when I was watching a program on TV which was the American equivalent of "Current Affair." The program was dubbed, so the voices didn't always fit. A young boy was seen riding a bicycle but pointing frantically to somewhere outside the camera frame. He was mouthing words but nothing was audible. There was a sense of drama and anxiety which I found really interesting. I'm interested in how the viewer identifies with the problems presented in the picture.

I like the purity of the two forms—text and photograph. One is completely different from the other. Viewers who are reading the text already create an image in their heads. On the other hand, the picture on the other side is received in text as well—a text is conjured up while looking at the picture. They imagine to themselves that the picture is about this thing or another. They identify with the picture through text and language. There is always a disjunction between the text which you conjure up and the image which you conjure up, and the actual image and text that is there. Because it isn't fixed, it creates this agitated resonating moment for all kinds of possible readings, and that's what I'm after.

It isn't interesting to depict someone just having a drink of coffee and not thinking about anything, but then if we were to depict the same guy drinking coffee and then added text, we could see that he's thinking about the fact that he's not doing well at work. Only then does it become a much more interesting image. I go to great lengths to stage these events. Why not just take a snapshot? Because I can't control it. I don't want a snapshot. If you can't control it, the reading of the work is not going to be directed. In that sense, I'm quite a conservative artist. —K.L.

Hum hum hummm
hum hummmm
Hum hummmm
hum hum hummm
Hum hum hummm
hum hummmm
Hum hummmm
hum hum hummm

Hello
How are you?
I am fine
My name is Fung
Hello
How are you?
I am fine
My name is Fung

What am I
doing here?
What am I
doing?
How'd I get
into this?
What am I
doing here?

Oh for crying
out loud!
where is he?!
Where is he?!
Where is that kid
of mine?!
Oh for crying
out loud!

Je
Je suis
Je suis Française
Je suis Americaine
Je suis Anglaise
Je suis Canadienne
Je
Je suis

give headaches!"

Uproarious laughter.

"Well, on that note we say thank you to Mr Osodi for a most entertaining evening."

13

One of the ~~very~~ many questions ~~which~~ (he had to field) ~~answered~~ in the course of ~~the~~ his lecture, ~~evening~~ some some briefly and some (spasmodic) at ~~great~~ length, ~~one had to~~ ~~do with~~ a ~~premium~~ ~~which~~ ~~comes~~ concerned (and ~~they~~) that the Central Bank of Kangan was ~~planning~~ completing plans to ~~print~~ the President's image on the nation's currency. ~~Was it true & if so~~ What did Mr Osodi think about ~~it~~ such an eventuality. Yes I heard of it like everybody else.

"My position is simple. ~~Fortunately I can~~ All I can say is I hope the rumour is unfounded. speak as a private citizen now. Any serious President foolish enough to lay ~~put~~ his head on a coin ~~should be~~ ~~I would be inclined~~ if people to take it off ~~the head~~ ~~should not be surprised~~ if he loses it, I mean the head."

This statement which was roundly applauded in the auditorium was to reverberate louder still through the country ~~beginning~~ from the very next morning when the National Gazette came out brandishing in the heaviest possible type the following headline: EX-EDITOR ADVOCATES REGICIDE!

A manuscript page from Chinua Achebe's *Anthills of the Savannah*.

Chinua Achebe

The Art of Fiction CXXXVIV

Chinua Achebe was born in Eastern Nigeria in 1930. He went to the local public schools and was among the first students to graduate from the University of Ibadan. After graduation, he worked for the Nigerian Broadcasting Corporation as a radio producer and Director of External Broadcasting, and it was during this period that he began his writing career.

He is the author, co-author, or editor of some seventeen books, among them five novels: Things Fall Apart, *1958;* No Longer at Ease, *1960;* Arrow of God, *1964;* A Man of the People, *1966; and* Anthills of the Savannah, *1987. He is the editor*

of several anthologies, including the essay collections Morning
Yet on Creation Day and Hopes and Impediments, and the
collection of poetry Beware Soul Brother. He is the editor of
the magazine, Okike, and founding editor of the Heinemann
series on African literature, a list which now has more than
three hundred titles. He is often called the father of modern
African literature. He is the recipient, at last count, of some
twenty-five honorary doctorates from universities throughout
the world and is currently the Charles P. Stevenson Jr. Professor
of English at Bard College.

The interview took place on two very different occasions.
The first meeting was before a live audience at the Unterberg
Poetry Center of the Ninety-second Street Y on a bitterly cold
and rainy January evening; the weather made the sidewalks
and roads treacherous. We were all the more surprised at the
very large and enthusiastic audience. The theater was almost
packed. It was Martin Luther King Jr.'s birthday; Achebe paid
gracious tribute to him and then answered questions from the
interviewer and audience. The interviewer and Achebe sat on
a stage with a table and a bouquet of flowers between them.
Achebe was at ease and captured the audience with stories of
his childhood and youth.

The second session took place on an early fall day at Achebe's
house on the beautiful grounds where he lives in upstate New
York. He answered the door in his wheelchair and graciously
ushered his guest through his large, neat living room to his
study, a long, narrow room lined with many books on history,
religion and literature. There is a small slightly cluttered desk
where he writes.

Achebe favors traditional Nigerian clothes and reminds one
more of the priest in Arrow of God than Okonkwo in Things
Fall Apart. His appearance is peaceful and his eyes wise. His
demeanor is modest, but when he begins to talk about literature and Nigeria, he is transformed. His eyes light up; he is
an assured, elegant and witty story teller.

The year 1990 marked Achebe's sixtieth birthday. His colleagues at the University of Nigeria at Nsukka, where he is a
professor of English and chairman emeritus of the department,

sponsored an international conference entitled Eagle on Iroko in his honor. Participants came from around the world to appraise the significance of his work for African and world literature. The conference opened on the day Nelson Mandela was liberated from prison, and the day was declared a national holiday. There was a festive mood during the week-long activities of scholarly papers, traditional drama, dancing and banquets. The iroko is the tallest tree in that part of Africa and the eagle soars to its height.

Scarcely a month later, while on his way to the airport in Lagos to resume a teaching post at Dartmouth, Achebe was severely injured in a car accident. He was flown to a London hospital where he underwent surgery and spent many months in painful recuperation. Although confined to a wheelchair, he has made a remarkable recovery in the past three years and, to the surprise of his family and many friends throughout the world, is beginning to look and sound like his old self.

INTERVIEWER

Would you tell us something about the Achebe family and growing up in an Igbo village, your early education, and whether there was anything there that pointed you that early in the direction of writing.

CHINUA ACHEBE

I think the thing that clearly pointed me there was my interest in stories. Not necessarily *writing* stories, because at that point, writing stories was not really viable. So you didn't think of it. But I knew I loved stories, stories told in our home, first by my mother, then by my elder sister — such as the story of the tortoise — whatever scraps of stories I could gather from conversations, just from hanging around, sitting around when my father had visitors. When I began going to school, I loved the stories I read. They were different, but I loved them too. My parents were early converts to Christianity in my part of Nigeria. They were not just converts; my father was an evangelist, a religious teacher. He and my mother traveled for thirty-five years to different parts of Igboland, spreading the gospel. I was the fifth of their six children. By the time I was growing up, my father had retired, and had returned with his family to his ancestral village.

When I began going to school and learned to read, I encountered stories of other people and other lands. In one of my essays, I remember the kind of things that fascinated me. Weird things, even, about a wizard who lived in Africa and went to China to find a lamp . . . fascinating to me because they were about things remote, and almost ethereal.

Then I grew older and began to read about adventures in which I didn't know that I was supposed to be on the side of those savages who were encountered by the good white man. I instinctively took sides with the white people. They were fine! They were excellent. They were intelligent. The others were not . . . they were stupid and ugly. That was the way I was introduced to the danger of not having your own stories. There is that great proverb, that until the lions have their own historians, the history of the hunt will always glorify the hunter. That did not come to me until much later. Once I realized that, I had to be a writer. I had to be that historian. It's not one man's job. It's not one person's job. But it is something we have to do, so that the story of the hunt will also reflect the agony, the travail, the bravery, even, of the lions.

INTERVIEWER

You were among the first graduates of the great University of Ibadan. What was it like in the early years of that university, and what did you study there? Has it stuck with you in your writing?

ACHEBE

Ibadan was, in retrospect, a great institution. In a way, it revealed the paradox of the colonial situation, because this university college was founded towards the end of British colonial rule in Nigeria. If they did any good things, Ibadan was

one of them. It began as a college of London University, because under the British, you don't rush into doing any of
those things like universities just like that. You start off as an
appendage of somebody else. You go through a period of
tutelage. We were the University College of Ibadan of London.
So I took a degree from London University. That was the way
it was organized in those days. One of the signs of independence, when it came, was for Ibadan to become a full-fledged
university.

I began with science, then English, history and religion. I
found these subjects exciting and very useful. Studying religion was new to me and interesting because it wasn't only
Christian theology; we also studied West African religions.
My teacher there, Dr. Parrinder, now an emeritus professor
of London University, was a pioneer in the area. He had done
extensive research in West Africa, in Dahomey. For the first
time, I was able to see the systems—including my own—
compared and placed side by side, which was really exciting.
I also encountered a professor, James Welch, in that department, an extraordinary man, who had been chaplain to King
George VI, chaplain to the BBC, and all kinds of high powered
things before he came to us. He was a very eloquent preacher.
On one occasion, he said to me, "We may not be able to teach
you what you need, or what you want. We can only teach
you what we know." I thought that was wonderful. That was
really the best education I had. I didn't learn anything there
that I really needed, except this kind of attitude. I have had
to go out on my own. The English department was a very
good example of what I mean. The people there would have
laughed at the idea that any of us would become a writer. That
didn't really cross their minds. I remember on one occasion a
departmental prize was offered. They put up a notice: Write
a short story over the long vacation for the departmental prize.
I'd never written a short story before, but when I got home,
I thought, Well, why not. So I wrote one and submitted it.
Months passed; then finally one day there was a notice on the
board announcing the result. It said that no prize was awarded
because no entry was up to the standard. They named me,

said that my story deserved mention. Ibadan in those days
was not a dance you danced with snuff in one palm. It was
a dance you danced with all your body. So when Ibadan said
you deserved mention, that was very high praise.

I went to the lecturer who had organized the prize and said,
"You said my story wasn't really good enough, but it was
interesting. Now what was wrong with it?" She said, "Well,
it's the form. It's the wrong form." So I said, "Ah. Can you
tell me about this?" She said, "Yes, but not now. I'm going
to play tennis; we'll talk about it. Remind me later, and I'll
tell you." This went on for a whole term. Every day when I
saw her, I'd say, "Can we talk about form?" She'd say, "No,
not now. We'll talk about it later." Then at the very end she
saw me and said, "You know, I looked at your story again,
and actually there's nothing wrong with it." So that was it!
That was all I learned from the English department about
writing short stories. You really have to go out on your own
and do it.

INTERVIEWER

When you finished university, one of the first careers you
embarked upon was broadcasting with the Nigerian Broadcasting Corporation.

ACHEBE

I got into it through the intervention of Professor Welch.
He had tried to get me a scholarship to Trinity College, Cam-
bridge, and it didn't work out. So the next thing was the
broadcasting department, which was newly started in Nigeria,
with a lot of BBC people. So that's how I got into it. It wasn't
because I was thinking of broadcasting. I really had no idea
what I was going to do when I left college. I'm amazed when
I think about students today. They know from day one what
they are going to be. We didn't. We just coasted. We just
knew that things would work out. Fortunately, things *did*
work out. There were not too many of us. You couldn't do
that today and survive. So I got into broadcasting and then
discovered that the section of it where I worked, the spoken

word department, the Talks department, as it's called, was
really congenial. It was just the thing I wanted. You edited
scripts. People's speeches. Then short stories. I really got into
editing and commissioning short stories. Things were happening very fast in our newly independent country, and I was
soon promoted out of this excitement into management.

INTERVIEWER

The titles of your first two books — *Things Fall Apart* and *No
Longer at Ease* — are from modern Irish and American poets.
Other black writers — I'm thinking particularly of Paule Marshall — borrow from Yeats. I wonder if Yeats and Eliot are
among your favorite poets.

ACHEBE

They were. Actually, I wouldn't make too much of that. I
was showing off more than anything else. As I told you, I
took a general degree, with English as part of it, and you had
to show some evidence of that. But I liked Yeats! That wild
Irishman. I really loved his love of language, his flow. His
chaotic ideas seemed to me just the right thing for a poet.
Passion! He was always on the right side. He may be wrong-
headed, but his heart was always on the right side. He wrote
beautiful poetry. It had the same kind of magic about it that
I mentioned the wizard had for me. I used to make up lines
with anything that came into my head, anything that sounded
interesting. So Yeats was that kind of person for me. It was only
later I discovered his theory of circles or cycles of civilization. I
wasn't thinking of that at all when it came time to find a title.
That phrase "things fall apart" seemed to me just right and
appropriate.

T.S. Eliot was quite different. I had to study him at Ibadan.
He had a kind of priestly erudition — eloquence, but of a different
kind. Scholarly to a fault. But I think the poem from which
I took the title of *No Longer at Ease*, the one about the three
magi, is one of the great poems in the English language. These
people who went and then came back to their countries were

"no longer at ease" . . . I think that that is great—the use of simple language, even when things talked about are profound, very moving, very poignant. So that's really all there is to it. But you'll notice that after those first two titles, I didn't do that anymore.

INTERVIEWER

I once heard your English publisher, Alan Hill, talk about how you sent the manuscript of *Things Fall Apart* to him.

ACHEBE

That was a long story. The first part of it was how the manuscript was nearly lost. In 1957 I was given a scholarship to go to London and study for some months at the BBC. I had a draft of *Things Fall Apart* with me, so I took it along to finish it. When I got to the BBC, one of my friends—there were two of us from Nigeria—said, "Why don't you show this to Mr. Phelps?" Gilbert Phelps, one of the instructors of the BBC school, was a novelist. I said, "What? No!" This went on for some time. Eventually I was pushed to do it, and I took the manuscript and handed it to Mr. Phelps. He said, "Well . . . all right," the way I would today if anyone brought me a manuscript. He was not really enthusiastic. Why should he be? He took it anyway, very politely. He was the first person, outside of myself, to say, "I think this is interesting." In fact, he felt so strongly that one Saturday he was compelled to look for me and tell me. I had traveled out of London; he found out where I was, phoned the hotel and asked me to call him back. When I was given this message, I was completely floored. I said, maybe he doesn't like it. But then why would he call me if he doesn't like it. So it must be he *likes* it. Anyway, I was very excited. When I got back to London, he said, "This is wonderful. Do you want me to show it to my publishers?" I said, "Yes, but not yet," because I had decided that the form wasn't right. Attempting to do a saga of three families, I was covering too much ground in this first draft. So I realized that I needed to do something drastic, really give it more body. So I said to Mr. Phelps, "Okay, I am very grateful, but I'd like to take this back to Nigeria and look at it again." Which is what I did.

When I was in England, I had seen advertisements about typing agencies; I had learned that if you really want to make a good impression, you should have your manuscript well typed. So, foolishly, from Nigeria, I parceled my manuscript—handwritten, by the way, and the only copy in the whole world—wrapped it up and posted it to this typing agency that advertised in the *Spectator*. They wrote back and said, "Thank you for your manuscript. We'll charge thirty-two pounds." That was what they wanted for two copies, and which they had to receive before they started. So I sent thirty-two pounds in British postal order to these people, and then I heard no more. Weeks passed, and months. I wrote and wrote and wrote. No answer. Not a word. I was getting thinner and thinner and thinner. Finally, I was very lucky. My boss at the broadcasting house was going home to London on leave. A very stubborn Englishwoman. I told her about this. She said, "Give me their name and address." When she got to London she went there! She said, "What's this nonsense?" They must have been shocked, because I think their notion was that a manuscript sent from *Africa*—well, there's really nobody to follow it up. The British don't normally behave like that. It's not done, you see. But something from Africa was treated differently. So when this woman, Mrs. Beattie, turned up in their office, and said, "What's going on?" they were confused. They said, "The manuscript was sent but customs returned it." Mrs. Beattie said, "Can I see your dispatch book?" They had no dispatch book. So she said, "Well, send this thing, typed up, back to him in the next week, or otherwise you'll hear about it." So soon after that, I received the typed manuscript of *Things Fall Apart*. One copy, not two. No letter at all to say what happened. My publisher, Alan Hill, rather believed that the thing was simply neglected, left in a corner gathering dust. That's not what happened. These people did not want to return it to me and had no intention of doing so. Anyway, when I got it I sent it back up to Heinemann. They had never seen an African novel. They didn't know what to do with it. Someone told them, "Oh, there's a professor of economics at London School of Economics and Political Science who just came back from those places. He might be able to advise you." Fortunately, Don Macrae was a very literate professor, a wonderful man. I got to know him later. He wrote what they said was the shortest report they ever had on any novel — seven words: *The best first novel since the war.* So that's how I got launched.

INTERVIEWER

Heinemann was also perplexed as to how many copies should be printed . . .

ACHEBE

Oh yes. They printed very, very few. It was a risk. Not something they'd ever done before. They had no idea if anybody would want to read it. It went out of print very quickly. It would have stayed that way if Alan Hill hadn't decided that he was going to gamble even more and launch a paperback edition of this book. Other publishers thought it was mad, that this was crazy. But that was how the African Writers Series came in to existence. In the end, Alan Hill was made a Commander of the British Empire for bringing into existence a body of literature they said was among the biggest developments in British literature of this century. So it was a very small beginning, but it caught fire.

INTERVIEWER

You have said that you wrote *Things Fall Apart* as a response to Joyce Cary's *Mr. Johnson*.

ACHEBE

I wish I hadn't said that.

INTERVIEWER

You made *Mr. Johnson* famous! But your most trenchant essay on the colonial novel is your subsequent essay on Conrad's

Heart of Darkness. I wonder what you think the image of
Africa is today in the western mind.

ACHEBE

I think it's changed a bit. But not very much in its essentials.
When I think of the standing, the importance and the erudition of all these people who see nothing about racism in *Heart
of Darkness*, I'm convinced that we must really be living in
different worlds. Anyway, if you don't like someone's story,
you write your own. If you don't like what somebody says,
you say what it is you don't like. Some people imagine that
what I mean is, Don't read Conrad. Good heavens, no! I *teach*
Conrad. I teach *Heart of Darkness*. I have a course on *Heart
of Darkness* in which what I'm saying is, Look at the way
this man handles Africans. Do you recognize humanity there?
People will tell you he was opposed to imperialism. But it's
not enough to say, "I'm opposed to imperialism." Or, "I'm
opposed to these people — these poor people — being treated
like this." Especially since he goes on straight away to call
them "dogs standing on their hind legs." That kind of thing.
Animal imagery throughout. He didn't see anything wrong
with it. So we must live in different worlds. Until these two
worlds come together we will have a lot of trouble.

INTERVIEWER

Have you ever taught creative writing?

ACHEBE

No.

INTERVIEWER

Why not?

ACHEBE

Well, I don't know how it's done. I mean it. I really don't
know. The only thing I can say for it is that it provides work
for writers. Don't laugh! It's very important. I think it's very

important for writers who need something else to do, especially
in these precarious times. Many writers can't make a living.
So to be able to teach how to write is valuable to them. But
I don't really know about its value to the student. I don't
mean it's useless. But I wouldn't have wanted anyone to teach
me how to write. That's my own taste. I prefer to stumble on
it. I prefer to go on trying all kinds of things, not to be told,
"This is the way it is done." Incidentally, there's a story I like
about a very distinguished writer today, who shall remain
nameless, who had been taught creative writing in his younger
days. The old man who taught him was reflecting about him
one day: "I remember his work was so good that I said to him,
'Don't stop writing, never stop writing.' I wish I'd never told
him that." So I don't know. I teach literature. That's easy for
me. Take someone else's work and talk about it.

INTERVIEWER

Has your work been translated into Igbo? Is it important
for it to be translated into Igbo?

ACHEBE

No, my work has not been translated. There is a problem
with the Igbo language. It suffers from a very serious inheri-
tance, which it received at the beginning of this century from
the Anglican mission. They sent out a missionary by the name
of Dennis. Archdeacon Dennis. He was a scholar. He had this
notion that the Igbo language — which had very many different
dialects — should somehow manufacture a uniform dialect that
would be used in writing to avoid all these different dialects.
Because the missionaries were powerful, what they wanted to
do they did. This became the law. An earlier translation of
the Bible into one of the dialects — an excellent translation,
by the way — was pushed aside, and a new dialect was invented
by Dennis. The way he did it was to invite six people from
six different dialectal areas. They sat round a table and they
took a sentence from the Bible: "In the beginning, God created
. . ." or whatever. "*In*. What is it in your dialect?" And they

would take that. *"The.* Yours? *Beginning.* Yours?" And in this way, around the table, they created what is called Standard Igbo, with which the Bible was translated. The result is incredible. I can speak about it because in my family we read the Bible day and night. I know the Bible very well. But the standard version cannot sing. There's nothing you can do with it to make it sing. It's heavy. It's wooden. It doesn't go anywhere. We've had it now for almost a hundred years so it has established a kind of presence; it has created its own momentum among our own scholars. There are grammarians who now sit over the Igbo language in the way that Dennis did in 1906 and dictate it into Standard Igbo. I think this is a terrible tragedy. I think dialects should be left alone. People should write in whatever dialect they feel they want to write. In the fullness of time, these dialects will sort themselves out. They actually were beginning to do so, because Igbo people have always traveled and met among themselves; they have a way of communicating. But this has not been allowed to happen. Instead the scholars are all over the place. I don't really have any interest in these translations. If someone said, I want to translate your novel into Igbo, I would say, go ahead. But when I write in the Igbo language, I write my own dialect. I write some poetry in that dialect. Maybe someday I will, myself, translate *Things Fall Apart* into the Igbo language. Just to show what I mean, though for me, being bilingual, the novel form seems to go with the English language. Poetry and drama seem to go with the Igbo language.

INTERVIEWER

How much do you think writers should engage themselves in public issues?

ACHEBE

I don't lay down the law for anybody else. But I think writers are not only writers, they are also citizens. They are generally adults. My position is that serious and good art has always existed to help, to serve, humanity. Not to indict. I don't see how art can be called art if its purpose is to frustrate humanity. To make humanity uncomfortable, yes. But intrinsically to be against humanity, that I don't take. This is why I find racism impossible, because this is against humanity. Some people think, Well, what he's saying is we must praise his people." For God's sake! Go and read my books. I don't praise my people. I am their greatest critic. Some people think my little pamphlet, *The Trouble with Nigeria*, went too far. I've got into all kinds of trouble for my writing. Art should be on the side of humanity. I think it was Yevtushenko talking about Rimbaud, the Frenchman who went to Ethiopia and came back with all kinds of diseases. Yevtushenko said of him that a poet cannot become a slave trader. When Rimbaud became a slave trader, he stopped writing poetry. Poetry and slave trading cannot be bedfellows. That's where I stand.

INTERVIEWER

Can you say something about the germination of a work. What comes first? A general idea, a specific situation, a plot, a character?

ACHEBE

It's not the same with every book. Generally, I think I can say that the general idea is the first, followed almost immediately by the major characters. We live in a sea of general ideas, so that's not a novel, since there are so many general ideas. But the moment a particular idea is linked to a character, it's like an engine moves it. Then you have a novel underway. This is particularly so with novels which have distinct and overbearing characters like Ezeulu in *Arrow of God*. In novels like *A Man of the People*, or better still, *No Longer at Ease*, with characters who are not commanding personalities, there I think the general idea plays a stronger part at the initial stage. But once you pass that initial state, there's really no difference between the general idea and the character; each has to work.

INTERVIEWER

What is the place of plot? Do you think of a plot as you go along? Does the plot grow out of the character, or out of the idea?

ACHEBE

Once a novel gets going, and I know it is viable, I don't then worry about plot or themes. These things will come in almost automatically because the characters are now pulling the story. At some point it seems as if you are not as much in command, in control, of events as you thought you were. There are things the story must have or else look incomplete. And these will almost automatically present themselves. When they don't, you are in trouble, and then the novel stops.

INTERVIEWER

Then, is writing easy for you? Or do you find it difficult?

ACHEBE

The honest answer is, it's difficult. But the word *difficult* doesn't really express what I mean. It is like wrestling; you are wrestling with ideas and with the story. There is a lot of energy required. At the same time, it is exciting. So it is both difficult and easy. What you must accept is that your life is not going to be the same while you are writing. I have said in the kind of exaggerated manner of writers and prophets that writing, for me, is like receiving a term of imprisonment: you know that's what you're in for, for whatever time it takes. So it is both pleasurable and difficult.

INTERVIEWER

Do you find a particular time or place that you like to write — a time of day, or a place in your house or your office?

ACHEBE

I have found that I work best when I am at home in Nigeria. But one learns to work in other places. I am most comfortable in the surroundings, the kind of environment about which I am writing. The time of day doesn't matter, really. I am not an early-morning person; I don't like to get out of bed, and so I don't begin writing at 5:00 A.M., though some people, I hear, do. I write once my day has started. And I can work late into the night, also. Generally, I don't attempt to produce a certain number of words a day. The discipline is to work whether you are producing a lot or not, because the day you produce a lot is not necessarily the day you do your best work. So it's trying to do it as regularly as you can without making it—without imposing too rigid a timetable on your self. That would be my ideal.

INTERVIEWER

Do you write with a pen, or a typewriter, or have you been seduced by computers?

ACHEBE

No! No, no—I'm very primitive; I write with a pen. A pen on paper is the ideal way for me. I am not really very comfortable with machines; I never learned to type very well. Whenever I try to do anything on a typewriter, it's like having this machine between me and the words; what comes out is not quite what would come out if I were scribbling. For one thing, I don't like to see mistakes on the typewriter. I like a perfect script. On the typewriter I will sometimes leave a phrase that is not right, not what I want, simply because to change it would be a bit messy. So when I look at all this . . . I am a preindustrial man.

INTERVIEWER

As the author of one of the most famous books in the world, *Things Fall Apart*, does it bother you that your other books are not discussed to the same extent as your first one?

ACHEBE

Well, sometimes, but I don't let it become a problem; you know, they're all in the family; *Things Fall Apart* was the first to arrive, and that fact gives it a certain position of prominence, whether in fact other books excel in other particular virtues. *Things Fall Apart* is a kind of fundamental story of my condition that demanded to be heard, to retell the story of my encounter with Europe in a way acceptable to me. The other books do not occupy that same position in my frame of thinking. So I don't resent *Things Fall Apart* getting all the attention it does get. If you ask me, "Now, is it your best book?" I would say I don't really know; I wouldn't even want to say. And I'd even go on and say, "I don't even think so." But that's all right. I think every book I've done has tried to be different; this is what I set out to do, because I believe in the complexity of the human story, and that there's no way you can tell that story in one way and say, "This is it." Always there will be someone who can tell it differently depending on where they are standing; the same person telling the story will tell it differently. I think of that masquerade in Igbo festivals that dances in the public arena. The Igbo people say: if you want to see it well, you must not stand in one place. The masquerade is moving through this big arena. Dancing. If you're rooted to a spot, you miss a lot of the grace. So you keep moving, and this is the way I think the world's stories should be told: from many different perspectives.

INTERVIEWER

I wonder if you would comment on any tension you see between aesthetics and being politically engaged as an African writer.

ACHEBE

I don't see any tension for myself. It has always been quite apparent to me that no important story can fail to tell us something of value to us. But at the same time I know that an important message is not a novel. To say that we should all be kind to our neighbors is an important statement; it's not a novel. There is something about important stories that is not just the message, but also the way that message is conveyed, the arrangement of the words, the felicity of the language. So it's really a balance between your commitment, whether it's political or economic or whatever, and your craft as an artist.

INTERVIEWER

Is there a difference between telling a story and writing a story?

ACHEBE

Well, there must be. I remember that when our children were young, we used to read them stories at bedtime. Occasionally I would say to them, "I want to *tell* you a story," and the way their eyes would light up was different from the way they would respond to hearing a story read. There's no doubt at all that they preferred the story that was told to the one that was read. We live in a society which is in transition from oral to written. There are oral stories which are still there, not exactly in their full magnificence, but still strong in their differentness from written stories. Each mode has its ways and methods and rules. They can reinforce each other; this is the advantage my generation has: we can bring to the written story something of that energy of the story told by word of mouth. This is really one of the contributions our literature has made to contemporary literature.

INTERVIEWER

Nigerian literature.

ACHEBE

Yes, yes. Bringing into the written literature some of that energy that was always there—the archaic energy of the creation stories.

INTERVIEWER

When you write, what audience do you have in mind? Is it Nigerian? Is it Igbo? Is it America?

ACHEBE

All of those. I have tried to describe my position in terms
of circles, standing there in the middle. These circles contain
the audiences that get to hear my story. The closest circle is
the one closest to my home in Igboland, because the material
I am using is their material. But unless I'm writing in the
Igbo language, I use a language developed elsewhere, which
is English. That affects the way I write. It even affects to some
extent the stories I write. So there is, if you like, a kind of
paradox there already. But then, if you can, visualize a large
number of ever-widening circles, including all, like Yeats's wid-
ening gyre. As more and more people are incorporated in this
network, they will get different levels of meaning out of the
story, depending on what they already know, or what they
suspect. These circles go on indefinitely to include, ultimately,
the whole world. I have become more aware of this as my
books become more widely known. At this particular time,
mostly the news I hear is of translations of my books, especially
Things Fall Apart . . . in Indonesia, in Thailand, Korea, Japan,
China and so on. Fortunately you don't think of all those
people when you are writing. At least, I don't. When I'm
writing, I really want to satisfy myself. I've got a story which
I am working on and struggling with, and I want to tell it
the most effective way I can. That's really what I struggle with.
And the thought of who may be reading it may be there
somewhere in the back of my mind—I'll never say it's not
there because I don't know—but it's not really what I'm thinking about. After all, some people will say, "Why does he put
in all these Nigerian-English words?" Some critics say that in
frustration. And I feel like saying to them, "Go to hell! That's
the way the story was given to me. And if you don't want to
make this amount of effort, the kind of effort that my people
have always made to understand Europe and the rest of the
world, if you won't make this little leap, then leave it alone!"

INTERVIEWER

Are you ever surprised, when you travel around the world,
by what readers make of your writings, or how they bond to
them?

ACHEBE

Yes. yes, yes, yes. I am. People make surprising comments
to me. I think particularly of a shy-looking, white American
boy who came into my office once — in the seventies, I think —
at the University of Massachusetts, and said to me, "That man,
Okonkwo, is my father"!

INTERVIEWER

You were surprised!

ACHEBE

Yes! I was surprised. I looked at him, and I said, "All right!"
As I've said elsewhere, another person said the same thing:
in a public discussion — a debate the two of us had in Florida —
James Baldwin said, "That man is my father."

INTERVIEWER

Okonkwo?

ACHEBE

Okonkwo.

INTERVIEWER

Did you ever know anybody named Okonkwo? When I was
in Nigeria visiting you some years ago, I met a small young
man who was a student at the university, who introduced
himself to me as Okonkwo. I thought he was an impostor! Is
it a real name?

ACHEBE

A very common name. Oh, yes. It's one of the commonest
names in Igboland because there are four days in the Igbo
week, and each of them is somebody's name. In other words,
you are born on Monday or Tuesday or Wednesday or Thursday, if you like, and you will be given the name — "The Son
of Monday," or "The Son of Tuesday," or "The Son of Wednesday," or "The Son of Thursday" — if you are Igbo. That's what
Okonkwo means: it means a man born on *nkwo* day. The first

day of the week. If you are not born on that day, you will be Okeke, Okoye, or Okafo. Not everybody answers to these. Your parents might give you another name, like Achebe; then you prefer to answer that. But you always have a name of the day of the week on which you were born. So Okonkwo is very common.

INTERVIEWER

One of the great women characters you have created, I think, is Beatrice in *Anthills of the Savannah*. Do you identify with her? Do you see any part of yourself in that character? She's sort of a savior, I think.

ACHEBE

Yes, yes, I identify with her. Actually, I identify with all my characters, good and bad. I have to do that in order to make them genuine. I have to understand them even if I don't approve of them. Not completely — it's impossible; complete identification is, in fact, not desirable. There must be areas in which a particular character does not represent you. At times, though, the characters — like Beatrice — do contain, I think, elements of my own self, and my systems of beliefs and *hopes* and aspirations. Beatrice is the first *major* woman character in my fiction. Those who do not read me as carefully as they ought have suggested that this is the only woman character I have ever written about, and that I probably created her out of pressure from the feminists. Actually, the character of Beatrice has been there in virtually all my fiction, certainly from *No Longer at Ease*, *A Man of the People*, right down to *Anthills of the Savannah*. There is a certain increase in the importance I assign to women in getting us out of the mess that we are in, which is a reflection of the role of women in my traditional culture: that they do not interfere in politics until men really make such a mess that the society is unable to go backward or forward. Then women will move in . . . this is the way the stories have been constructed, and this is what I have tried to say. In one of Sembene Ousmane's films he portrays that same kind of situation where the men struggle, are beaten and cannot defend their rights against French colonial rule. They surrender their rice harvest, which is an abomination. They dance one last time in the village arena and leave their spears where they danced and go away—this is the final humiliation. The women then emerge, pick up the spears, and begin their own dance. So it's not just in the Igbo culture. It seems to be something which other African peoples also taught us.

INTERVIEWER

You wrote a very passionate piece a year or so ago in *The New York Times* op-ed page about the present status of life in Nigeria. Are you pessimistic or hopeful about Nigeria's return to democracy?

ACHEBE

What is going on is extremely sad. It's appalling. And extremely disappointing to all lovers or friends or citizens of Nigeria. I try as hard as possible not to be pessimistic because I have never thought or believed that creating a Nigerian nation would be easy; I have always known that it was going to be a very tough job. But I never really thought that it would be *this* tough. And what's going on now, which is a subjection of this potentially great country to a clique of military adventurers and a political class that they have completely corrupted— this is really quite appalling. The suffering that they have unleashed on millions of people is quite intolerable. What makes me so angry is that this was quite avoidable. If a political class—including intellectuals, university professors and people like that, who have read all the books and know how the world works—if they had based their actions on *principle* rather than on opportunity, the military would not have dared to go as far as they are going. But they looked around and saw that they could buy people. Anybody who called himself president would immediately find everyone lining up outside his home or his office to be made minister of this or that. And this is what they have exploited: they have exploited the divisions, the ethnic and religious divisions in the country. These have always been serious, but they were never insurmountable with good leadership. But over the last ten years these military types have been so cynical that they didn't really care what they did as long as they stayed in power. And they watched Nigeria going through the most intolerable situation of suffering and pain. And I just hope, as nothing goes on forever, that we will find a way to stumble out of this anarchy.

INTERVIEWER

Do you miss Nigeria?

ACHEBE

Yes, very much. One reason why I am quite angry with what is happening in Nigeria today is that everything has collapsed. If I decide to go back now, there will be so many problems, where will I find the physical therapy and other things that I now require? Will the doctors, who are leaving in *droves*, coming to America, going to everywhere in the world—Saudi Arabia—how many of them will be there? The universities have almost completely lost their faculties and are hardly ever in session, shut down for one reason or another. So these are some of the reasons why I have not yet been able to get back. So I miss it. And it doesn't have to be that way.

INTERVIEWER

I wanted to ask, how are you coming along? Have you been able to resume writing since your accident?

ACHEBE

I am feeling my way back into writing. The problem is that in this condition you spend a lot of time just getting used to your body again. It does take a lot of energy and time, so that your day does not begin where it used to begin. And the result is that there are very few hours in the day. That's a real problem, and what I have been trying to do is reorganize my day so that I can get in as much writing as possible before the discomfort makes it necessary for me to get up or go out. So, I am beginning—

INTERVIEWER

What advice would you give to someone with literary promise? I would assume that you are constantly being asked by
budding novelists to give them advice, to read their manuscripts, and so on.

ACHEBE

I don't get the deluge of manuscripts that I would be getting
in Nigeria. But some do manage to find me. This is something
I understand because a budding writer wants to be encour-
aged. But I believe myself that a good writer doesn't really
need to be told anything except to keep at it. Just think of
the work you've set yourself to do, and do it as well as you
can. Once you have really done all you can, then you can show
it to people. But I find this is increasingly not the case with
the younger people. They do a first draft and want somebody
to finish it off for them with good advice. So I just maneuver
myself out of this. I say, "Keep at it." I grew up recognizing
that there was nobody to give me any advice, and that you
do your best, and if it's not good enough, someday you will
come to terms with that. I don't want to be the one to tell
somebody, "You will not make it," even though I know that
the majority of those who come to me with their manuscripts
are not really good enough. But you don't ever want to say
to a young person, "You can't," or, "You are no good." Some
people might be able to do it, but I don't think I am a police-
man for literature. So I tell them, sweat it out, do your best.
Don't publish it yourself—this is one tendency which is becoming more and more common in Nigeria. You go and find
someone—a friend—to print your book.

INTERVIEWER

We call that vanity press here.

ACHEBE

Yes, vanity printing, yes. That really has very severe limita-
tions. I think once you have done all you can to a manuscript,
let it find its way in the world.

—Jerome Brooks

Two Poems by Marie Ponsot

For My Old Self, at Notre-Dame de Paris:
fluctuat nec mergitur

The dark madonna cut from a knot of wood
has robes whose folds make waves against the grain
and a touching face — noble in side view,
impish or childish seen head-on from above.
The wood has the rich stain of tannin, raised
to all-color lustre by the steep of time.

The mouths of her shadows are pursed by time
to suck sun-lit memories from the wood.
Freezing damp and candle-smut have raised
her eyebrows into wings flung up by the grain,
caught in the light of bulbs plugged high above.
She stands alert, as if hailed, with beasts in view.

Outside on the jeweled river-ship, I view
a girl's back, walking off. Oh. Just in time
I shut up. She'd never hear me shout above
the tour guides and ski-skate kids. How I would
have liked to see her face again, the grain
of beauty on her forehead, her chin raised

startled; her Who are you? wild, a question raised
by seeing me, an old woman, in plain view.
Time is a tree in me; in her it's a grain
ready to plant. I go back in, taking my time
leafy among stone trunks that soar in stone woods
where incense drifts, misty, lit pink from above.

She's headed for her hotel room then above
Cluny's garden. She'll sit there then, feet raised,
notebook on her knees, to write. Maybe she would

have heard, turned, known us both in a larger view,
and caught my age in the freshness of its time.
She dreads clocks, she says. Such dry rot warps the grain.

They still say mass here, wine and wheat-grain
digest to flesh in words that float above
six kneeling women, a man dressed outside time,
and the dark madonna, her baby raised
dangerously high to pull in our view.
Magic dame, cut knot, your ancient wood

would reach back to teach her if it could. Spring rain.
Through it I call to thank her, loud above
the joy she raised me for, this softfall. Sweet time.

Evening the Ark

After judgment & the wet sacrament of slaughter,

greener than Eden, a shock of bliss to see
just past the stew and suck of reeking waters,
the earth ate sunshine under the olive trees.

Noah, his wife, their sons, their daughters
rushed to lower the gangplank. Awkward, long doubled,
unboxed & jostling, the passengers suddenly freed
hustled uncoupling ashore to uncouple, suddenly free.

Henry Sloss

Between Lives

> If you were fired and were free to go
> From Appalachia to
> The Apennines, would you
> Think twice before you flew,
> With wife and child in tow,
> To the old world and to a new
> Life at Lake Trasimeno?

As his cohort brushes up
on Customs, readies baby, passport, map,
terra firma rushes up,

Jolts a soldier from his nap—
the hero of lost battles and failed wiles—
lands him in the old world's lap

Roughly, say, a million miles
from where, like spring's first pitch, he was thrown out
to the crowd's contagious smiles.

Partisans appear to sprout
from Rome's mobbed airport's tangle and to sweep
three tired troopers from the rout

Through the sunset to a steep
starlit road, winding up somewhere above
scenes unseen except in sleep.

One of them is dreaming of
a world as precious to him as his breath,
lost as causes, job, and love,

When he wakes gasping for air, scared to death.

How far we go, how little we know
Of even the world we leave;
How easy to believe
The new will be a breeze,
Or at worst a three-day blow,
Above the gray-barked olive trees
And ash-white Trasimeno.

After an half hour of steam,
the hand at his throat, foot pressed to his chest
were removed and he could dream

Things had worked out for the best;
but when the windows showed the world immersed
still in darkness, he confessed

Things had worked out for the worst.
History was the nightmare he had read
it was; politics were cursed;

Even Revolution bred
more fat cats by transmogrifying mice,
who had better have been dead,

Into felines, vice by vice,
felonious appetite for power by lust . . .
—cheese he tasted once or twice.

Whether the closed house's must
and dust, or sunset's rust, choked him, a yawn
cleared the way for him to just

Surrender to suggestions of a dawn.

Although this took place years ago,
September of '72,
That ageing *ingenu*,
At ripe old thirty-one,
Knew everything I know
Except that his life had just begun
At gray-green Trasimeno.

Soon as he had left the chill
of the box-like cottage, copses of pine
drew his eye far down the hill.

'Cloudy mass without outline',
he began, 'if you are Lake Trasimene,
will you favor our design?

Can a simple change of scene,
a year's lease on a house in paradise,
matter? What does pretty mean?

Justice has been my device
for so long, how can olives, tree by tree
brought to light by the precise

Fingering of dawn, touch me?
What has a world of beauty to do with
war, racism, poverty?

Or is equity a myth?
Candor and independence variegation
for self-interest's monolith?'

The wilderness is no place for vacation.

What becomes of the injured ego
Without the aid of others
When bathing one another's
Wounds had seemed so ideal?

Can poetry bestow
What never was—the power to heal
On milky Trasimeno?

Gentle Reader, if you are
there at all, can you see me as I am
figured in these lines, so far

Gone on innocence, a lamb
thrown to the lions could not feel less guilt?
Notwithstanding the enjamb-

Ment of a late (sticky) gilt-
edged love interest's blurring the period,
righteousness remained unsplit.

Actually I felt an odd
comfort in culpability, saw even
there the even hand of god.

Some impurity would leaven
the hell I would describe in poetry,
once we settled into heaven.

Other people seem to see
the comic features of our self-conception
much more easily than we,

For whom self-knowledge is of self-deception.

Again at ripe old fifty or so,
Where ripeness shows as gray,
An ageless naivete
Makes me feel like a dope.
Do you, do others go
Through lives as free of muddying hope
As transparent Trasimeno?

Tasteless as this self-abuse
may seem, what would self be without its spice?
Piquancy is my excuse

For browbeating someone twice
as well-meaning as I could ever be
again; someone just as nice

To friend as to enemy;
a man whose faults were generous in kind
as mine are in quantity.

Out of it, where 'it' is mind,
he thinks his suffering in a good cause should
be rewarded. Is he blind,

Or am I? I know I would
not tell him everything I know today,
even if somehow I could.

He will learn along the way
the wages of his virtue, and the cost
comes to more than I dare say

To anyone so proud as he and lost.

Two Poems by Steve Kronen

Autobiography: The Early Years

"Bring out your dead!" and I did, roadside
service; Auntie Mame and Uncle Joe, (and Little Timmy)
    hauled away —
my childhood stacked like cordwood
on the rickety cart with the huge
wooden wheels half sunk in the muddy lane,
but turning still, round and round.

And spring once more, the sun made its rounds
over the mountainside
above our drafty house where the weak had lain
all season. How they weighed
upon me, their presence huge
in the small room of thatch and wood

and shuttered windows which would
not keep out the wind or the rounds
sung over the sour beer in the huge
outdoors beyond our door. Mame, lying there, sighed
just to hear their harmonizing way
down the treeless lane.

Oh I was sad seeing where the three had lain
pitching back and forth all winter on their slatted, wooden
beds, but figured there was no way
I, a small boy with small hands, could bring them round,
though I rubbed Mame's feet once, turned Timmy on his side.
But their intransigence was huge

and I busied myself before the huge
blue light of the television, the laying
of my small hands upon it brightening my side

of the room where I sat each morning, wooed
by the shimmer of the round
test pattern and the farm report all the way

from Iowa City. But that light convinced me of a better way
and during commercials I wrapped Mame's huge
shawl, the one from Paris she said, around
her skinny body as I kept an ear cocked to the lane,
placed the flap of his hat over Joe's wooden
gaze, and tucked Timmy's arms to his side,

glancing sidelong from screen to lane
where the cart would come our way and those voices
call us to the huge world still turning round and round.

The World Before Them

Actually, it was sweet and heavy with juice
and we passed it back and forth, a river
of nectar running down her chin and mine
until we were full and our faces shone
and could not tell receiver from giver.
I loved its weight in my hand, bruised
just a little from having fallen
from those high, green limbs. And we took its seed
and planted more when we left that place
so we'd always be sure to have its taste
upon our tongues. That was her idea, freed
us from worrying about the future. And all in
all, we didn't. We ate them to the core.
It's as though we'd been provided for.

Mary Maxwell

Beckett in Roussillon

His difficulties the danger putting one
  foot past the other impossible
    the downcast eye captured by
      blood-red coloring mined ochers
tender heel pressed against leather
  rubber rock verb mortal flesh
    up against bullet-like nails of
      a sole *profugus* refugees
fato surrounding German legions
  Romance etymologies *Guillems*
    de Cabestaing his heart *lo cor*
      consumed *wie Wasser* his steps
von Klippe zu Klippe geworfen such hurling
  uncertainties each rust foothold his fate
    the incipient footfall placement one
      word one more word down the page

Alicia Ostriker

The Boys, the Broomhandle,
the Retarded Girl

Who was asking for it—
Everyone can see
Even today in the formal courtroom,
Beneath the coarse flag draped
Across the wall like something on a stage,
Which reminds her of the agony of school
But also of a dress they let her wear
To a parade one time,
Anyone can tell
She's asking, she's pleading
For it, as we all
Plead—
Chews on a wisp of hair,
Holds down the knee
That tries to creep under her chin,
Picks at the flake of skin, anxious
And eager to please this scowling man
And the rest of them, if she only can—
Replies *I cared for them, they were my friends—*

It is she of whom these boys
Said, afterward, *Wow, what a sicko,*
It is she of whom they boasted
As we all boast

Now and again, as anyone might reach
Across that oaken bench to touch for luck
The flag hung in law's hall, but avoid
Touching the girl.

Two Poems by John Gery

Lie #1: That Penelope
Resisted Scores of Suitors

I'm not convinced that woman wanted him
ever to come back home. She had her business
in tapestries, those three-hour meals with men,
and Telemachus, who it's true was dim
and narrow, some said not unlike Ulysses,
but still his mother's toy. And after ten

or more years, don't all lovers seem the same
in memory? One man surmounts the teeming,
well-meaning invitations, only to pout
when she, like Hera, claims she's not to blame
for his interminable lust and dreaming.
The man wants her to take him; she wants out

of the question of desire altogether,
on his terms. So she starts to count completely
not on Ulysses' missing, but on facts
like ships we watch crossing against the weather
toward the world's edge, which shimmer discretely,
then disappear when some small flick distracts

our curious eyes. You couldn't pin her down,
not that one. Cooler to the touch than the prick
of a needle, she had mastered her delay
with vague unweavings, building her renown
on nothing but a calculated trick
to cover black and white with seamless gray,

to keep the fools like me coming around
drooling like basset hounds. It's often so:
The facts protect the ones who want to lie
alone, while those for whom nothing is sound
muddle, splash and drown. Sometimes, though,
we also sail, blindly, into the sky.

Lie #2: That Parkman Almost
Died on the Oregon Trail

The Ogillallah Village, 1846

My mind is mush. Three days without a thought
but how to tell them I can't eat their corn
again, nor smoke that pipe that tastes like silt,
nor drink the soot in the water bags we brought
from Boston. Why do I think I was born
for something better than this bile I've spilt

on prairie grass, which dies only to sprout
hardier than before? My education
seems now mostly an exercise in tact
and confidence, as though to conquer doubt
I talked myself into thinking a whole nation
of Sioux, Dahcotah, and Blackfeet could be tracked

like body parts drawn in some medical book.
Mornings I read, when I'm not on the trail,
or talk with trappers come down from the Black Hills;
by noon, whatever meaning I mistook
for fact fades, like the buffalo or whale,
so that by night the dark sends up my back chills

worse than a seasick sailor's. *Write it down*,
I keep reminding myself, *Write it down*,
and pray ideas will shoot forth from the earth
I lie on, shivering in my dressing gown.
But nausea engulfs me and I drown
in ignorance and colic fits not worth

Harvard Library's crowded shelves of lies:
Even the idea I do not belong here,
once noted, seems banal against this beauty
I couldn't have predicted would hurt my eyes,
and dreading what I'm eating seems the wrong fear.
Maybe a lack of sleep has made me moody

or working hard to mispronounce their words,
to prove myself both flexible and stable,
has skewed the reason why I came: for truth.
I'm small. We're all small. Hardly more than birds.
Whatever I write is nothing but a label
to identify my corpse by, like a tooth.

Philip Kobylarz

The Insubstantial Pageant

My Christian name you ask? It is Joseph Ignace.
I fell from my mother's womb while she walked,
a nightly stroll around the neighborhood
in the city of nights and splendid catacombs.
She dropped into a fit of hysterics and labor
and bore me into the sewer among the fallen leaves
rainwater, urine and sweetmold, at the sound
of a man's scream — baby Asreal delivered
in cobblestone and steam. The town's priest
drunk on spirits blessed the child and took him
under his fourteen feathered wing. Boy of the altar
the cherubs sang, who would wear the absent square
in his collar like a lost ring on a missing finger.

●

Docteur or docte, I am no longer sure . . . What I do
remember is a toy from my youth not soon after . . .
a poupée, the figurine of a young man, black mop
of hair, Italianate, a twine bearing from his shoulder —
with a pull, off popped its head, with the expression
of no expression and the grimace of something felt
not on its face, not gone, nor missing.
                                        Where there's
nothing lost, all is found. The laws of physics
are laid to live for. There is the great architecture
of science and technology. The criminal in a coat
is an easy catch. If the physicians cannot kill death,
we shall execute him plain and simple. Quick
to the cut, bone sliced from bone.

•

                    This will be
the end of our grand halls decked in satin curtains,
an epoch orchestrated on the crooked steps
of the Ministry. In the courtyard I will unveil
my finite motion machine, my Louisette,
my picture window of infinity with its singular
drape of razor. The stories from the scaffold
told will be mythology.

•

                    A head severed
from the body speaking an encore of last words.
A face without blood blushing when it's slapped.
The light of the soul cannot linger in the skull
as the living perceive the phantom of a flame
in the darkness after it has been snuffed out.
What isn't cannot remain. Even a King won't be
immune to the lightning flash of truth. Envelopes
from the officers standing guard dabbed in blood
and raised to pike-point. Heads falling to the rhythm
of drumbeat at a quarter past the hour of each hour
of the day. Pools of blood staining the bricks copper.
Those guilty of their crimes will be immortalized
in woodcut and buried headless in the ossuary
one stacked upon the other as limestone accretes
in layers, foothills forgotten in time.

•

                    Death as banal
at the symmetry of the gallows, the hangman's knot
unraveled. Flags unfurled in my name, a name
embedded in history. For I am he, I am Guillotine —
who is absolutely sure — both the man and the machine.

Three Poems by Kathleen Peirce

Figure with Trees

One shoulder breaking the tension of a satin slip,
making the strap fall loose inside the dress.
Bend of the gesture sliding the strap back, into place,
one frond of the mimosa.

Something hurts her. Or, head bent, she's sleeping
sitting up. Heavy beauty in the curved, lax hands,
two gold bracelets crossed. But her knees have fallen
open under the stitched cloth, and her mouth has. Red
edge of one ear, red five-petaled hand. The one shoulder
brought outside the bodice of the dress.

Wind is a kind of looking, different in a cedar
than a sycamore. Hundreds of cedar on this hill. Rare
    sycamore,
common wind. Four pretty mimosa.
Her human shoulder moving as she breathes.

Height

What I thought was stillness
was not stillness. What else would
a tall girl love but hills to stand on
and look out from? Why shouldn't it have begun
in Lincoln Park, straddling the cannon, or
in Long View Park, straddling the bronze lion,
or in my first true place, the 38th Street cemetery?
What did I know, pinching the best flowers from
dead bouquets, having my first kiss? I thought my mind was

made of what I liked to see, and why not endlessly pretend
to be on camera? After marriage, I watched my husband
run uphill through head-high corn to see me. Who wouldn't
mistake that happiness for power since it seemed there was
a stillness in it that must be what the powerful feel
when what they want moves closer. Who would have thought
that moving to the mountains with my darling
and my broken back and our beautiful tall son would show me
so clearly and so soon how long I was terrified?

Mother and Son

When his arms raise it's all he knows of how
a body opens. Light and full,
his body in the moment just before she touches him
knows to meet and fill the contours of the day, so that her
hands, cupping his sides, duplicate his sides
to make him twice contained. He is not less
when she lets go because the day receives him
with brief obedience in ways too various to count,
if he could count; daylight rakes the barrier
she's put him on, a cemetery wall, with stripéd giddiness.
Cars passing make the darker stripes, the stripes of sound.
He can't tell if he finds things or they come to him.
If he looks further on, the narrowing wall seems pulled out
    of itself,
so he looks where he stands. Pebbles make the wall's top
lion-colored. Pale upright stones align in the interior,
a field for the greater presences: calm blue hydrangea,
angel with hard hands, wings, and face held out,
stuck in radiance. These worlds are shapely and occasional
as she is now, who lifts him down.

Open House

Charles D'Ambrosio

The last time I'd seen my father he behaved like one of those wolf-boys, those kids suckled and reared in the wild by animals, and I was never sure, during the ten confusing minutes I stood on the lawn outside the house, whether or not he recognized me. The security chain on the back door remained slotted. Inside, through the crack, he asked me when I was going to relinquish my disease, which made me think either he was speaking rhetorically or confusing me with my brother Miles, who is schizophrenic and lives in a halfway. Then he seemed to have a moment of lucidity and called me a loser for dropping out of college. He had trouble breathing and rasped and swore like someone twitched by demons on a down-town corner. All the flowers, in the hanging baskets, in the clay pots, in the whiskey barrel, were dead and hissing dryly in the wind, so it was true, apparently, that he had watered the garden with gasoline. He gasped, he yelled, he mixed the latinate with potty talk, calling my sisters complicitous cunts and my mother a vituperative bitch. His shouting had always had the effect of diminishing me, the sheer volume of it taking away the ground I stood on, for it would sound as if he were screaming across the country or into the past, to someone, at any rate, who was not present, and the longer I remained there, listening, the more invisible I felt. He had a certain emotional vigor that turned his head purple, and all during that most recent visit his head was purple. When I was a kid he'd put that purple head in my face and grab my jaw and tell me, "If you were me you'd be dead because my father would have killed you." Driving away, I had that feeling, of echoes within echoes.

Certain he was finally and forever crazy, and in need of professional help, I called his shrink, Dr. Headberry, but that poor, harassed pill-dispenser had been fired, or dismissed, and then, about a week later, my father tried to take his suffering public. He came to church dressed in his version of sackcloth and ashes — tin pants, snake boots, a wool coat with suede ovals at the elbows and a plaid cap with foam earflaps. These things had long ago been banished to hooks in the garage, and smelled, I knew, of motor oil and grass clippings and dusty, forgotten fabrics that have gone damp and dried, then gone damp again and dried again, endlessly over the years. He'd locked away his guns after my brother Jackie (as my father liked to say) sucked a barrel — shoved a twelve-gauge Mossberg back in his tonsil-area and opened his skull against the bedroom wall. While both my older brothers were evidently fucked up, I, as the baby of the family, was luckily buffered by my four sisters. If it wasn't for them, I knew I'd be way more of a mental clodhopper than I was, or dead or crazy like my brothers. Karen, Lucy, Meg and especially Roxy, they all had this special way, this oddball interest in good places to paddle canoes, and herb remedies, and parks where you could take safe walks in the dark, and sardonyx and black fire opals, and weird healing practices, and crow feathers and chips of eggshells, and numerology, and playing records backwards, and food that didn't come out of a can or box. My father thought they were witches. Roxy carried a bull thistle in a tea infuser chained around her neck. The Salish believed thistles would ward off back luck, and the Scots believed they would keep away the enemy. Roxy gave me a thistle of my own and once she gave me a pomegranate. I'd never seen one before, and I was shocked that someone could think of me, sitting downstairs in Jackie's room, on Jackie's old bed, and bring me a gift out of nowhere, and for no reason. A pomegranate. *Out of nowhere, and for no reason*! Isn't it perfect, she asked, and it was.

I watched my father from across the aisle. He knelt in a pew with his head bowed, and his hands hung limply over the backrest as though he'd been clamped into a pillory. Lawyers for both sides had called me, asking if I'd testify if the divorce went to trial, but I had no idea what I'd say if I were being deposed. He looked drunk and sleepy and wired, and also penitent in this odd, remembered way, as if he were still trying to fool some buzzard-backed nun from his childhood. He wiped sweat from his brow with a wrinkled hanky, mopped the back of his neck, held the thing like a flag of truce as he folded his hands for prayer. During the offertory he began crying or weeping — weeping, I guess, because there was something stagey about it. He beat the butt of his palm against his head, lifted his eyes to the cross, and said, "Oh God, oh God, my God."

"I wish I could be crucified," my father had told me over the phone, the day after he was served papers. "That's really the only way to settle these things."

Despite the lunacy of pitting his agony against the agony of Jesus Christ, I now decided he wasn't crazy. This was calculated. He'd come to menace and harass my mother. For years church had been her only bastion and retreat and he'd come as a trespasser to violate it, to pollute its purity and calm, to take it away from her, and make it ugly like everything else in our life, and that's what I'd tell the lawyers. I was no disciple or defender of the church and no big fan of the snobs who weekly attended mass. With its pale green walls and polished pine benches and high windows of distorted glass it seemed a place for lame rummage sales, a place where fussy old men sold boxes of yesterday's best-sellers, soup ladles and wide neckties. The young seemed old, and the old seemed ancient — widowers in pleated pants who had retired into a sallow golden age, bereft men with nothing to do but sip their pensions like weak tea in a waiting room whose only door opened on death. And the women — some so fanatically dedicated to a pre-Vatican II universe they still wore hats within the nave, and if they'd forgotten a scarf or hat, they'd unclasp their purses and find a Kleenex and bobby-pin that to their hair. Arranged in the pews these women with toilet paper on their heads looked like planted rows of petunias. Yet that Saturday, as my father crudely interrupted the service, I considered the possibility that the heart and soul of any faith is absurdity, and that these ridiculous, otherworldly women, with their silly gestures, might just be saints.

The mass stopped and everyone turned from the altar and stared at him. Everyone — the Greys, the Hams, the Wooleys, Mrs. Kayhew and the Grands and the Stones. Also the priest, the altar boys. It was a caesura that filled with whisperings of disbelief and doubt, and only my mother, who was the eucharistic minister and sat in the sanctuary, remained quiet and calm. She laced her hands together and set them like a dead bird in her lap. Sitting in her chair, icily withdrawn, she looked as she did when I was a child and dinner was not going well, evenings when my father occupied the head of the table like a cigar-store Indian and silence settled in our bones and we could hear little else but the tink-tink of fork tines and the sound of chewing and it was painful to swallow. Those nights I wouldn't eat the hard things, the raw carrots or breadsticks, for fear of making a noise, and my mother wouldn't eat at all. My mother liked to say that silence had made her a very slender woman, and it was true, she was slim and at sixty still looked girlish in blue jeans.

The priest drank wine from the chalice and, wiping the rim, held the cup to my mother's lips. He leaned toward her, whispered something in her ear, and she nodded her head deliberately. Together they stepped down to the communion rail. My father waited until the line dwindled down, then lifted himself awkwardly, stumbling up the aisle alone. I saw Mrs. Grand lay a hand on her husband, restraining him. My father stood, swaying a little, before my mother. Later, after my mother returned from her trip to Texas, she would tell me it was not her place to judge, and certainly not her role as the morning's eucharistic minister. Her faith gave her the ability not to judge anything, even movies. To me, as an outsider, and someone without any faith at all, the scene at the communion rail seemed a show of profound strength, but my father, later, would say he only went up there to prove what a chickenshit she was. The church was dead quiet. My mother lifted the eucharist as you would a bright, promised coin, holding it slightly above eye level, and my father looked up. "Body and Blood of Christ," she said, and he responded, "Amen," and then she very carefully set the host on his waiting tongue.

After the blessing my mother left the sanctuary and knelt in the front pew. The door in the vestibule had been jammed open with a rubber wedge and a cool wet wind circulated through church, stirring the lace edge of the altar cloth and the sprigs of white gladiolas in their fluted gold standards. Her friends filed out, and cars left the lot. She remained kneeling on the padded hassock and prayed with her eyes shut and with her eyes shut she heard, from the vestibule, the ruffle of the priest's soutane as the black skirt swept the floor, and then the hurried, heavy steps of my father. She remained still and continued to pray.

"She denied me and she denied me," my father said to the priest. "She denied me even the simplest things a husband requires."

The priest gestured helplessly toward the confessionals—the penalty boxes, my father called them, those two upright coffins in the corner of the church. Probably it crossed the priest's mind that the formality of this arrangement might help contain my father's apparent madness. A closed door, at the very least, might muffle his complaint. My father didn't often go out in public because he thought people didn't like him, and when he did socialize, out of nervousness and excessive drinking, he was a terrible gas bag, and most people did try to avoid him, and so the fact that he'd come to church, and made such an awful ruckus, now swayed me back in the direction of the idea that he must be crazy. I was about to step in, but the priest waved me away.

"Even bedtime pleasures."

The priest said, "I'm sure there's more to the story."

"Don't tell me about stories," my father responded. "Calumny is one of the seven deadly sins."

"No it isn't," the priest said, firmly.

My father ignored him, shouting at my mother.

"How dare you judge me! You call yourself Christians!"

The altar boy returned to snuff the candles and collect the cruets of wine and water. My mother could smell the curls of black smoke rising from the burnt wicks. With her eyes closed, she felt as though she could lift herself up, she could rise away and soar, as she said her prayers, on the whispered fluttering wingbeat of words, away, away, away . . . while my father stared after her from what then seemed a lifetime of hatred. She did not move. Her skin was pale to the point of appearing blue. Her fingers, interlaced, were delicate and weak. She was as still in her pew as the pale crucified Christ floating high above the sanctuary, but she was gone.

"Goddamn you to hell," my father screamed on his way out the door.

I hadn't dropped out of school. In early March the bursar asked me to withdraw until the outstanding balance on my tuition bill was paid. I stuffed a rucksack with clothes and left campus that night. I was relieved. My lisp made me quiet and shy, embarrassed at the sound of myself, and also something of a hostile shit. People gathered in their dorms, smoked bong hits under batik bedspreads that breathed and endlessly analyzed their families. I couldn't get into it. The soft sibilance of my voice didn't square with what I had to say, and I felt paralyzed by a pressure, a sense that if I started talking there was a good chance I'd never stop. To cure this, or get around it, I had signed up for a writing course, but dropped it when I couldn't figure out the economy of a story, the lifeboat ethics of it—who got pitched in with the sharks, who got rescued. By the end of January I had stopped attending classes, and only turned in the written assignments, and sometime in February I pulled the curtains and lay in bed for a week.

I left school without telling anyone, in part because as a rule, a policy, I never say good-bye. The night I walked off campus was quiet, I remember, that country quiet where every sound seems to have a distinct place in the world, and by the next morning I'd hitched to Altoona, Wisconsin. From there I hopped a freight train home to Seattle. Twice, as the train crossed trestles over the Yellowstone and then later over the Clark Fork, I considered jumping off to do some fishing, but the divorce was already in progress and I was convinced my father was going to destroy the contents of our house. (He did: he burned the christening dress we'd been baptized in, he tossed our photo albums.) Back in Seattle I rented a shoe box room and got a job busing tables at a restaurant owned by two lesbians I knew from day one would eventually fire me. (They did.) I spent most nights hunched over my vice, drinking beer and tying flies, filling one box with hare's ears and pheasant tails, and another with size 16 blue-winged olives and pale morning duns. My only plan in the world right then was to hop a train to Livingston, head into the park and fish the Firehole near the west end of Fountain Flats, a place that was a favorite of both Miles and Jackie. After that, after Memorial Day, I planned to take my tent and stove and live in the park all season. (Which I did, until in mid-October I woke one morning with my tent sagging like a collapsed parachute and was driven out by snow.)

The only things I wanted out of our house were Miles's old fly rod and the original fifteen and a half pages of Jackie's suicide note.

Realtor's signs had been staked into the front and side yards, and a sandwich board stood spraddled on the sidewalk. OPEN HOUSE, it said, SUNDAY, and the lead agent's name was Cynthia. My father's beat spy car was parked in the drive, the passenger door lashed shut with loops of clothesline, the landau top half-scalped, peeling back to raw metal. For weeks he'd been tailing my mother around town in this battered, rust-bitten Plymouth. Was this corny or dangerous? In the last days, as the end drew near, he'd thrown her down the stairs, grated her arm with a grapefruit knife—but the end had been drawing near regularly for twenty years; my entire life, and the tragic end of it all was the very rhythm of all our hearts, and if two of my sisters, Roxy and Karen, hadn't finally abducted my mother, hadn't dragged her out of the house, she would have stayed, I bet, and would still be getting chased around the house with knives and screamed at.

As the youngest of seven children, my family's history had always been my future, a past I was growing into and inheriting, a finished world, a place where the choices had been made, irrevocably. As a result I was never very interested in the riddle of heredity or the way dysteleology can become design. I arrived too late to believe any other world existed. I was fourteen when Miles started living either on Western Avenue behind the Skyway coat factory or at the V.A. or in a series of ratty halfway houses, and by now I just assumed the voices Miles heard would speak to me also. I was sixteen when Jackie killed himself. At twenty, I assumed madness would visit me, and so would suicide. I assumed they would approach quietly and hold out their hands and claim me and take me where they had taken my brothers. Miles had tried to kill himself too, driven by his voices to jump off the Aurora Bridge, but he'd survived. Frequently, obsessively, I fantasized sitting on the bridge railing and shooting myself in the head. That way in one moment I'd bring my brothers together in me. I was convinced I'd know them in that way. And my father? Would I know him? Could I even describe him? Often my father couldn't take a shit unless my mother held his hand. But I couldn't really imagine that.

I looked up, and there he was, framed in the open window of Miles's old bedroom.

"You can't come in," he shouted. "My lawyer guy said nobody can come in the house. Not you, not anybody. I'm sorry, I know it sounds stupid, but too many negative things redound in my direction."

"I came to get my stuff," I said.

"I have to insulate me totally."

He disappeared from the window and reappeared at the back door. He opened it a crack, steel chain still slotted.

"We did this last week," I said.

"You can't come in. I'm sorry, too many negative things. You're all complicitous with your mother. I didn't want this. It wasn't my idea. I wanted to work it out. There's family solutions to family problems, but this, this is appalling and obscene, it's immoral."

"I have a key," I said.

"Not any more you don't. I changed the locks."

The back porch was lined with clay pots full of dead marigolds, woolly brown swabs on bent black stalks.

"What's wrong?" I asked.

"Wrong? Nothing's wrong except your mother's got me by the fucking balls. She's got her hooks in me, but I'm fine."

I picked up one of the clay pots and put my nose to the soil and it had the cold smell of gasoline.

"Did you pour gas on the flowers?"

"That's just more of your mother's calumny."

"I think we should call Dr. Headberry," I said.

"Headberry? I just talked with him. Headberry says I have no real problems. He's got your mother analyzed perfectly, though. It's ugly. She's got control of my life."

He was lying about Headberry, of course, and unless something happened we were going to continue having the kind of conversation that you have when there's only one seat left on the bus.

"Let me in."

"I don't understand the ugliness — the enormity of the entire process. So many hooks there — they've got control of my life."

I dropped the pot, letting it shatter on the porch, and started walking back out to my truck.

"This is against my better instinct," my father said. He closed the door and slipped the chain off. "It's against everything I know and against my lawyer's advice too."

"Thanks," I said. I nodded out toward the Realtor's sign. "There's an open house tomorrow."

"Yeah, yeah," he said. "Well, I guess you're here and you're coming in and we'll talk and maybe have a drink and then you'll leave. So let's start. Come on in."

Except for boxers drooping off his ass, he was naked. His hunting outfit was piled on a shelf in the kitchen.

He shook his head, and scratched the thick, knotted hair on his chest, then rubbed his arms, his stubbled face.

"Feel like my veins are turning into worms," he said.

"Why'd you come to church?"

"Hey, don't forget I let you in," he said. He fumbled inside his coat and pulled out a piece of paper. "I got the restraining order right here. I take it with me everywhere I go. I felt the need to talk to a priest." He scratched the pale insides of his arm, and examined the legal document. "I don't think the law applies to a church," he said. "Once you get inside you get asylum."

He returned the paper to his coat pocket and then picked up the kitchen garbage can, reached his hand in, and pushed aside newspapers, a tuna can, a melon rind.

"See?" he said.

He meant to show me a prescription bottle at the bottom of the can. I lifted it out, gave it a rattle, and held it to the light.

"There's one left," I said.

"I quit," he said. "Thirty-five years and now I've kicked 'em cold turkey."

My father never talked about his own father, and the oldest story he ever told me about himself was of the way snow whipped off Lake Erie in August of 1953, great blinding gusts and rolling drifts, the summer landscape sculpted into a sea of white. Fantastic! A miracle! Naturally, of course, it hadn't been August. He'd been hospitalized, locked up in a Cleveland sanatorium and then shocked out of his mind for six months, and it was January, the day of his release. Why, in telling me this, had he left the story in its state of confusion? Now I thought of the snow in August. At the time, electroconvulsive therapy was an experimental procedure and current thinking called for barbituates in long-term intractable cases.

That, then, was science and the bold sci-fi future. My father, the day of his release, filled his prescription at a corner druggist and renewed it regularly, like his subscription to the *Wall Street Journal*, for the next thirty-five years.

"When d'you quit?"

"It's a booger, man," he said, clawing at his arms and again at the matted hair on his chest. "I tried watching TV. Then I tried taking a shower and banging my head against the wall."

"You just now tossed these," I said.

"Why the fuck do you think I'm traipsing around the house naked?" he shouted. "My clothes were driving me crazy, that's why."

"I'd like to call Headberry."

He scratched himself some more. "Worms, man. I feel like I could explode. You want a drink?"

The gin and limes and a tray of melting ice were already out on the sink counter. He fixed us two drinks and we sat at the dining table. Across the street the Grand and Wooley families walked out onto their adjoining lawns. A badminton net was strung across the property line on metal stakes. The kids, some of them my age, stood on one side, and the parents stood on the other. Everybody carried rackets and Mr. Wooley, in chinos and a pink shirt, opened a cannister of birdies. Bill Grand said something and Bill Wooley leaned back and aimed a silent laugh at the sky.

"I hate those redundant bastards," my father commented.

"You don't even know them."

"Sure I do, you know one you know 'em all." He sipped his drink with fine relish. "Where's your mother going?"

It surprised me that he knew she was going anywhere, and I was caught off guard.

"I'm not saying," I said, and now there was a secret between us.

"She's having an affair."

"Mom? Mom's not having an affair."

"What makes you so sure?"

"Who with then?"

My father looked away, out the window. "Jesus Christ, probably." He sucked an ice cube out of his drink and bit it, spitting glassy splinters. "She's got me by the nuts."

"Hardly," I said. "You're free."

"Free? Free my ass. You know, I've never been to the rainforest—isn't that a phenomena? She's mortgaged my work effort."

For the longest time I thought this was an old bromide all fathers told their kids. Don't mortgage my work effort. No one in this house is going to mortgage my work effort. Roxy took me to the dictionary and explained. *Mort*, she said, means dead. And *gage*, she said, means security.

"That doesn't make any sense," I told him now.

"No? Okay, fine. What's up with you?"

I guessed we were going to ignore the scene at church. Somehow we had agreed to forget it.

"I had a dream about you last night."

"Other people's dreams are boring."

"I was over here, in the kitchen. You were trying to give me some medicine, like when I was a kid, with a squeeze dropper. Like liquid aspirin. But I wasn't a kid anymore. You were holding the back of my head and telling me to open my mouth. Open up, you said, and when I did, you put a gun in my mouth and kept saying, take your medicine. Take your medicine, you'll feel better."

"Goddamnit," he said.

"It's just a dream."

"Let's talk about something else. You hear the latest about Mr. Kayhew?"

"No, what?"

"You knew a blood vessel popped in his head? Up in an airplane, up there behind the curtain, first class, knowing the Kayhews. He wasn't dead, just in a coma. I heard they rented him his own apartment and he lived there in a coma."

"I didn't know."

"I'm practically there myself."

I must have made a face.

"What? I'm serious. When I die I'll be exploded to shit.

People'll look in the box and say, 'Good God, what the hell killed him?'"

My dad sipped his drink again, keeping an eye on me over the lip of his glass.

"Just everything," he said, answering himself. "Anyway, Kayhew's out."

"Out?"

"He was in a coma."

"You told me that," I said. "So he's out of it now?"

"I guess. I guess you could say that. He's dead."

"That's not what people usually mean when they say someone comes out of a coma."

"Well, it's a little discussed medical fact, but dying is the other way out."

After a moment, he said, "We were friends, you know, me and Kayhew. Not great friends, but I liked him all right, and he liked me. I think he liked me. He never actually said he liked me, but—anyway, the point is, I read his obit—he was much beloved, survived by, et cetera—and only sixty-five years old. Sixty-five. That's five years older than me. You know how many days that is?"

"Do you?" I said.

"2,190," my father said. "Given my habits, I figure I've got 2,000 days left." He raised his eyebrows. "This is one of them." He shrugged. "How's your drink? You want another? I'm having another."

"I'll hold off," I said.

But he made me a drink anyway. When he returned to the table, a cigarette dangled from his lips.

"Smoking?"

"2,000 days, man. Who gives a crap?"

I left the split seeds and floating pulp of my old drink and started the new one. I held the glass to the light and the fresh gin at that moment seemed to be the clearest thing I'd ever seen in my life.

"Miles used to say certain streams were gin clear," I said, "That's how he'd describe them."

"I hate fishing."

"I was only remembering. It was just something to say."

"I've worked in insurance all my life," he said. "The actuarial tables are incredibly accurate. They'll nail you to the wall just about every time. You can read those things and then call a mortician and make an appointment. Like Jackie."

Jackie's last day, his last hour, was an obsessive concern of mine. I'd reconstructed it. I knew where he went, who he talked to, the last tape he played in his stereo ("Johnny Was," by Stiff Little Fingers). The night Jackie shot himself my mother had come into his bedroom. He was at his desk, writing. It was shortly after 8:30. He wore a green and gray flannel shirt, blue jeans with blown out knees, black army boots. Jackie wouldn't turn around and face her. She went back upstairs to tell my father something was strange, that Jackie had a shotgun in his room. "I'm watching a TV show," he said, "don't interrupt me. And close the door when you leave." But that doesn't really explain. What he told my mother that night he told her every night. Without the punctuation of Jackie's death the night of November 26, and all the information I'd gathered about it, would mean nothing. But at 4:30 in the morning, when the police lights pulsed in the graying air and a couple cops stood on the lawn discussing the case, I ran out there in my pj's. "It wasn't suicide," I screamed at them. "It was murder!"

"You want a smoke?" My dad waved his pack of Pall Malls at me. He went to the kitchen and fished in the garbage can and set the tuna can between us. "No ashtrays. I quit these buggers to save money. I calculated it out that I was spending two hundred bucks a year on cigs. That was when I only made two hundred a month. A whole month's salary. So I quit."

"Where's the rug?" I asked.

I had just felt with my feet below the dining table that the oriental rug wasn't there.

"What? The rug, I don't know."

"That's weird," I said. "All my life it was under the table and now it's gone."

"Crazy, huh?"

I finished my drink, stood and said, "I'm gonna split. First I want to get some stuff."

"Stay here," my dad said. "I can't having you running around the house."

"It's my house too."

"On what piece of paper does it say this is your house?"

"There's only two things I want."

"Look, sit down. Okay? Sit down. Let's have another drink."

"I want Miles's fly rod. You don't fish and I want it."

"It's yours, you can have it. Okay? Jesus. I hate fishing. Fishing makes me feel fucking hopeless."

"And the christening dress, I want that too."

"I'm not sure where that is," my dad said.

"Crazy, huh?"

"It's fucking nuts," he said, "the way things get lost."

Out the window the Grands and Wooleys were still playing badminton in the lowering light. I could faintly hear their shouts and cries as they chased the birdie. The gray air seemed to be filling the house like rising water.

My dad said, "It's wild."

I waited for him to say what was wild, but he only looked out the window.

"What?"

"I can't make the data stand still."

My father sipped his drink meditatively and watched.

"So what's your mother doing in Texas?" he asked.

"How do you know she's going to Texas?"

"She went to the travel agent. She used our credit card to charge the ticket. That's how."

"You put on quite a show at church this afternoon."

"A show?"

I was starting to feel hazy, blurred. "Yeah, a show. You almost looked like somebody in need of pity."

I shook a Pall Mall from the pack, lit it. My dad watched the badminton game wind down. The Wooleys and the Grands seemed to be running around their lawn swatting flies. Cheers went up, moans, cries, but I could no longer see what they were chasing. It was too dark. A clock ticked in the living room and the refrigerator buzzed and a wind must have risen because behind me a branch scratched the window. A car passed.

"I'll get that stuff," I said.

"You know what the agent told me? Cynthia—that's her name, Cynthia—she told me the place had bad vibes."

"I don't get it."

"We'll have to sell below the appraised value," my dad said. "We won't get near the asking price. They all know Jackie killed himself in the basement, they know Miles is crazy, they know all that shit."

"They? Who's they?"

"People." He looked at me. He smiled, grimly. "Do what you have to do. I'm having another drink. This gin is something, huh?"

Our basement was a museum housing a collection of all the usual artifacts. In bins and racks, we had baseball bats, broken skis, tennis rackets with warped guts, wingless gliders, golf clubs, aquariums, hula hoops, a bowling ball and several orange lifejackets my dad had purchased at a lawn sale, along with an old O'Brien waterski and a gas can, all with the idea, a very sudden, impulsive idea, that he'd buy a boat, too. For weeks after we saw boats gleaming in showrooms or parked on trailers in someone's driveway or heading out to sea or docked at a slip in the Union Bay Marina. I don't know what happened to that idea, but here were four faded lifejackets, hooked on tenpenny nails. Along a rickety wooden shelf were cases of canned peas and corn and thirty-weight oil, a box of powdered milk, several bottles of novitiate wine—bulk items of a big family. In boxes were tools, tools to fix everything, from loose chair legs to leaky faucets. C-clamps, crimpers, a circular saw. With a tool in his hand, my dad was no better than a caveman. He couldn't fix anything. He usually ended up clubbing whatever wouldn't work, breaking it worse. But he loved tools, he strolled through hardware stores handling trouble lights and blue hacksaw blades with the enthusiasm other people might reserve for the Louvre.

I found what I was looking for: a polished cherry wood case, narrow and about two and a half feet long. I brought it upstairs and turned on a light. I popped the hasp, and opened the box. The inside was lined with crushed velvet, and hand-carved bridges at either end held the rod in place. I lifted the butt end out, cradled the sanded cork in my hand. The cane was pale blond, unmarred by knots or coarse grain, and the lacquer, gin clear, seemed only to draw out the bamboo's simplicity; the reel seat was rosewood, the fittings nickel plated; the guides gleamed; the ferrules were wrapped in blue and green thread, winding in a spiral pattern. I heard the ice in my dad's glass clink, and then he was there, looking at the rod over my shoulder. I turned the rod in my hand. Miles had called us all down to his workbench in the basement the day he signed it. He used a Chinese brush from which he'd clipped all but a single horsehair. I remember watching him do it, the way he held one hand steady with the other while, miraculously, his name looped across the cane in a single stroke.

"That's art, man. That's a piece of work," I said.

"Not bad for a crazy fuck," my dad said.

"He wasn't crazy then." I angled the rod in the light. "It's just the opposite of how he is now. It's simple."

"Have another drink?"

"No thanks," I said.

From the kitchen, Dad said, "You planning a trip?"

"Wyoming," I said. "I'm gonna live in the park all season."

"That's stupid," Dad said. "Here's your gin."

"I said no. What's stupid about it? I go there every year."

"What about school?"

"What about it?"

"Don't look at me that way," my father said. "I'm broke."

"Anyway, it's where I tossed Jackie's ashes," I said. After he'd been cremated, we were each given an envelope of ashes, just a pinch—you'd throw more oregano in a pot of spaghetti sauce.

"Where?"

"Well, you've never been there, so it's hard to describe."

"Hey guy," my father said, "it's good to see you."

"You're drunk."

"Sure. Been drunk. I don't think I've talked to anyone for ten days, two weeks."

"You're talking pretty good tonight."

"I guess I am. Imagine if you were God and had to listen to all this."

And then I must have said yes. I should have gone back to the shoe box, and there were four or five opportunities to say I'd had enough, I got what I wanted, see you. But the evening kept opening up, wider and wider, accepting every vague word and half-assed idea. Everything was finding a place; there was a room at every inn. The night became like a fairy tale in which every juncture is answered with a yes, and the children hold hands and merrily march down the dark trail into a furnace. The gin ran clear, the tuna can was full of stubbed Pall Malls, I was drunk and awake and my dad was drunk and awake, and the space was there, yawning, and something had to happen.

"Tell me where your mother is?" Dad was saying.

"No way," I insisted.

"Tell me."

"Okay," I said. I squinted a teasing look across the table. "I'll trade you."

"You already got the fly rod."

"I want the original of Jackie's letter."

"Can't do it. I don't know where it is."

"Oh well—"

"All right."

"Get it," I said.

"You don't trust me?"

"Oh, I don't think so."

When he brought the letter back I checked to make sure all fifteen and a half pages were there, licking my fingers and counting them like bills.

Then I said, "She's gone to see an angel."

"An angel huh?"

"In the bark of a tree, a cottonwood. In the middle of a

junkyard somewhere in Texas. There's been reports, so she's going to see for herself."

"It's been in the papers. I've read about that angel." He lit a cigarette, waved the smoke from his face. "Hey, we got coffee stains in the carpet look like angels. We got angels in this house."

A bus passed out front. An old habit, I looked through the window to see if any of my brothers or sisters were coming home.

"Your mother was never anything but a whore. She got me fired off my job. All slander."

"The reason you were fired is because no one likes you. You're an asshole—that's actually a quote."

"Who said that? Markula?"

"I'm not telling."

"I got something else to give you," my father said.

He disappeared again and when he returned to the table he set the shotgun and a box of shells in front of me.

I said, "That's the gun."

"Cops took this as evidence," my father said. "Suicide's a crime. Evidence? Heigh-ho—but I got it back."

In the garage we gathered up gunnysacks, some twine and a flashlight, and loaded everything into the Plymouth.

"Me and Miles used to do this," my dad said, as we drove away.

Again I thought he was confusing me with my brother. "I'm not too big on guns," I reminded him.

"Neither was Jackie. You took after him on that."

I thought there was a joke in there somehow, but I couldn't find it.

"A gun doesn't mean anything."

"Huh?"

"Take a caveman," my father said. "You put a short-arm of some sort, a .38 or what have you, you put it on the ground with some other stuff, like a rock and a sewing machine and a banana. Ordinary things. What's the caveman going to do? Huh? He's not going to look at the banana and think, Oh, this'd be good on cornflakes. He's not going to take the sewing machine and stitch up a tutu. And he's not going to look at the gun and think, Maybe I'll blow my head off. You see what I'm saying."

I thought I did, and then I was sure I didn't.

"I'm nearly broke," my dad said.

"No you're not."

"I thought I'd be living with more dignity by this time, but it's not turning out that way."

"You're lying," I said again. It wasn't an accusation, more like a statement. We were stopped at a four-way intersection. My father curled his hands tightly around the wheel to steady them.

"Maybe I should do the Jackie thing," he said.

"Fuck you," I said. The words just popped out of my mouth, like a champagne cork. Now my hands were trembling, and I put them in my coat pocket. "Don't ever say that again."

"Why are you so pissed all of a sudden?"

"Let's just go. Let's get those birds."

I've read and reread Jackie's letter to us, I've searched the final paragraph for a summation. Now I had the original. The letter is long. In it he lists the things he likes: wolves and trains, the Skagit River, coasting a bike down Market Street in Ballard. He talks about my mom, Dad, my four sisters and Miles, but at no time does he mention me. Toward the last few pages I sense a creepy mortmain, as if my father's hand is folded over his, guiding the pen across the page, line by line, word by word. Is he trying to say something about himself, or about my father? I look at the last word and think of the moment when he put down the pen and picked up the gun and pulled the trigger. How much time passed? Had he been thinking it over? To pull the trigger he would have used the same finger he used to press the pen against the paper. What went on in that space? Between the pen and the gun?

Under the freeway we found a cement ledge. A sleepy cooing came from the recess, the occasional flutter of beating wings. It sounded like a nursery at nap time.

"You stay down here," Dad said. "I'll hand the birds to you."

He chinned himself onto the ledge, grunting loudly. He wiped shit off his hands, and I passed him the flashlight. He aimed the beam at the birds, a row of them squatting along the ledge. The first bird was mottled gray and brown with beady eyes like drops of melted chocolate. Its eyes remained wide open, stunned and tranced, staring into the beam, unable to move or turn away from the white light. Dad stroked the bird's throat gently. "Come to papa," he said, and when he'd soothed it somewhat he grabbed it by the neck and passed it down to me. I could feel its heart beating in my hand. I slipped the bird into the gunnysack. The pigeon flopped around, trying to orient itself. Dad jacklit another and another. Some were white, others black as crows. After we'd bagged five birds I tied off the first sack with twine and started a new one. Dad handed me five more paralyzed pigeons and then jumped down.

"That ought to do it," he said. He brushed molted gray feathers from his face, from his arms. "Look at that," he said.

The sacks were alive with confused pigeons, two blobs rolling down the hill. You could see the birds struggling to take off, stupidly beating against the burlap. We ran after them, two drunks at a pigeon rodeo, each grabbing a sack.

We put the birds in the back seat of the car. I picked a downy feather from my father's ear.

"You still pissed?" he said.

"Don't make hollow threats."

"You think it was hollow?"

"I've heard it before."

"Feel like it was just yesterday I was driving around the woods with the Beauty Queen, trying to get my hand up her skirt."

My father laughed. The Beauty Queen was my mother. She'd been Miss Spanaway in 1954.

"Well," he said, gesturing broadly with a sweep of the bottle, "I did. Seven kids. One dead, one crazy. Four girls who don't want a damn thing to do with me. Then you. What the fuck's wrong with you, I wonder?"

"We going?"

The pigeons were insane, jumping around inside the sacks. A crazy burlap aviary. My father got out of the car, took the sacks, and spun the birds in circles. When he put them back in the seat, they were quiet.

"You're the only one left. You'll bury me," my father said. "You'll write my obituary."

Generally my father was what people call a paper killer. He drove to a firing range and clamped on ear protection and stood in a port lined with blue baffle shield and shot two-bit targets. Bull's-eyes, black silhouettes, now and then the joke target of a dictator's face in profile. At the end of an afternoon of shooting, he'd roll up and rubber band his targets, tacking the best to a wall in his den, like trophies. "You shoot against your old self," he'd told me. Of the boys, it was my crazy brother Miles who enjoyed guns. Jackie hated them. The first and only time he'd ever fired a gun, the barrel was in his mouth. Obviously, you don't need to be a sharpshooter to kill yourself. Even before Jackie, I'd never liked guns. My father sensed this hesitance, and took me out to the woods, trying to teach me to see things and then trying to get me to shoot them out of the trees. Squirrels, robins. The only time I'd actually fired a gun with him was at a gravel pit. He stood behind me and watched as I leveled his bolt-action .22 at a row of pop cans. He calmly gave me directions, but I quickly aimed high and pinched off a round, missing, then chambering another round and missing again, spent shells skittering at my feet in brassy flashes, until I dry-fired and knew the gun was empty. I was ten years old, and it was the first time I'd ever felt like I was not in control of myself. I'd been feeling the urge to turn around and shoot my father.

It was near dawn when we parked at the gravel pit. I hadn't been there in ten years and it was now abandoned, a maze of packed dirt roads, each ending in a cul-de-sac of bitten earth. I carried the pigeons and Dad carried the gun. The sky was just beginning to pale with a metallic dawn light outlining a dark fringe of trees. We sat down.

"Can't drink like I used to," Dad said.

I raised an eyebrow. "How'd you used to?"

"I didn't mean I don't drink like I used to," he said. "Just I can't." He coughed up a laugh, breathing in short, swift rasps. He lit a cigarette. "My lawyer call you?"

"He did."

"You gonna testify?"

I though about it, briefly, as shapes in the gravel pit took on solidity. People were using it as a dump. Washing machines, the odd chair, boxes and lawnbags, bent and twisted gutters, a suitcase.

"I wouldn't let it go to trial," I said.

"You mean I don't have a chance?"

I imagined my father's life caught up in the snare of the law, the courts, in the web of family history, in all those things whose severest weapon is consistency, and I knew he would not fare well.

"I'd settle."

My father nodded. He pointed the shotgun at the gunnysack of pigeons.

"Better than skeet," he said.

"I'll release them."

"You don't want to shoot? You want, you can go first."

I looked at the gun, resting across my father's lap. I knew no magic inhered in the piece itself, that it was just a shotgun, but even though I could convince myself that the thing housed no resident bogey, I wouldn't touch it.

"I'll just do the birds," I said.

I carried both sacks about fifty yards away, intensely aware that my back was turned to my father. A spot at the base of my neck grew hot. My heart beat in a way that made me conscious of it. I untied the knot on the first sack and gently cradled a pigeon in my palm. I covered its eyes and looked at my father. He nodded. I spun the bird in circles, round and round, and then I set it down. It fell over. The next few moments were kind of vaudevillian. The pigeon flapped its wings, raising a cloud of dust, scooting sideways over the ground, pratfalling, and then it took flight, rising drunkenly in the air, executing a few goofy loops and turns. By instinct the pigeon appeared to know it was supposed to fly, but couldn't figure out the up and down of it. It smashed to the ground, leaden, then rose again. Before it could gain equilibrium and fly level, I heard the deep percussive blast of the shotgun, and the pigeon jerked back, propelled by the impact, and fell like a limp dishrag from the sky. Immediately I grabbed another bird. Its heart raced in my palm. Dad nodded. I spun it around and released it, watching as it rose so far and then exploded in a flakburst of gray feathers. Each time, for the moment I held the bird, I could feel its life, the heart and the breast bones and the soft cooing in its throat, but there really was no moment of decision on my part, no hesitation, as I released the bird. I tossed another into the air, watching it struggle wildly against falling, then rise erratically, lifting above the trees, and get blown out of the sky.

"Take a shot," my Dad said.

"No thanks," I said.

He came to me, and we sat down again. He drank from the gin and passed the bottle.

"This used to be open country out here," he said. "But I think we're inside the city limits now. I think we're in the suburbs."

I took a drink, and said, "You know the christening dress? All of us were baptized in that. Mom was, and grandpa too."

"Yeah, so?"

"Where is it?"

"She'll get an annullment. Everything to nothing in the eyes—" I interrupted.

"But we'll never see it again, right?"

When he didn't answer, I said, "Let's head out."

"There's one more pigeon left."

I folded open the sack and let the bird go. It walked around, head bobbing, among the dead ones.

My father, on thorazine, always became childlike. He walked in slanted, headlong, stumbling bursts that ended when he smacked into walls or collapsed in a heap on the carpet. He hid in closets, he broke his head open falling down stairs. We cleaned up after him, we mopped piss off the bathroom floor, we helped my mother wipe his muddied ass. At dinner, we wrapped a bedsheet around his neck and spoonfed him pureed carrots and canned spaghetti and pale green peas we mooshed with a fork. We fought over the chance to feed him, played airplane games with the zooming spoon. He babbled and sputtered and sometimes through the thorazine fog the rudiments of language bubbled up. Once, while the nine of us sat at the table, silently eating our dinner, he began to mumble, and we all leaned forward to listen. "Fuck you," he said. "Fuck you. Fuck you. Fuck you." My mother pushed another spoonful of mashed potato in his mouth, and it burbled back out in a fuck you.

As the youngest I was never left alone with my father, never left to care for him by myself — except once, and briefly. Everyone was out and I remember the strangeness of being in the house alone with him. I asked him, did he want to watch TV? When he was crazy, the television ran constantly. I flipped the dial from sports to cartoons to network coverage of the last lunar mission, Apollo 17. Then he spoke — it was a miracle, like hearing a child's first words. He wanted me to go through the house and gather up all the sunglasses I could find. Despite his ongoing bouts of insanity, he was still my father, no crazier than the dads in the Old Testament, and I obeyed him. I thought it was a game. I tore through the house. "Thataboy," he shouted whenever I found a new pair of glasses. I gathered up Jackie's wire rims, a pair of aviators and blocky tortoise shells, the girls' red and yellow and green plastic Disney glasses. Ski goggles, protective eyeware. My father arranged them on the floor, shuffled them one way, then another way, and then he asked, "Who do you think we can call about these glasses?" I said I didn't think there was anyone. And he said, "Well, I guess we're sitting ducks then. I guess there's no hope. Isn't there anybody we can call?"

This memory came back to me at the open house. My father had put on his good suit and Sunday shoes but perversely decided not to wear his glasses. Immediately he looked lost. He stumbled around the house, filling shallow dishes with salted nuts, setting out a cardtable with potato chips and pretzels and pop. There were so many things missing from the house — things like family photos and favorite sympathy cards, things that had earned their places on the wall, on the fireplace mantel, simply by virtue of having always been there — that my father seemed spatially confused and kept rearranging his dishes of nuts, putting them down on the coffee table, then the end table, then setting them back in their original spots.

"Sit down," I said.

"I'm not supposed to be here," my father said. "Cynthia asked me to vacate for a while."

Cynthia, the agent, was openly miffed when she saw my father. She introduced prospective buyers to me, and then quickly moved on. I tagged along. She had a proprietary air as she showed the first few strangers through the house. She took a young, childless couple upstairs and showed them the master bedroom. She stood by the window and pointed to the view, the long sloping hill, the mountains in the west, offering this vista as a possibility for the future. We toured the kitchen, the livingroom. Then we all went downstairs, to the basement. Half of it was unfinished and the other half was panelled in knotty pine. While the Realtor talked about turning the basement into a rumpus room, I lifted the lid of an old Te-Amo cigarbox and found some pennies and pen caps, a few buttons, a harmonica and several hypodermics. When he was fifteen and sixteen, Jackie had been a junkie, and he'd shoot up in the basement. I'd find him downstairs, nodded off, a needle dangling from his arm. It felt like ages ago now, my childhood. I closed the box.

The most earnest and eager buyers showed up early, followed by a few dreamers who obviously couldn't make a reasonable offer. By afternoon, though, the tone of things changed. I was standing at the picture window when I saw Mrs. Wooley stroll up the walkway. She was wearing a short skirt and heels. She rang the doorbell, and I let her in.

"Bobby," she said. "I'm surprised to see you."

She was an intimate of my mother and had to have known, of course, that I'd left school. She had a daughter my age finishing up at Yale.

"Nice to see you Mrs. Wooley," I said.

"Call me Lois," she said. "I think you can do that now."

I offered her a drink. She looked at her watch and said, "No, thank you."

She bit her lip, and a little pink came off on her teeth.

"Last time I saw you," she said, "was at the funeral."

"You thinking of buying the house?"

"I was just in the neighborhood."

"Yeah, well, you always are. You live across the street. You're our neighbor."

"Lois, Lois," I heard my father say. He clasped her hand and smiled warmly. "It's been forever. How are you?" He looked down at this feet. "Things have been crazy."

"So I've heard," Mrs. Wooley said.

"Can I show you around the house?" he asked her.

Mrs. Kayhew tottered across the street and walked up the stone steps to our porch as if avoiding cracks. And shortly after, Mrs. Greyham followed, along with several other women from the neighborhood. My father greeted each of them with the same warm somewhat chastened smile and then, like a docent, he led the entire group on a tour of our house. He was especially kind to Mrs. Kayhew. He took her arm in his and was guiding her up the stairs. Mrs. Kayhew turned her yellow face toward my father, holding it up at a precise angle, as if her blue eyes were pools of water she didn't want to spill.

The little group stood on the upstairs landing. All the bedroom doors were closed, and the thickly coated brown paint gave them a certain feel, as if they'd been sealed shut a long time ago.

My father nudged a crucifix with his foot. He'd knocked it off the wall the day he came home to find my mother gone. The brass Jesus had come un-nailed, and was wedged between two spikes in the bannister. Mrs. Greyham looked at the cross and then at my father. I waited to hear the lie he would tell.

"I knocked it off the wall," Dad said.

My dad hitched his trousers and bent down on one knee. He picked up the cross and the Jesus and held them, one in each hand, and then tried to fit them together.

He opened his bedroom door, and all the women stepped in. He showed them the deck and the half-bath and the big closet still filled with my mother's clothes. The big king bed still held the outline of my father in the wrinkled sheets, an intaglio of a head and legs and an arm stretching out toward the other pillow. He looked down at the impression, as if he might slip right back into bed, occupying the mold of himself.

My father offered to make a pot of tea.

"Tea?" I blurted out.

"That's okay," my dad said.

But none of these women had come to see the house, which was unexceptional; they'd come to see him. Now they were ready to leave.

When they left, I asked my father if he'd like to have a drink. The last light faded from the day and the streetlamps were flickering to life. My father seemed dispirited.

"I think I'll just sit," he said. He pointed to his chair in the living room and then followed his index finger. He sat down and removed his wingtips, his navy socks, and began massaging his feet.

"Boy, they're sore," he said, squeezing his toes.

He sat in the dark, very quietly, as if he'd discovered a still point.

"Any buyers?"

"Huh? Oh, maybe."

I went to the kitchen and fished my dad's last barbiturate from the garbage can. I rattled the amber bottle and popped the top and dry-swallowed the pill. I used to steal them out of his medicine cabinet all the time. The thing about barbiturates is they make you feel caressed or gently held, your skin humming all over with the touch of a thousand fingers. I sat at the dining table and took apart Miles's old reel, dabbing drops of Remington gun oil on the pawls, and then went outside and rigged up the fly rod, drawing the line through the guides. I stripped out twenty-five feet of line and began false casting. At first I was out of practice, throwing wide loops that dipped low on the backcast and piled up on the forecast, but with each stroke I made a minor adjustment and soon I could feel the rhythm, marking time. To Mrs. Wooley across the street I might have looked like a man sending semaphore to a distant ship. I worked the line until I was casting forty, fifty feet, and the back and forth motion felt substantial, bending the rod down to the butt. I took up a couple extra coils in my left hand and shot those forward. The line sailed smoothly through the guides and unfurled across the street.

Holding Miles's rod in my hand I thought of him, my living, wrecked brother. A few weeks after he jumped from the Aurora Bridge, I decided, one night, to walk out there. I'm terrified of heights, and I walked slowly out onto the bridge, step by step, my hand rubbing the dirty railing, until I'd made it midway onto the span. My legs weakened, my hands shook and burned with sweat. I had not yet looked down but I didn't need to; the fear rose toward me. I closed my eyes and felt the gritty wind suctioned by oncoming traffic. I heard the clack of tires over the concrete, the screech of a seagull. When I looked down, some three hundred feet, where the black water of Union Bay glinted with city lights, I couldn't move, I froze. My legs wouldn't work. I felt the fall in my stomach, an opening up and a hollowing out. I couldn't move forward up the bridge, or back where I'd come from. I couldn't let go of the rail. I might have been there for an hour, easy, when a woman, out walking her dog, came by. My fear of heights overcame my normal fear of speaking to strangers, and I told her I couldn't move. "I'm afraid," I said, pointing over the edge. She switched the leash to her other hand. "I thought I could cross," I explained. The woman took my hand. She talked us across, I know, because I remember the sound of her voice, but I have no idea what she said, and on the other side of the bridge I thanked her ridiculously, over and over, and the next day I rode the bus to pick up my truck.

My father came out. He was barefoot, but still wore the suit. He scratched the back of his hand, and looked over his shoulders at our house. I lifted the line off the street and started casting again.

"I'll never settle," he said.

"Your choice, I guess."

I kept casting, working the rod back and forth, the line flowing gently in watery curls, whispering over our heads.

"It's beautiful," my father said. "Like haiku."

"Let me give it a try," he said.

I let the line fall and stood behind him, closing his hand around the cork, then closing my hand over his.

Two Poems by Edward Hirsch

Idea of the Holy
New York City, 1975

Out of the doleful city of Dis
rising between the rivers

Out of the God-shaped hole in my chest
and the sacred groves of your body

Out of stars drilled through empty spaces
and Stones in My Passway at four A.M.

All those hours studying under the lamp
the First Cause and the Unmoved Mover

the circle whose circumference is
everywhere and whose center is nowhere

the Lord strolled under the oak tree at Mamre
at the hottest moment of the day

the Lord vacated a region within himself
and recoiled from the broken vessels

a God uncreated or else a God withdrawn
a God comprehended is no God

Out of subway stations and towering bridges
Out of murky waters and the wound of chaos

Out of useless walks under fire escapes
Be friends to your burning

I saw the sun convulsed in clouds
and the moon candescent in a ring of flame

souls I saw weeping on streetcorners
in a strangeness I could not name

O falling numinous world at dusk
O stunned and afflicted emptiness

After three days and nights without sleep
I felt something shatter within me

then I lay down on my cot motionless
and sailed to the far side of nothing

The Burning of the Midnight Lamp

Listening to Purple Haze and The Wind Cries Mary,
Let Me Stand Next to Your Fire and Manic Depression,

I am drifting undersea toward strobe lights
and feedback, the dreamy, acoustic waves of 1969.

Remember how you explained those dirty sounds—
the two-note riff banned by the Spanish Inquisition,

the hammer-ons and pull-offs, the sharpened ninth?
Is it tomorrow or just the end of time?

I've forgotten nothing. Any moment I'll cross
the campus near the dormitory where you've moved in

with another man; I'll pause under the window trembling
with volume—a betrayer betrayed and turned back

to the raw, metallic, bristling taste of wind.
The morning is dead and the day is too

There's nothing left here to lead me, but the velvet moon
(you always liked the wah-wah pedal on that song).

• • •

Someone is playing *Voodoo Child* and *House Burning Down*,
checking the chord progression in *Spanish Castle Magic*

and the octaves in *Third Stone from the Sun*.
Another is blasting *Crosstown Traffic* from a lounge

where darkness branches into maroon rivers
and cigarette butts flare into the stars.

No more parties with our friends eating seeds
and lacing punch, smoking joints in a dim room

where you go on talking about sinister bent strings
and dive-bombing sounds, the devil invoked

in the interval of a tritone or flattened fifth.
No more waiting for you to return to me

(*that forgotten earring lying on the floor*)
through a downpour of left-handed notes.

But sometimes when I close my eyes
I see your body fading back into shadows.

• • •

As a child, Jimi Hendrix watched his soul floating
away from his torso, looking down at himself

from a different realm. He was awake but slipping
mindlessly through another dimension, the astral plane.

That's how you felt about LSD and STP,
those ten-milligram doses of the sublime.

We were looking for fire escapes: ladders
and watchtowers spiraling up from the ground.

But that year as I smoldered within my body
and you tripped through the acid nights

Orpheus stomped microphones and humped speakers,
smashing amplifiers on stage after stage

as though he could whammy the Underworld
into submission and subdue the Furies

while darkness vibrated around him
and electric guitars exploded in flames.

Judy Longley

from Matisse in Morocco

I. Landscape from a Window

Two vases of flowers squarely on the ledge
stare out as though they regret the countryside,
mean to ignore you squinting above the edge
of your canvas, generating color that slides
over the sill, pours into the valley an intense
hue. Though you mean only dusk under eucalyptus,
buildings loom like sepulchers sinking in a dense
wave of cobalt. Was this how Atlantis drowned?
Scattered islands of light, cedars at attention,
the palace consumed by dark. Unable to stem the flood
from your palette, the impulse of creation,
you urge a donkey to safer ground and would
save Tangiers poised by the sea on high cliffs
from which minarets signal the sky for relief.

II. Zorah in Yellow

She's wiser now but still at sea. Moon-
faced, she floats on an aqua wave,
the night's pale disc reflected at noon,
docile, accepting whatever is asked, grave
even when you joke, call her your Russian egg
encased in her decorative wrapper.
For she knows you take what's left of her, beg
what she can least refuse, knows your canvas captures
her the way water holds the moon's image, white vessel
caught on the tide, shattered, made whole,

shattered again. So at night in the brothel
she thinks of you, Matisse, thinks how her soul,
diminished by your painting, wanes and tires,
a sickle moon awash in men's desires.

III. The Moroccans

It's the Morocco you will dream for a lifetime,
pared to geometric figures lapped
by black so deep it embraces, defines
how water gives a form to this land.
A single turbaned male, back to the viewer,
represents his people, religion a ritual
reduced to his left arm swelling like prayer
out of the dark, as a crab claw might signal
from a tide pool. Oranges bob and glow,
buoys anchored to trees that lift, sway
with the current. Over all, the tomb of a holy
hermit. From the tower dome, beams displace
the night. Brush stilled, you lean, peer
into the wet, wait for creation to clear.

Bin Ramke

As If the Past

I am weary of repenting.
—Jeremiah

Some sad Greek said the atoms swerve
and that's how anything happens, "anything" meaning not nothing. The nerve

of us to live it through, the many
and the few of us, just and unjust alike
sitting on the curb being cold ("Come in" he

told the young one leaning her bike
on her hip as we imagined perversions afoot
but lacked the will to salvation—like

what you like, it's all taste, good
or bad. Then the parade turned a corner
abandoned our nice neighborhood

to devices. Someone should inform her
that the man is famous among boys,
but whose business is it?) She's torn her

tight little dress, oh dear. Toys
in the window. Remnants of someone's youth
make the rest of us sick. All the joys

are out today, the sun and wind and truth,
the kind of wisdom you pick up on the street
being what passes in this kind of uncouth

colloquia. The parade's over; no beating
even in the distance of drums. No need
to linger. The day is doomed to retreat

into itself, or night. Let's eat—
before the pigeons get it. Popcorn, birdseed,
all the same allegorical need.

●

"With lots of pictures and good stories too
and Jack and jiant killers high renown" he wrote,
young John Clare, who also surely knew

streets like this and neighbors more remote
than moonmen watching us walk and hating us
for reasons too complex to chart but note

how often we pull the shades at midday thus
proving our evil intent. I was married,
faithless husband I, and she took it just

as far as she could, then turned and carried
herself inward until we were both old
and on the street the little children scurried

away from our steps passing. Oh how cold
it has become. I need more words like birds
falling at my feet, I once knew old

words like some know wines; would sniff
them into memory—white lines on mirror
sniff sniff. To train the words to lift

themselves into lyrical lines, to fear or
at least obey me—on the other hand
noble aspirations seemed to come no nearer.

What's the matter with, what is the matter
which makes, the substance of, the bland
smooth sentence I see before me shattered

by the brutal pigeon's coo? Fury and
sound, the iridescent bird makes his
two-note poem until the lady birds demand

his feathery favors. What a life his is—
nor could Shakespeare have remotely
written it better. Successful business.

●

It's all political: she hates me
and I, I can't remember what living skin
feels like. When did I last see

the fond shadow of my own thin
hand dance across the delicate tight
boundary of a human actual body when

even in accident I swerve like light
caught against the gravity of stars;
on the bus I back into corners tight

to myself because I want some warmth
and there it is before me so there
I cannot be, oh man oh woman, what harms

●

us makes us mean. Vacuum genesis—stars:
Think for a moment about the beginning, a spot
appears and from nothing anything, wars

among the particles (who cares?) let us not
to the marriage of true kinds make
impediment/love/sport of. All is fraught

with anger. So we're riding the wake
with our little surfboard self, we're balanced
on the Big Bang hurtling through quaking

time and I am crying over spilt youth. Lanced
boils and stitched split lips, semi-health
surrounds us. It'll pass. Time pranced

past us all decorated as if work stealthily
were happening but it was only luck
happening happily, full of imaginary wealth.

•

Do certain things to him and he will follow
you anywhere. Such knowledge is highly
dangerous: the uneasy erotics of tall, low

stooping women, for instance inflame him nightly
his thin sleep. He remembers the sound of the Latin
fading and the years passing—the incitements unsightly

and the furious fasting for Holy Mother Church, satin
lined and coffin-cool. To atone for suffering
children this good boy would refrain from Matins

till dawn from food and water. Around him a ring
of shadows arrayed themselves: a sun to himself
he walked in imagined holiness, for all the things

he did he thought were good. For all the good health
left to his sense of the world: on snow all shadows
are blue, but some are bluer than others. Wealth

naturally evaded such men. For all he knows
the morning still comes heavily draped
in Olympian intention, and hope falls with snow.

•

Those pigeons: they neither toil nor spin
and they are rather ugly to the untrained
eye. They live on garbage as if when

hard edged life turned poignant and refrained
from killing small beings it was nothing
more than justice. They are wise and tame.

They know something no man can ignore
and they fill the streets with arrogance
during every inaugural parade. No more

nature than this, it is enough. Let every
creature crawl back into the slime,
give us two of each for every zoo and see

what else we can do with our time
than sit contemplating nature-navels
to remind us of all species before crime

cast out the pearls of wit and swine
aligned themselves with mud and bliss.
Take what's yours and make it mine.

•

And yet you love a fellow human
and think about her/him as if some flaw
in the brain were curable with too many

rapt minutes expended upon the virtue
and too few hours upon the vice
and beauty, beauty is a food to you

and beauty is so lovely and nice
hollowing out a nest of nerve
while you live on air and ice.

Jordan Smith

After *Die Walküre*

It is all death, right from the start,
That fluttering agitation in the violins.
Even the love duet, by nightfall
Given over to iron and fire,
Those mediocrities,
The will's forgeries of affection.

So here is my hand, love, a tremolo,
Unsteady around my morning cup of coffee.
And here is the list of what we have to do today,
The discardings, the patchwork,
And the blanks of the seed catalogue—
An order to be filled,

Every day, every day. *Du bist der Lenz*
Soars from the stereo,
The tenor so confident
He must believe the song goes on forever
Like this work of spring,
Which is endless and all preparation.

There is a raw wind
In the bare branches of the maple, the cherry,
A trembling, which is neither will nor its absence
Nor a wish that anything be otherwise
In a world of love than

Mandatory, temporary.

Artis Bernard

Securing Yellow

Check yellow. It must be kept for the center
of flowers and
other intense moments, not
spread across walls, neither those interior that face
dust and shadows, nor exterior that
fade from sun's continuous puzzlement.
Pierre is visiting his paintings

in the museum with wholehearted regard,
as if they were
relatives. He has brought for
them a new yellow paint he's discovered and a fine
camelhair brush to serve it with. It's in
his pocket. He must wait until the guard
turns his back. Just a little touch here

where light throws the face into darkness and there
under the lampshade.
Emily has placed yellow
at the whip edge of day, in the pockets of the sun,
counting it up with care, yellow being
as costly as lovers' words. Vincent weights
his doubt with yellow sunflowers, sun

pungent yellow. Frieda's yellow contains
her body's scream.
Mark will shore up one yellow
with yellow. Dark yellow claims the center over light
yellow that imprisons dark yellow. Size
regulates power. Their intense desire
to dominate one another keeps

them uneasily in place. Restrain yellow.
Do not let it
wander sprawling over large
spaces to scare attention, anyone's shrill. Let it
be well defined, but in place precisely,
like an oriole in flight, or on a far
hillside a field of mustard in bloom.

Joyce Carol Oates

Like Walking to the Drug Store,
When I Get Out

Dear Joyce Carol—

This is the 5th time for me to be writing to you
& I promise it is the last.
I know your reading this Joyce Carol
but I cant prove it can I!

I saw your picture in the paper here.
Maybe you were in Iowa City.
I told you I have a story to tell you
you could write up but you let that opertunity pass.
That's tough shit for you Joyce Carol
only one day you'll know how much.

I'm locked up here for child molestation.
I wont tell you whether I'm guilty or innocent
on account of I've already done 6½ yrs
& guilt or innocence doesnt matter to me now.
I know your asking do you have remorse,
well remorse for what?
Do YOU have remorse?

You people have done everything you want
to me, doesn't that give me equal right.
If you spit in my face & insult me & throw me in solitary
what do you think you will be repaid
when I get out of here?

Look, I never did anything I'd feel guilty about.
I wouldn't do anything I'm ashamed of.
You don't know me, Joyce Carol but thats not my nature.

If youd taken down my story then youd know.
But you wouldnt give me shit & now it's too late.
Maybe I haven't done enough, maybe
that's what I'm ashamed of.

Maybe I should have killed four or five hundred people!
I think now I would feel better.
When I had the chance, but now I don't.
Then I would know I really offered society something!
I'd know I made my mark, like you.
If I wanted to kill somebody
I'd just grab a baseball bat and I'd beat you
till your brains leaked out.
& I wouldn't feel a thing.
I'd be just like walking to the drug store, when I get out.

What do you want to call me a child molester for?
I never molested anyone.
I don't need to molest anyone.
You capitalist swine are molesting your own sons & daughters
& the Constitution says every bit of it is O.K.!
In my whole life I burglarized a 7-11, some nickels & dimes
& busted open a stamp machine
& some cars & cashed a couple checks.
All of which shit I was never caught for & thus
no record of proof available.

I am not a child molester.
I like pussy with hair on it.
Lots of hair on it.
I saw your picture in the paper & your too old for me.
Believe me if I started murdering people
there'd be none of you left.

PS. The U.S. started World War II.

Michael White

The Woman on the Steps of the *Bella Vista Apts*.

I followed her gaze past rooftops of tin, fired-clay
and tar, to the lake's far sleights of vision — its gulls
blown sideways and backwards in flight, its islands floating
in their reflections — with lightning rippling the nerves
of distance, and thunderheads massing across the west. . . .

And then, for more than an hour, wherever I looked —
the stoplights bleeding like watercolors across
the glass of buildings — she was fixed in the fringe
of sight, her right hand absently clasped in her left:
the woman, the desert, the cloudcover closing off.

Slicked down with a shadow of rain, the streets were strangely
deserted; starlings and litter kept disappearing
through clearings of sky. An occasional passerby
lurched past in the flat relief of a paper cutout
beneath the heaves of storm. And over and over —

until I was home in the solitude of my dark
apartment — I kept seeing flashes of basin and range
unreeling beneath the first cold stars. . . .

                                        What is it
drawing us out like moths, in shivers of sunlight
sweeping the lake? Why do we give ourselves

to the wind, to vapory helixes of dust,
the longer we live our lives? These are the hours
we recognize our thirst for brokenness,
for lit-shale dusks arrayed on the lavish scale
of our looking, when only the half-healed cut in your palm

can call you back to your body. These are the hours
rain turns the air it dries in iridescent,
lingering like a taste on the tongue, for as long
as this moment lasts, there is no other end
to it, there is no other end in sight

but iron skies, and the irised glow of the moon.

Masks

Flavia Gandolfo

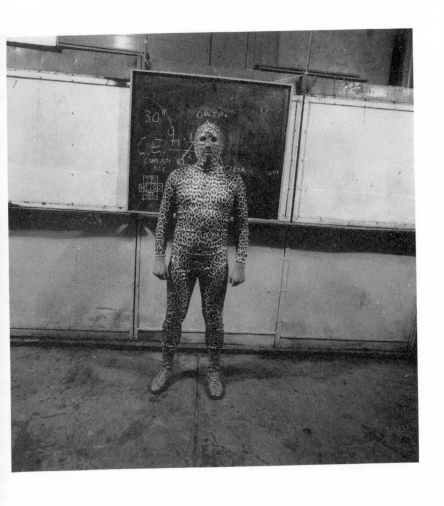

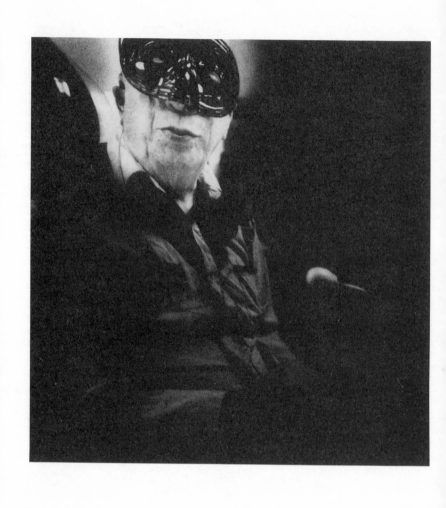

A manuscript page from one of Czeslaw Milosz's notebooks.

Czeslaw Milosz

The Art of Poetry LXX

A loss of harmony with the surrounding space, the inability to feel at home in the world, so oppressive to an expatriate, a refugee, an immigrant, paradoxically integrates him in contemporary society and makes him, if he is an artist, understood by all. Even more, to express the existential situation of modern man, one must live in exile of some sort.

— Czeslaw Milosz
"On Exile"

Though Nobelist Czeslaw Milosz considers himself a Polish poet because he writes in that "native mother tongue," he was not born in Poland, nor has he lived there for over half a century. Nonetheless, the poems of this sensuous mystic are inscribed on monuments in Gdansk as well as printed on posters in the New York City transit system.

He was born in 1911 in Szetejnie, Lithuania, the impover-ished estate of his grandfather, a gentleman farmer. Milosz remembers the rural Lithuania of that time as a "country of myth and poetry." His childhood world was broken by World War I when his father, Alexander, a road engineer, was re-cruited by the Czar's army. Milosz and his mother accompa-nied his father on dangerous bridge-building expeditions near Russian battle zones.

The family returned to Lithuania in 1918. For several years Milosz enjoyed youthful solitude before beginning a rigorous formal education in Wilno, the capital of Polish Lithuania. In his early twenties he published his first volume of poems, A Poem on Frozen Time. Three Winters, his second volume, appeared in 1936. Milosz received a law degree from the uni-versity in Wilno and spent a year in Paris on a scholarship, where he met his distant cousin Oscar Milosz, the French poet who became his mentor.

The Soviet regime in Wilno eventually forced Milosz to flee the city of his youth to Nazi-occupied Warsaw, where he joined the socialist resistance. Milosz's anthology of anti-Nazi poetry, The Invincible Song, was published by underground presses in Warsaw, where he also wrote "The World (A Naive Poem)" and the cycle Voices of Poor People. After the destruction of Warsaw he lived for a while outside of Cracow. The state publishing house brought out his collected poems in a volume entitled Rescue.

The end of the war brought more dislocation. Milosz worked as a cultural attaché of the Polish communist government, serving in both New York and Washington over a period of years. He broke with the Polish government in 1951 and sought political asylum in France, even though it meant virtual disconnection from Polish readers. His ten years in France found him at odds with the strongly pro-socialist and commu-nist intellectual community. He wrote two novels during this period, Seizure of Power and The Issa Valley, as well as his most famous book, The Captive Mind, a study of the danger-ous appeal of totalitarian thought, along with portraits of friends who had been seduced by it. An exponent of Simone

Weil, he translated her essays into Polish. He also wrote two
volumes of poetry and an intellectual autobiography, Native
Realm: A Search for Self-Definition. *Banned in Poland, Mi-*
losz's poetry was published in Paris by the Instytut Literacki.

Milosz moved yet further west when, in 1961, at age fifty,
he began a new career as a professor of Slavic languages and
literature at the University of California at Berkeley. Though
an unknown member of a small department, he eventually
became popular for his courses on Dostoyevsky and, to those
outside the university, as a translator of the poems of Zbigniew
Herbert. Milosz's Selected Poems *were not published in En-*
glish until 1973. In 1978 his collection Bells in Winter *ap-*
peared, and Milosz was awarded the Nobel Prize for literature.
In 1981 he visited Poland for the first time in thirty years and
in 1992 saw his native Lithuania again after a fifty-two year
absence.

Since winning the Nobel Prize, Milosz has published many
volumes of prose and poetry. His prose collections include
Visions from San Francisco Bay, Beginning with My Streets,
The Land of Ulro *and his Charles Eliot Norton lectures,* The
Witness of Poetry. *His* Collected Poems *appeared in 1988 and*
included portions of Unattainable Earth. *It was followed most*
recently by another collection, Provinces. *A diary of the year*
1988, A Year of the Hunter, *was published in 1994 and an-*
other volume of poetry, Facing the River, *is due out in 1995.*
Milosz resides in Berkeley most of the year but spends portions
of his summers in Cracow.

This interview was conducted primarily at Milosz's home
in the Berkeley hills overlooking San Francisco Bay, where he
lives with his wife, Carol, and a cat named Tiny. Other portions
were recorded before a live audience at the Unterberg Poetry
Center of the 92nd Street YMHA in New York. The first
part of the conversation in Berkeley lasted four hours without
interruption, until the poet looked at his watch and then,
somewhat sympathetically, at his exhausted interlocutor to
ask, "It is six o'clock, time for a little vodka?"

INTERVIEWER

You returned to Lithuania recently for the first time in
fifty-two years. How was it?

CZESLAW MILOSZ

It was a moving experience. I was received very cordially as
a native son. I was given an honorary degree at the University
of Kaunas. Then I visited my county, where I was greeted by
a border delegation in peasant costumes—quite a big event
in the region. I was made an honorary citizen and attended
a mass in the wooden church where I was baptized. But many
villages have disappeared. I have to presume enormous numbers of their inhabitants were deported to Siberia. Instead
there are neat little red brick towns. I visited the place where
I was born, but there was no house, only the bare remnants
of a park, and the river is polluted.

INTERVIEWER

What literature shaped your imagination as you grew up
in Lithuania?

MILOSZ

Imagine a world without radio, without television and without film. That was my childhood in a provincial part of Europe.
At that time, the impact of books was much greater than it
is now, and I profited from the library of my grandfather,
which was largely composed of books from the nineteenth
century. The only atlas was so outdated that it had a big white
spot in the middle of Africa. The mystery of time was revealed
to me not by Marcel Proust but by James Fenimore Cooper.
Authors like Fenimore Cooper were very popular at the time
in abridged and somewhat garbled versions for children. For
instance, all the volumes of the epic *The Deerslayer* were con-
densed into one. Still, it made a tremendous impression upon
me, because it was really the story of a young hunter gradually
changing into maturity and then into an old man as he slowly
moved from the East to West. His tragedy was that he was

an exile, but could not escape civilization. I also read authors who have never been heard of in the United States, like Thomas Mayne Reid. He was an Irishman, who spent some time in America as a hunter, teacher, and who then made a career as an author of children's books while living in London. His books were filled with all kinds of plants, animals and birds—each identified with a Latin name. That was crucial for me, for at the time I wanted to become an ornithologist. I knew all the names for birds and their Latin equivalents. I also read Karl May, who was beloved by little boys all over Europe and translated into all European languages but unknown in America. He was a German who wrote novels of adventure sitting in a debtor's prison.

Later, when I lived in Wilno, I saw films. My education in this respect was like that of contemporary American children. Mary Pickford, Lillian Gish, Buster Keaton, Charlie Chaplin and later Greta Garbo, all made an impression on me. It's very difficult to draw a line between childhood reading and the beginning of reading more mature books. But because of my rural and provincial childhood and because of those books from the library of the nineteenth century, I was always entranced by books on nature, especially those with illustrations and colored woodcuts—Audubon, Alexander Wilson and so on. These books defined my attitude toward nature.

INTERVIEWER

What fascinated you about nature?

MILOSZ

Well, my great hero was Linnaeus; I loved the idea that he had invented a system for naming creatures, that he had captured nature that way. My wonder at nature was in large part a fascination with names and naming. But I was also a hunter. So was my father. Today I am deeply ashamed of having killed birds and animals. I would never do that now, but at the time I enjoyed it. I was even a taxidermist. In high school, when I was about thirteen or fourteen, I discovered

Darwin and his theories about natural selection. I was entranced and gave lectures about Darwin in our naturalists' club. But at the same time, even though it was a state school, the priests were very important. So on the one hand, I was learning about religion, the history of the Church, dogmatics and apologetics; on the other hand I learned about science, which basically undermines religion. Eventually I turned away from Darwinism because of its cruelty, though at first I embraced it. Nature is much more beautiful in painting, in my opinion.

INTERVIEWER

Can a connection be made between the naturalist's and the poet's appreciation of nature?

MILOSZ

David Wagoner has written a poem called "The Author of *American Ornithology* Sketches a Bird, Now Extinct." It's a poem about Alexander Wilson, one of the leading ornithologists in America, shooting and wounding an Ivory-billed woodpecker, which he kept to draw because it was a specimen that was new to him. The bird was slowly dying in his house. Wilson explains that he has to kill birds so that they can live on the pages of his books. It's a very dramatic poem. So the relation of science to nature, and I suspect also of art to nature, is a sort of a meeting of the minds of both scientist and artist in that they both have a passion to grasp the world. I am more concerned with the erosion of the religious imagination because of the impact of science. It goes to the root of one of the essential problems of our time—the incapacity of contemporary man to think in religious terms. I have also been influenced by Thomas Merton, with whom I corresponded for many years. We mostly discussed religion and nature. I reproached him for his optimistic and largely American attitude toward nature.

INTERVIEWER

So the Catholic faith in which you were raised overrides the impact of science?

MILOSZ

Oh, yes. But the trouble is that writing religious poetry in the twentieth century is very difficult. We are in a largely post-religious world. I had a conversation with the present Pope, who commented upon some of my work, in particular my "Six Lectures in Verse." "Well," he said, "you make one step forward, one step back." I answered, "Holy Father, how in the twentieth century can one write religious poetry differently?"

INTERVIEWER

And how did the Pope respond?

MILOSZ

He smiled.

INTERVIEWER

In your book *The Land of Ulro*, you address these problems and the importance to you of your older cousin, Oscar Milosz. To what extent did he influence your work?

MILOSZ

As far as style was concerned, I was aware that his influence was dangerous. His style was late symbolist, something I felt should not be imitated at that time. But the essence of his mystical writings, "The Epistle to Storge" and "The Ars Magna" — namely that the world was created through a transmutation of non-physical light into physical light — that was very important to me. He intuitively conceived, indeed before Einstein, a cosmology of relativity — a moment when there is no space, no matter, no time; all three are united in his imagination with movement.

INTERVIEWER

You once wrote a poem dedicated to Einstein.

MILOSZ

I knew Einstein. In fact, I worshipped him. My cousin Oscar Milosz believed that his theory of relativity had opened a new era of mankind — an era of harmony, reconciliation between science, religion and art. The positive consequence of Einstein's discoveries was the elimination of Newtonian time and space as infinite and the introduction of the relativity of time and space that underlies our cosmology and its concept of the big bang. I approached Einstein with enormous reverence. So I wrote a poem about him. At the time he was convinced that the world was moving toward destruction because of atomic weapons, and that the only solution was to create a world government to control the weapons. In 1948, he wrote a paper in that spirit and sent it to the World Congress for Intellectuals in Wroclaw, Poland. The Congress was just a front for Stalin's armaments policy, and the Russians opposed reading that memo. Around that time I asked Einstein whether I should go back to Poland or stay abroad. He thought I should return and was very frank about it.

INTERVIEWER

What were the circumstances of your meeting him?

MILOSZ

I was working as an attaché at the Polish embassy in Washington. That was a difficult period for me, deciding whether or not to break with the communist regime in Poland. Einstein was, of course, in exile in America, and I sought him out as an authority. One day instead of driving directly from New York to Washington, I turned off and went to Princeton. Of course, I knew Einstein lived there. Despite my sense of irony, my nature sought someone to revere, to praise. Einstein's white hair, his gray sweatshirt with the fountain pen clipped to it, his soft hands and voice all appealed to my need for a father figure, a leader. He was an absolutely charming, warmhearted person. He was opposed to my becoming an émigré. He responded to me on an emotional level, saying, You can't break with your country; a poet should stick to his native country. I know it is difficult, but things have to change. They won't go on like that. He was optimistic that the regime would pass. As a humanitarian, he assumed that man was a reasonable creature, though my generation saw man more as the plaything of demonic powers. So, I left his house on Mercer Street and drove away somewhat numbly. All of us yearn for the highest wisdom, but we have to rely on ourselves in the end.

INTERVIEWER

When did you first think of becoming a writer?

MILOSZ

I started to write when I was in high school, though it was not an effort to express myself—exercises of form, very cool, and I guess influenced by the French poets of the sixteenth-century school La Pléiade that I read in my French textbooks—Joachim du Bellay, Remy Belleau, Pierre de Ronsard and others. It would be inaccurate to say that I wanted to be a poet. I wanted to be in conflict with my surroundings, to take on a negative attitude, what Flaubert referred to as a hatred of the bourgeois. I wanted to have a different style, live a different way of life.

INTERVIEWER

Wilno was the city of your youth and it recurs in your writing.

MILOSZ

It had a very durable effect. I see enormous advantages of growing up in a provincial town. It gives a different—perhaps, a better—perspective. When I found myself abroad, I tried to introduce Wilno and Lithuania to Western readers, which was difficult to do because the city has changed hands thirteen times in this century. With its various nationalities, denominations, languages, it was like Sarajevo. I have been deeply moved by what is happening in Bosnia because I understand all those ethnic conflicts.

INTERVIEWER

But in your poetry in recent years, there is much less interest in history.

MILOSZ

Yes, definitely. At the time of Solidarity in Poland when martial law was proclaimed, I published an article called "Noblemindedness, Alas," in which I warned that unified resistance to martial law created a certain highfalutin, noble-minded ethos in literature and art that was dangerous because it pushed aside any other human concerns and concentrated on the struggle of the moment. At the time, a kind of pact existed between the intellectuals and the church, which had been giving refuge to many literary and artistic enterprises. My article has become somewhat prophetic because that national unity has unraveled in the last several years. The young generation cannot stand any appearance of appealing to lofty moral ideals. I am in sympathy with idealists, and I define my religious position as a Catholic. But I am not very much in love with the Church as a political institution.

INTERVIEWER

Early on, you were part of a literary group known as Zagary, whose worldview and poetic practice became known as "catastrophism."

MILOSZ

I was a cofounder of that group. We didn't know that we were catastrophists. That was a name applied later by literary critics. Those years — 1931–1933 — were years of despair. I now wonder whether a dark vision of history is a result of a personal inclination to pessimism or if one's pessimism reflects the aura of an historical period. Whatever, that was a horrible period in Europe. The literature from Weimar Germany was nihilistic, sarcastic, full of hatred. The literature from the Soviet Union of the 1920s before the introduction of socialist realism was also extremely cruel and negative. There were writers like Seifulina and Ilya Ehrenburg, who lived at that time in Paris. Ehrenburg's nihilistic novels were immediately translated into Polish. So the mood of literature was very pessimistic, very negative; at the same time the political news was awful— Stalinism in Russia and Hitler coming to power in Germany. Understanding all that, of course, influenced our group. So did the rector of our university, an old professor, Marian Zdzie-chowski, who was an utter pessimist. He wrote a book entitled *Facing the End* in which he predicted that Europe would soon be destroyed by two forces, nationalism and communism. Fortunately for him, he died in 1939 just before the war started. There were also extremely pessimistic Polish authors, especially Stanislaw Ignacy Witkiewicz, a catastrophist in outlook. So our poetry expressed foreboding—a kind of surrealistic prophecy of horrors to come. It was like the voice of Cassandra. We conceived a cosmic catastrophe rather than a clearly defined political catastrophe. Later, under the Nazi occupation of Warsaw, there was a group of very young poets for whom, of course, the culmination, the Apocalypse, was the Nazi occupation. For us it was not; it was simply part of a larger picture.

INTERVIEWER

You were part of the resistance in Warsaw. You published— or contributed to—a clandestine anthology of poetry against the Nazis. What effect did the war years have on your poetry?

MILOSZ

I was uneasy as a poet because I had come to understand that poetry could not depict the world as it was—the formal conventions were wrong. So I searched for something different. But at the same time, I wrote a long work consisting of short poems, entitled "The World (A Naive Poem)" a sequence— though I was not aware of it at the time—like Blake's "Songs of Innocence." I considered the world so horrible that these childish poems were answers—the world as it should be, not as it was. Written in view of what was happening, "The World" was a profoundly ironic poem.

INTERVIEWER

That's the significance of the subtitle: "A Naive Poem."

MILOSZ

This poem is as much pure fiction as a book for children about Teddy bears. It makes me uneasy when critics and readers take those so-called "positive" poems about love, faith, hope and prescribe them for schoolchildren in Poland. I receive letters from children who read these poems in school and learn them by heart—poems which were actually written tongue in cheek.

INTERVIEWER

In one of the poems from "The World" you wrote, "We and the Flowers throw shadows on the earth. / What has no shadow has no strength to live."

MILOSZ

There is some Thomas Aquinas behind those lines. He asserts belief in the objective existence of things. It's a sort of naive poem—a belief in the reality of a flower, of a river and a garden. My poems of that era contain a double search: one, a search for the grace of innocence—the "naive" poems—the other, the cycle "Voices of Poor People," a search for a means of how to deal directly with the Nazi occupation. There is also the influence of the Chinese poetry that I was reading then for color, pure color.

INTERVIEWER

How did you happen upon Chinese poetry?

MILOSZ

In Warsaw, I bought an anthology, *The Chinese Flute*, which was a translation not from Chinese but from the French. The poetry provided clear images and, particularly, strong colors which I could inject into a dark, black and red world of the Nazi occupation. Since that time, the two-color combination of black and red has always been ominous for me.

INTERVIEWER

Which Asian poets interested you most?

MILOSZ

At that time, I didn't know much about individual poets. That came later through my interest in American poetry. As you know, translations from old Chinese and Japanese poetry played an eminent role in its development. Ezra Pound was a pioneer in this respect: the Imagists were strongly influenced by Asian literature. So, it was a gradual influence and developed largely because of some of the philosophical premises of my work.

INTERVIEWER

Such as?

MILOSZ

Well, I don't want to sound too theoretical, but I was reacting to certain tendencies in modern poetry towards complete subjectivization. In Asian poetry there is a certain equilibrium between subject and object rarely attained in the West. I come from a poetic tradition in which history plays a great role, my poetry involving to a large extent the transposition of certain major events, tragedies of history. The tradition in Central Europe is that the individual is weak, quite different from the West, which is very strong in its emphasis on the individual. After I stopped dealing with the big tragedies of the twentieth century, I wanted to find a balance. I didn't want to write purely personal perceptions, which is typical of so much of the poetry today—seen through a very personal perspective, and thus very often difficult to decipher. I realized that the weakness of the individual is no good in poetry, and that an excess of individualism is a danger as well.

INTERVIEWER

Yet, in *Unattainable Earth* you express your admiration for Whitman, a strong egoist, by including translations of many of his poems. How do you feel about his presentation of self?

MILOSZ

Whitman is a very peculiar case because he creates a persona. That persona speaks; yet a certain distance exists between Whitman and the complex persona that he impersonates throughout his poetry, which is different from a poet who naively believes that everything he feels and perceives at a given moment interests the reader. Of course, Whitman is an extremely complex poet, mixing good and bad, which, as my cousin Oscar Milosz used to say, is a prescription for great poetry. When we read the large sweep of Whitman today we skip many naivetés, particularly those enumerations, the long lists. For me, Whitman is a poet out of whom you can carve so many excellent short poems—an extremely rich poet.

INTERVIEWER

You also have an admiration for a modern inheritor of the Whitman tradition—Allen Ginsberg.

MILOSZ

My poem "To Allen Ginsberg" is tricky. He came up to me after a reading of his and said, "Well, I guess you are not as much of a square as you present yourself." My attitude toward Ginsberg is contradictory. His "Kaddish" is, in a way, a horrible piece of writing but extremely daring. To speak of one's mother's insanity, describing its various phases . . . that's incredible. I have always denounced that sort of personal indiscretion. So, I'm shocked and somewhat envious of Ginsberg's daring, and that is what I have expressed in my poem about him.

INTERVIEWER

I noted you included Whitman's poem "Sparkles from the Wheel" in *Unattainable Earth*. Whitman uses a wonderful word in that poem, "unminded," suggesting both the state of being unnoticed but also of detaching one's attention. This is something you do in your own poetry.

MILOSZ

Yes. A kind of irony. Let's call it romantic irony. One partici-
pates and observes at the same time: while falling down the
stairs one sees the situation as funny. I feel that when a poem
becomes too general, and it moves toward some sort of sentimental confession, I want to introduce additional commen-
tary—not a formal device but rather a search for honesty. That
kind of irony is so integral to my writing that I can hardly
even separate it from the process.

INTERVIEWER

In your poem "*Ars Poetica?*" you stated that the purpose
of poetry is to remind us how difficult it is to remain just one
person.

MILOSZ

My poetry has been called polyphonic, which is to say that
I have always been full of voices speaking; in a way I consider
myself an instrument, a medium. My friend Jeanne Hersch,
who introduced me to the existentialism of Karl Jaspers, used
to say, "I have never seen a person so instrumental," meaning
that I was visited by voices. There is nothing extraterrestrial
in this, but something within myself. Am I alone in this? I
don't think so. Dostoyevsky was one of the first writers, along
with Friedrich Nietzsche, to identify a crisis of modern civilization: that every one of us is visited by contradictory voices,
contradictory physical urges. I have written about the difficulty
of remaining the same person when such guests enter and go
and take us for their instrument. But we must hope to be
inspired by good spirits, not evil ones.

INTERVIEWER

You have called yourself a medium, but a suspicious one.
What do you mean by this? Of what are you a medium?

MILOSZ

I suppose, looking back, that everything was dictated to
me, and I was just a tool. Of what I don't know. I would like

to believe that I am a tool of God, but that's presumptuous. So I prefer to call whatever it is my "*daimonion*." I have written a new poem that describes this relationship:

> Please, my Daimonion, ease off just a bit,
> I'm still closing accounts and have much to tell.
> Your rhythmical whispers intimidate me.
> Today for instance, reading about a certain old woman
> I saw again—Let us call her Priscilla,
> Though I am astonished that I can give her any name
> And people will not care. So that Priscilla,
> Her gums in poor shape, an old hag,
> Is the one to whom I return, in order to throw charms
> And grant her eternal youth. I introduce a river,
> Green hills, irises wet with rain
> And, of course, a conversation. "You know," I say,
> "I could never guess what was on your mind
> And will never learn. I have a question
> That won't be answered." And you, Daimonion,
> Just at this moment interfere, interrupt us, averse to
> Surnames and family names and all reality
> Too prosaic and ridiculous, no doubt.

So, this voice involves my purification from the past by time and distance. It interferes and stops me from writing about my life too realistically, too prosaically. I am able to move to another dimension.

INTERVIEWER

To go back to your earlier years, you were a witness to the Warsaw uprising and the Holocaust, but have written relatively little about them.

MILOSZ

From time to time I am asked to read my poem "Campo dei Fiori," which is about that suffering. Recently, I refused a request for permission to reprint my poems about those events. I do not want to be known as a professional mourner.

INTERVIEWER

You lived in Paris as an émigré. In your poem "Bypassing Rue Descartes," you describe Paris as a city where many espoused what you called "beautiful ideas" — ideals both naive and cruel.

MILOSZ

Paris was certainly not a place for somebody who came from Eastern Europe. I lived through two phases in Paris. In 1950, I was an attaché of the Polish embassy and attended parties with Paul Éluard and Pablo Neruda. The following year, after breaking with the Polish communist regime, I came to live there as a refugee. At that time, French intellectuals were completely in love with communism and Stalin. Anyone who was dissatisfied and who came from the East like myself was considered a madman or an agent of America. The French felt that their so-called "ideés générales" were valid for the whole planet — beautiful ideas, but hardly realistic. At that time the political climate of Europe was dismal; millions of people were in gulags; their suffering contaminated the aura, the air of Europe. I knew what was going on. The West had to wait for Solzhenitsyn to write *The Gulag Archipelago* to learn about it.

INTERVIEWER

Did your views get you into trouble?

MILOSZ

This isn't a secret. When I returned to Warsaw the government took my passport. They didn't want me to return to Paris for my diplomatic job. It was eventually restored to me, but then I broke with them and became an exile. A Russian woman, the wife of the Minister of Foreign Affairs, a very zealous communist, said, In my opinion, a poet should stay with his country, but since you have decided otherwise, remember that you have a duty to fight against him. Against whom? Stalin, she said; the executioner of Russia. To say such a thing then was very dangerous. But I too felt an obligation to speak out. I was on friendly terms with Albert Camus at the time Jean-Paul Sartre and his crowd were after him, trying to destroy him because in *The Rebel* among other things he had mentioned that there were concentration camps in the Soviet Union. Because of my views, people who could have translated me refused. They said that they would be ostracized if they did so. So I was in a difficult position then.

INTERVIEWER

Is poetry the proper realm for philosophy?

MILOSZ

It depends what kind of philosophy.

INTERVIEWER

What kind have you found appropriate for your poetry?

MILOSZ

There are some kinds of philosophy which remind me of the circumstance of driving at night and having a hare jump in front of the lights. The hare doesn't know how to get out of the beam of light, he runs straight ahead. I am interested in the kind of philosophy that would be useful to the hare in that instance.

INTERVIEWER

Not much hope for the hare. When you were a student you carried a history of the Church in your knapsack, and you seem particularly interested in the Manichaean heresy.

MILOSZ

Well, Manichaeanism was not just a heresy. It was an established religion for a long time. Basically, it recognizes the considerable power of evil, and counteracts the classical, theological explanation that evil is the lack of good. In these times the power of evil is widely recognized as a collective creation of human society and an element of the individual human soul. The argument of contemporary atheists — that a benevolent god couldn't have created the world such as it is — is essentially neo-Manichaean. Though not necessarily my view, I recognize it as a valid argument; I am very concerned in my poetry with the existence of evil. Simone Weil, who was a very strong determinist, recognized the power of evil as well, which is the source of my great interest in her thinking. She went on to say that there is only a "mustard seed of grace" in man.

MILOSZ

In your poem "The Song" the woman longs for "one seed without rust." You and Weil both seem to be referring to the mustard seed in the Gospel of Saint Mark.

MILOSZ

Yes. The little grain of mustard seed is really the kingdom of God, grace and goodness — small when compared with the evil in the world. That was Weil's belief. Another writer who attracted me around that time was Lev Shestov, who saw the whole world as ruled by laws of necessity. He opposed stoicism. A stoic, whether ancient or modern, would say, "Grin and bear it." But why should we? Shestov's view was that, on the contrary, we ought to rebel, scream no! His powerful book *Athens and Jerusalem* depicts Job, in contrast to Greek stoicism, as screaming.

INTERVIEWER

Do you think God's answer to Job from the whirlwind is adequate?

MILOSZ

It is not adequate. It is not adequate.

INTERVIEWER

Do you regard Job's God and the God of the New Testament as two different gods?

MILOSZ

I don't know. I guess we have entered the realm where there are no answers.

INTERVIEWER

Gnosticism dealt with the complexities of early Christianity by emphasizing salvation through knowledge rather than faith. How does your interest in gnosticism relate to your own poetry?

MILOSZ

In the first centuries of Christianity, the new religion proved insufficient for the educated people in many ways, and so gnosticism became widespread. Gnosticism did then what poetry does today for educated people. But poetry should not be reduced to mere aestheticism. In its most important instances, poetry is an exploration of man's place in the cosmos. Good and evil have been attributes of man since the Fall. The big question is: What state did Adam and Eve live in before that moment? Original sin is an enormous and extremely difficult philosophical problem. Lev Shestov said, and I agree, that it is remarkable, indeed hardly conceivable, that primitive shepherds were able to come up with a myth so enigmatic that the generations who have sweated over it to this day still do not understand it.

INTERVIEWER

You have grappled in your poetry with the question of how a good god can permit evil in the world. Can we justify God through reason, through poetry?

MILOSZ

Shestov said that there are questions that shouldn't be asked because we have no answers. Simone Weil defended contradiction by what she referred to as a "lever of transcendence." I myself have been all contradiction; I am composed of contradictions, which is why poetry is a better form for me than philosophy.

INTERVIEWER

Weil was skeptical about the facile comfort that can be found in religion.

MILOSZ

She was a very severe person with little tolerance for human weakness, especially so with herself. In a way she was a pure ascetic. For instance, she dismissed as diabolical workings of the imagination the illusions of terminally ill people who think they are going to get better. Well, it's very human to have a hope of miraculous healing. Why deny them that? In everything that is human we should allow for that solace.

INTERVIEWER

Your friend Witold Gombrowicz once wrote in his diary, "Milosz experiences strife, torment, and doubts that were completely unknown to writers formerly." Do you agree with him?

MILOSZ

Yes, I agree. He refers especially to my book *The Captive Mind* and to my struggle with the demon of this century—the Hegelian belief in historical necessity, that history develops along preordained lines. I wrote *The Captive Mind* in order to liberate myself, to find arguments against that philosophy. That's probably why he says my struggle was previously unknown to writers.

INTERVIEWER

What do you think helped that liberation?

MILOSZ

My novel *The Issa Valley*, which has nothing political in it. The action takes place in the Lithuanian countryside about 1922. It's about a priest who has a mistress who commits suicide and starts to haunt the parish. I visited the parish recently in my first trip back to Lithuania in more than fifty years. The girl's grave is in the local cemetery near the same church where

I was baptized and where many of the things I describe in the novel happened. But the novel is not a mere reminiscence of childhood, but rather a philosophical novel about devils and my desire to liberate myself from historical necessity and the cruelty in Nature.

INTERVIEWER

Since then you have been uninterested in writing novels. You seem to have a quarrel with the genre. Why?

MILOSZ

It's an impure form. I taught Dostoyevsky at Berkeley for twenty years. A born novelist, he would sacrifice everything; he knows no obligations of honor. He would put anything in a novel. Dostoyevsky created a character in *The Idiot*, General Ivolgin, who is a liar and tells stories—how he lost his leg in a war, how he buried his leg, and then what he inscribed on the tombstone. The inscription is taken from the tomb of Dostoyevsky's mother. There you have a true novelist. I couldn't do that.

INTERVIEWER

Though the genre of the novel doesn't suit you, you admire Thomas Mann and even wrote a poem called "A Magic Mountain."

MILOSZ

When I was a student I was very much impressed by *The Magic Mountain*. There is a character in it, Naphta, who is a Jesuit priest, a totalitarian, an enemy of the Enlightenment. I was fascinated with him. I had strong leftist totalitarian tendencies myself and was drawn to Naphta's skepticism of the Enlightenment. Today though, I would side with Naphta's antagonist in the novel, Settembrini, who represents the spirit of the Enlightenment. But my vision of humanity is much darker than Settembrini's.

INTERVIEWER

During the occupation you translated Eliot from English into Polish. What attracted you to his work?

MILOSZ

The Waste Land is filled with elements of catastrophe. At the time, in occupied Warsaw, it had a certain power, filled with images of collapsing cities. It made weird reading as the glow from the burning ghetto illuminated the skyline. It is a deeply satiric poem, however, even a sarcastic poem. That is alien to my vision. But in the *Four Quartets* we have the exceptional and rare case of someone who, after much struggle, has succeeded in reconciling his return to faith with his art. I met Eliot in London, and he gave me a warm reception. Later I saw him in America and translated more of his poems into Polish.

INTERVIEWER

Do you feel, as Eliot did, that poetry is an escape from personality?

MILOSZ

This has been a constant problem for me. Literature is born out of a desire to be truthful — not to hide anything and not to present oneself as somebody else. Yet when you write there are certain obligations, what I call laws of form. You cannot tell everything. Of course, it's true that people talk too much and without restraint. But poetry imposes certain restraints. Nevertheless, there is always the feeling that you didn't unveil yourself enough. A book is finished and appears and I feel, Well, next time I will unveil myself. And when the next book appears, I have the same feeling. And then your life ends, and that's it.

INTERVIEWER

There are confessions in a number of your poems. Do you feel that confession leads to anything?

MILOSZ

I don't know. I have never been psychoanalyzed. I am very skeptical as far as psychiatry is concerned. My dream is to be on a couch and to tell everything, but I wouldn't be able to, probably, and besides it wouldn't lead anywhere.

INTERVIEWER

What is your writing process like?

MILOSZ

I write every morning, whether one line or more, but only in the morning. I write in notebooks and then type drafts into my computer. I never drink coffee and never use any stimulants when I write. I do drink moderately, but only after my work. I probably don't fit the image of the neurotic modern writer for those reasons, but who knows?

INTERVIEWER

Do you revise your poetry a great deal?

MILOSZ

There is no rule. Sometimes a poem is written in five minutes, sometimes it takes months. There is no rule.

INTERVIEWER

Do you write first in Polish and then translate it to English?

MILOSZ

I write only in Polish. I have always written only in Polish, because I think my mastery of language is greatest when I use the language of my childhood.

INTERVIEWER

Do you think your poetry can be translated well?

MILOSZ

I translate myself and then friends of mine, mostly Robert Hass these days or Leonard Nathan, correct it. But the basic rhythms are determined by me, because they don't know the Polish language. I didn't believe my poetry could be translated. I feel very privileged that I can communicate with American audiences. Half of them are usually aspiring poets. They appreciate me more as a poet. For Poles I am more than anything a famous personality.

INTERVIEWER

You have called yourself a hermetic poet. Don't you imagine an audience?

MILOSZ

I write for an ideal person who is a kind of alter ego. I don't care about being more accessible. I assess whether my poems have what is necessary, what is proper. I follow my need for rhythm and order, and my struggle against chaos and nothingness to translate as many aspects of reality as possible into a form.

INTERVIEWER

In a recent poem, "Spider," you refer to poetry metaphorically as "building diminutive boats / . . . for sailing beyond the borderline of time." Is this how you view your own work?

MILOSZ

I prefer to use the metaphor of shedding skins, which means abandoning old forms and assumptions. I feel this is what makes writing exciting. My poetry is always a search for a more spacious form. I have always been in conflict with those theories of poetry which concentrate on the aesthetic object. Yet I have been pleased, in a way, how well some of my old poems stand on their own, separated from me and the act of making them.

INTERVIEWER

Then why do you so often express misgivings when a poet or artist is admired and held in high regard?

MILOSZ

The problem is that the public usually wants a well-painted portrait of an artist, deprived of all contradictions and more monumental than life allows. The disparity between such a portrait and the subject can be depressing. If a poet has renown limited to a narrow circle, it's more probable that his image will not be distorted. The larger the circle, the greater risk of distortion.

INTERVIEWER

What distortion of yourself do you find most troubling?

MILOSZ

The image of me as a moralist. When the ban on my poetry was lifted in Poland after I won the Nobel Prize, I became for many people a symbol of freedom from censorship, and thus a moral figure. I don't know whether I have retained this image, it's probably gotten a bit shoddy already. Let me show you something. *[Milosz searches his pockets and retrieves a small medallion.]* This is a replica of a monument in Poland. It has four symbols: the insignia of Pope John Paul II, the miter of the Polish archbishop, the tools of the electrician — that's Walesa — and a book, which represents me.

INTERVIEWER

You're in good company.

MILOSZ

Not bad for a poet of the twentieth century, especially in light of all the lamenting about the place of poetry in human society. But I am rather skeptical about this. I don't want to be thought of as part of a great moral movement in Polish history. Art is not a sufficient substitute for the problem of leading a moral life. I am afraid of wearing a cloak that is too big for me.

INTERVIEWER

Do you think it is better for a poet to work in obscurity?

MILOSZ

I worked for many years in a state of nearly total obscurity. My years in Berkeley were a time when I had practically no audience here, and very few people in America on whose judgment I could rely. I had a couple of friends in Paris and Poland, so correspondence played an enormous role for me: letters received from a few friends were my only sustaining force. I was publishing my books of verse in Polish. They had to be smuggled into Poland so I did not know the reactions of readers in Poland.

I knew who I was, and I knew my worth, but I was completely unknown to almost all my colleagues at Berkeley except, of course, the Slavic languages professors. I was an obscure professor in an obscure department. I became well known to students only when I started to teach Dostoyevsky. There is a story which summarizes those years. I was at a literary dinner at Stanford with Jerzy Kosinski and, of course, he was quite famous. There was a woman, a fan of Kosinski's, who was my neighbor at the table. She felt obliged to be polite and asked, "What do you do?" And I said, "I write poetry." She snapped in reply: "Everybody writes poetry." I didn't mind that much but it still hurt. It represented my situation for years, the sufferings of ambition.

INTERVIEWER

How do you account for your relatively large audience?

MILOSZ

There was a period long ago when I tasted recognition due to my writing things that pleased people, but that period is long gone. When you write political poems, as I did during the war, you always have clientele. Today, I am surprised and uneasy about the recognition I receive because I would like to know that the response is genuine and not because I am a Nobel Laureate. On the other hand, I don't think that the Nobel Prize has affected me or my work.

INTERVIEWER

How do you regard Wallace Stevens's notion that the modern poem is "the poem of the act of the mind in finding what will suffice"?

MILOSZ

Literature and poetry today are under enormous pressure from the scientific mode of thinking, an empirical way of thinking. Wallace Stevens has a penetrating, dissecting mind, which I think applied to poetry is wrong. If we take Stevens's poem "Study of Two Pears," it seems an attempt to describe the pears as if to a Martian, to a creature from another planet. That's dissection. I feel that things of this world should be contemplated rather than dissected—the kind of detached attitude towards objects one finds in Dutch still lifes. Schopenhauer considered these to be the highest form of art. That contemplation is also in Japanese haiku poems. As Basho said: To write about the pine, you must learn from the pine. This is a completely different attitude from dissecting the world. Schopenhauer, I feel, is really the artist's, the poet's, philosopher.

INTERVIEWER

Why?

MILOSZ

Because he stressed the need for distance. In the workings of the universe, we are in that infernal circle of passions—striving and struggling. Schopenhauer was influenced by the religious writings of India; for him liberation meant to stand outside of the wheel of eternal birth and death. Art should also stand outside that turning wheel, so that we can approach an object without passion, without desire and with a certain detachment. Life's passion can be eliminated through detached contemplation, which is a good definition of art: "detached contemplation." That is why Schopenhauer's epitome of art was the still life, the Dutch still life.

INTERVIEWER

In two poems, "To Raja Rao," which was a response to a conversation, and a recent poem entitled "Capri," you make reference to waiting for "the real presence," the mystery of divinity in the flesh. Does this suggest that poetry is a sacramental act through which we can invoke this presence?

MILOSZ

Yes, I personally believe that the world we know is the skin of a deeper reality, and that reality is there. It cannot be reduced to mere words, and this is my basic disagreement with some writers of this century. There is a difference between a man who focuses on language, on his inner life, and the hunter—like me—who grieves because reality cannot be captured.

INTERVIEWER

How do you feel about Larkin's poem "Aubade," in which he views religion as a kind of trick and calls it "That vast moth-eaten musical brocade / Created to pretend we never die"?

MILOSZ

I know Larkin's "Aubade," and for me it's a hateful poem. I don't like Larkin. He was a wonderful craftsman, very good indeed. As a stylist I rank him very high, because he exemplifies precisely my ideal—to write clear poetry with a clear meaning, and not just an accounting of subjective impressions; but I don't like his poetry, which I consider too symptomatic to be liked.

INTERVIEWER

Symptomatic of?

MILOSZ

Symptomatic of the present, desperate worldview, or weltanschauung. It seems to me that there is no revelation in his poetry. Even his letters dismay his friends because they are full of hatred, especially racist hatred for blacks, Indians, Pakistanis and so on. He was a very frustrated and very unhappy, desperate man. He proposes a sort of desire for nothingness as opposed to life—which didn't bring him much. I'm afraid we have completely lost the habit of applying moral criteria to art. Because when somebody tells me that Larkin is a great poet, and that it's enough to write great poetry by forsaking all human values, I'm skeptical. Probably that's my education and instincts speaking. My motto could be that haiku of Issa— "We walk on the roof of Hell / gazing at flowers." It's a little cheap to fall into sarcasm, irony. That emptiness and cruelty, which is the basis of Larkin's weltanschauung, should be accepted as a basis upon which you work *towards* something light.

INTERVIEWER

Well, how closely is language able to capture the world?

MILOSZ

Language does not capture everything, nor is it purely arbitrary. Certain words have a deeper meaning than in purely conventional usage. So, I reject calling language arbitrary, but I also would not reduce language to *écriture*, to writing in and of itself.

INTERVIEWER

In a prose poem in *Provinces* entitled "A Philosopher's Home" you attribute "the passionate zeal of a photo-reporter" to God. Does this describe your ideal of God as witness, and is it an ideal of what the poet can try to do?

MILOSZ

Yes. Though I should also say that the poet is like a mouse in an enormous cheese excited by how much cheese there is to eat. As I mentioned, Whitman was a poet who exerted a very strong influence upon me. Whitman wanted to embrace everything, put everything into his poetry, and we can forgive

him his infinite streams of words because he strove so hard
to embrace as much reality as possible. I guess it is somehow
connected with my image of life after death, which should
be—as in Blake's phrase—"infinite hunting."

INTERVIEWER

You have called poetry "the passionate pursuit of the real"?
Have you ever in your work attained "the real"?

MILOSZ

The real, by which I mean God, continues to remain
unfathomable.

—Robert Faggen

Cook's Joy

Romesh Gunesekera

We drove for hours; whistling over a ribbon of tarmac measuring the perpetual embrace of the shore and the sea, bounded by a fretwork of undulating coconut trees, pure unadorned forms framing the seascape into a kaleidoscope of bluish jewels. Above us a tracery of green and yellow leaves arrowed to a vanishing-point we could never reach. At times the road curved as though it were the edge of a wave itself rushing in and then retreating into the ocean. We skittered over these moving surfaces at a speed I had never experienced before. Through the back window I watched the road pour out from under us and settle into a silvery picture of serene timelessness. We overtook the occasional bus belching smoke or a lorry lisping with billowing hay; we blasted through bustling towns and torpid villages. We passed churches and temples, crosses and statues, grey shacks and lattice-work mansions. Mister Salgado only slowed down when we came to the skull-heaps of petrified coral—five-foot pyramids beside smokey kilns—marking the allotments of a line of impoverished lime-makers, tomorrow's cement fodder, crumbling on the loveliest stretch of the coast. "Look at that stuff," he said to Dias, "Goes by the ton."

When we got to the bungalow—his observatory on the beach—I spent the rest of the day doing what I always did: putting things away, making the beds, getting the food ready, serving, clearing, cleaning, sorting, shutting up. But every time I looked out of the windows, it took my breath away. The bungalow itself was shrouded with huge green leaves luminous with sunlight, shading yet illuminating. The sand garden, the clumps of crotons, the vines around the trellises by the kitchen, all seemed to breathe with life. Inside, the rooms were small; the walls were painted a cool green and the floors had turned dark. Even the furniture seemed stained by the shade, but when I looked up again I would glimpse the sea between the trees bathed in a mulled gold light. The colour of it, the roar of it, was overwhelming. It was like living inside a conch: the endless pounding. Numinous. You couldn't get away from it. No wonder Mister Salgado said the sea would be the end of us all. During those two nights we spent on tour I felt the sea getting closer; each wave just a grain of sand closer to washing the life out of us. They say the sea air makes you feel better, but I reckon that must be to lull us to sleep; it made me feel helpless. After a while it terrified me. And it was no comfort when we eventually got to see Mister Salgado's instrument that was going to save us all from a watery grave. A black plastic binder filled with grids and numbers that his assistant, Wijetunga, recorded twice a day after measuring the tidemark on the beach and counting the corals, sea-slugs, angel-fish, urchins, groupers and barracudas he happened to see as he snorkelled along a buoy-line stretched between two posts stuck in the sea. This seemed feeble in the face of the ocean's huge ripples, but I didn't say anything to Mister Salgado or Dias at the time. I asked Wijetunga, later in the evening after I had fried the fish, whether that was all there was to it. Numbers on a slate at the seaside. But having spent so much time underwater examining convoluted prehistoric life-forms, he seemed unable to speak. It looked as though his heart were full of desire—a need—for expression, but his mouth permanently corked; holding in his breath. He was an educated man, with neat, tiny handwriting. He wore black trousers when Mister Salgado asked him to join them at mealtimes. But he always looked uncomfortable, as if choking on his own thoughts. When I spoke to him, he rubbed his broad rubbery nose with the palm of his hand and sighed noisily, thinking, I suppose, of how impossible it was to deal with my ignorance. He mumbled through his hand something about timing and diving.

Dias was also, I think, not entirely convinced. After tucking into my fish-balls and a huge helping of red rice, he washed his fingers in a bowl of lime-water and said, "I don't know, *men*, I am not much of a sea-bather, but I find this ocean is very big, no? Isn't it? I mean for us to really do anything?" Faced with this sea he was not keen even on a boat trip.

Mister Salgado drew in his breath. Whenever he felt threatened he drew breath. His chest would inflate and his hands would swell up. He crossed his arms. "The ocean?"

Dias lit a cigarette and puffed vigorously, building up a good head of smoke. "I mean this dipping a stick in here and there, how will it tell you what is happening when thousands of miles away, like in Australia, a whole bunch of whales may be humping or something. That'll make this millimetre here and there all cock-eyed, no?"

"Whales don't go in for orgies."

"I know, I know. But you know, no, what I mean? A bit of hanky-panks."

I could see the shape of Mister Salgado's tongue as it traveled around his mouth, running over his teeth just under the lips making the skin ripple. "Wijetunga here is not measuring millimetres. He is examining samples. You can tell a helluva lot from a sample, if it is thoroughly observed. You know, as if I sliced just a tiny bit of skin from your finger, or took just one strand of your hair . . ." He reached forward as if to pluck it.

"Oy! Thank you, thank you, but leave my hair out of this. Precious bloody few here as it is." Dias patted his polished forehead.

"But really, just with one strand, or a bit of tissue, we can analyse it and tell you everything about your biological history."

Dias laughed, "Uh-huh-ha, yes, yes. That I can believe. Let me tell you I also, as an accountant — even a government accountant — can tell you a helluva lot: one helluva lot. If I know a man's salary and his age I can tell you his whole biographical history — his life story past, present and future, you know." He pursed his lips.

Wijetunga looked flustered, but he said nothing. Mister Salgado chuckled, "That's it. Same thing. Imagine the globe as a head. You see, you only need a tiny bit of information to build the whole picture. And the most important bit of information is in movement. The motion of a wave." He relaxed now. "The tiny vibration, the sound wave for example, that might take centuries to evaporate. If we had the instruments sensitive enough to measure it, that wave could tell us the conversation your great-grandmother might have had with your great-grandfather on their wedding night a hundred years ago."

"You mean that naughty talk is still going round?" Dias twirled his finger in the air, sloshing the arrack in his glass and giggling. The sea was booming so loud I reckoned every wave, sound or otherwise, would be obliterated forever. "So, you have this kind of instrument for the ocean?"

"It's an idea. We are working on it. But we have no fancy lab yet."

"Bullshit, *machang*, bullshit."

Mister Salgado laughed.

I was working on the curry rings on their dirty dinner-plates, scientifically applying a tuft of coconut hair and lime-water to the yellow grease. I was scrubbing my heart out. It was no joke.

Two Poems by Pattiann Rogers

The Fallacy of Thinking Flesh Is Flesh

Some part of every living creature
is always trembling, a curious
constancy in the wavering rims
of the cup coral, the tasseling
of fringe fish, in the polyrippling
of the polyclad flatworm even under the black
bottom water at midnight when nothing
in particular notices.

The single topknot, head feather,
of the horned screamer or the tufted
quail can never, in all its tethered
barbs and furs, be totally still.
And notice the plural flickers
of the puss moth's powdery antennae.
Not even the puss moth knows how
to stop them.

Maybe it's the pattern of the shattering
sea-moon so inherent to each body
that makes each more than merely body.
Maybe it's the way the blood possesses
the pitch and fall of blooming grasses
in a wind that makes the prairie
of the heart greater than its boundaries.
Maybe it's god's breath swelling
in the breast and limbs, like a sky
at dawn, that gives bright bone
the holiness of a rising sun.
There's more to flesh than flesh.

The steady flex and draw of the digger
wasp's blue-bulbed abdomen — I know
there's a fact beyond presence
in all that fidgeting.

Even as it sleeps, watch the body
perplex its definition — the slight shift
of the spine, the inevitable lash shiver,
signal pulse knocking. See, there,
that simple shimmer of the smallest
toe again, just to prove it.

The Singing Place

For the orange, saucer-eyed
lemurs indri of the family sifaka,
it is the perfect forest of the hot,
humid zones. There, at sunset and dawn,
they all pause arboreally and chorus,
howling, hooting, shaking the shadows
overhead, the fruits and burrowing
beetles inside the many-storied
jungle. They are the ushers,
the chaperones, the screaming
broadcast of darkness and light.

The house cricket, the field cricket,
the dead-leaf cricket make song places
of the warmest, darkest niches
they can find, at the bases of stones,
in grass stem funnels, the mossy
underbark of southside tree trunks.

For the sage grouse, male, the real
singing place is where he actually sings,
there inside the thimble-sized, flesh-
and-blood place of his voice, that air
sac burbling and popping, puffing
through the morning as he struts
and bows before his hens on the open
spring lek. Breath, I believe,
is place.

And maybe even the bulb and tuber
and root suck of the big black slug
of wet pastures could be called a long,
slow mud music and meter of sustenance,
by those lucky enough to be born
with a pasture sense for sound.

The whine and wind of heat
through ragged gorges make sandstone
and basalt a moving song. And place,
I think, is moments in motion.

As on the white-statue plains
of the moon's most weird winter
where no dusk scream or lingering suck
or floosing air sac of song has ever
existed, utter stillness is a singing
place too, moments where I first
must find a shape of silence,
where I then must begin
to hum its structure.

Rika Lesser

Epilogue: *Dödsdansen*

I. After the Fall

Standing in the midst of my illness
alone. Psychiatrist gone. The work
undone. The incident, the "fall" — deadly,
yes, but hardly suicidal — comes
in disparate forms, whose outlines blur:

There may have been gunshots.
A woman says I jumped.
I sleeprode to the subway stop
called East New York, near where
I grew up (my father says
there the platform rises 50
or 60 feet). To hit the street
where I did, transit police claim
I had to climb over two large
obstacles. Can this be believed?
In the gym when I mount the Gravitron
and the platform hoists me to
the chinning bars, unstable,
my legs shake.

           I recall nothing past
the day before. I couldn't tell I was verging
on mania. Whatever else took place, I lost
control. Whether I fell, jumped, or was
pushed, from iliac crest to acetabulum,
my pelvis broke (a big white pretzel snapping),
as did a bone in the wrist on the same side.
I could have died, but healed, and almost

painlessly. There was, of course, an injury
to my head. The worst harm done was to my
psyche. Psyche, I say, not pride—that comes
before a fall.

              That I am back on
lithium now is quite all right, but how
to see myself the whole of the prior
year? How to look at you now disappeared,
invisible doctor?

II. Parting

Once I could walk again, I had to know
what had happened to you. Your office tape
had gone six months unchanged. To get your
"covering" doctor to reveal anything
    (back in the fall, she was incompetent;
    doesn't a pro return an urgent
    call in under 48 hours?)
my new psychiatrist had to say I would sue;
myself tell her I dared not presume
she gave a damn whether I lived or died.

You have ovarian cancer.
                         Inside,
something dissolved, allowed me to feel
for you. More like a friend than a doctor?
Close in age, five months into our fifth year
together, we both knew how many deaths
I'd survived. In the end (*What does "End" mean?*)
Death is the side of life *that is turned
away from us.* Where are you? What gives
you the right to turn away before I've
said goodbye?

And the fall? you ask.
Whether or not this fall's fall was a leap
to a conclusion Life won't let me make,
there's now a crack, a parting in my life,
a fissure in what I termed my "progress."
To heal it is to get bone knit back to bone.

Which slowly I do (it is hardly
possible to imagine how slowly),
watch the white fibers bridge the dark rift
until solidly my whole skeleton
can bear weight, stand, and bid *Farewell*.

Richard Lyons

The Black Venus: For Max Ernst

1.

Max, I lean a photo of Josephine Baker
in this box lined with black construction paper,

it looks like a miniature dollhouse
lined with morose wallpaper that would caution
even the young Mark Rothko.
But, as in his work,
we must distinguish the shapes of panthers
in the black expanse—her emblem—

as she poses in Miss Bricktop's new *boîte de nuit*,
her hair oiled flat against her skull like a Black Venus.

Maybe you saw her dance—all lips & hips—
her skin one shade darker than honey
turning in the hot lights the ghostly shade
of Lalique glass. I imagine you two
passing in the street, her entourage parting for her
behind the leash her leopard Chiquita draws
as the crowd leans from the cat
and back again toward her.

Fifteen years her senior,
you will die within months of her—
that year I chucked my job counting numbers
to follow your ghost through the sandstone
of Sedona, Arizona, with a blank book for poems.

Didn't we emerge from the same prehistoric egg
amid sparks of jet & obsidian embedded in the hills
of Montmartre? "Only Negroes can excite Paris."
Fernand Léger said to Daven, who marveled

at black women dancing the quai of Gare St.-Lazare,
their *feu d'artifice* under sooty gray glass.

2.

One night upstairs in her room at the theatre
off the Champs-Elysées,
watching the letters *Citroën* flash the Eiffel Tower
with the sensational new effect called Néon

she whispers it's a new age, baby, damn straight.

And the next night
as she weaves with "the speed of a hummingbird"
through the tree-trunk legs of the giant Joe Alex,
you can't keep your eyes off her.
Later, schnitzel burning on an illegal hot plate
in your room above the Pantheon,
you begin your first paragon Afrique
born from a pair of lovebirds, a pink macaw.

In my photograph of her,
she's playfully staring down the replica of an elephant,
already imagining her failure
in your country & hers,

her girdle of phallic bananas turned to the tusks
poachers hack from elephants.

3.

Does what is dark & magnificent
require we hack it,
the way the words of the American tourist
in the fashionable restaurant

hacked a silence: *Back home, a nigger woman belongs in the
    kitchen.*
In my mind, as in a movie, you stride out of the dark
like a Hollywood hero & bash the man on his ear bone,
the blood like a snail trail on his collar.

Years later, during the occupation,
my movie's still running:

your small round head buried in her breast
as the car swerves south. She's telling you
how every night she dreams about her half-sister
Willie Mae peering in between the blinds
at the late night doctor's office
above a drugstore in St. Louis

where the girl bled to death from a botched abortion.

She tells you how the Hotel St. Moritz hailed her
by asking she give the lobby a wide berth
and use the service elevator,

all the while your heart about to explode with love & fear
as you pass another checkpoint,
the contraband petrol in champagne bottles
in the trunk of the car.

4.

                    Ah, to explode
with Josephine in the final number of *très sauvage*
in an egg-shaped gold cage of fire,

to transcend the world she saw as the horror of men
returning home from war with only one arm, one leg, one
    eye. . . .

Today I read that the cop who bludgeoned Rodney King
over fifty times will get a reduced sentence.

I imagine this man bent over a slab of meat
as the black brothers in the maximum security
lean against the walls, stretching their Achilles'
   & gesticulating.

But just as surely as she had to leave again her country
these cops will serve a few months in a condo.
One of Gauguin's dark maidens,

she will climb the stairs, much older now,
radishes from the garden trailing from her hands.
With their fronds she'll tickle awake her adopted children
in the many bedrooms of the house in the Dordogne.

She is the pure black shape of a panther
undiscovered in Lascaux.

In my box, this *boîte de nuit*,
I've juxtaposed her image with an overexposed picture
of a black cat. Eight different edges of the same cat
stare straight ahead, as if on stage

but the ninth stares off across her dark skin
to a box with slats I've turned on its side
to stand for a jail made of blond pine.

Inside is a demonic clown-head on a spring:
a jack-in-the-box the size of a swollen thumb.

I call this "Homey the clown incarcerated
for wearing whiteface, August 1993" after a popular

black television figure,
not Step'n Fetch It, Hannibal above the ruins of Rome.

Two Poems by Jim Moore

The Young Men

My father naked in the photo, young
again, crouched among rocks and water. It's an island,
a time so long ago he is thin,
buttocks tense with the pleasure
of climbing down towards beach and sea.
Who is this man who so loved sunlight,
bare skin? Somewhere inside
all the fathers
are these young men:
virginal, unburdened of thoughtful,
mysterious sons and stubborn, principled daughters.

I have the photo to prove it:
they are climbing down rocks
towards the sea. They are almost
on the beach. They are naked
and happy, filled with delight
to be crouching on the coastlines of uninhabited islands.

Freshman Papers

Like orange candywrappers, writes
the daughter now, describing the time
years ago when the goldfish
were thrown into the street
after her mother died.
*Like litter, but still
trying to swim.* And then,
there's the young man
whose father flew over Hiroshima,
just afterwards. My student wanders
around in prose until
he discovers why his father never speaks
of what he feels: *Maybe he saw
too much death even before
I was born.* The son tries to forgive
the father in paragraph eight.
Title: *My Father The Stranger.*

If I only had
one mistake to take with me, red pen
in hand, into the grave, I'd choose
surprise: those misspelled words that drop
the undeserving reader
without warning into *hys-
terical*, rather than *historical*, or it's a *doggy
dog world.* And truly, it's a dog
eat dog world. Take the daughter
who just last year
remembered the neighbor's zipper
when she was six, then seven, then eight,
how it scratched her cheek, how carefully
he dried her face.

Daily,
I spoil their terrors
by pleading in the margins
for more or less.
I grade what I can and leave
the rest to them to revise
as they must, these sons
and daughters with their lost subjects
and ruinous verbs, their bent heads
just inches above the paper
when they write in class,
free hand cupped around the words they form
so that no one will see before
they do, how it is their lives
turn out, now that I have asked.

Three Poems by Thomas Pfau

The End of the Private Self

came as a surprise, even beyond astonishment,
turned into a monument carved in rock
like Ozymandias, a hard fact. The self's
song had become foreign as an ashen bird's.

The self had lounged around in backyards for all
too long, smoking, bored and boring, whiling
away those afternoons when there was still time
enough to think. The labor of our apprenticeship

to inwardness had come to nothing. We had been
looking at a landscape still overfamiliar,
an alphabet so well known that we no longer
perceived the letters. Once it had seemed a truth,

like Euclidean space, or the theory of lying alone
on our backs in the dark. It's as if it never
existed, the TV on as always, the parking lots
eagerly overstudied, the world filling up

with empty glances. No nostalgias could save it,
no deliriums of rearrangement; the loss might
not even have been one. Now it's a museum piece,
stupid as porcelain, on long-term display

in the new conceptual wing, where the loose
bandages of late autumn light swirl
around its pedestal, and where, occasionally,
a few observers can hear it whisper.

Suburban Exquisites

We had been waiting on the porch at evening
in thought. Uneventful winds dropped down
from the green park of rock west of town —
we didn't understand.

The lawn outlined in light. The wine was good.
Bodies languidly flung to admit things
in the blond ease of wicker chairs, we figured
we were parts of a cloud.

We used phrases like "what use is understanding?"
We wanted everything to be casual, effortless,
a rescue. The fading sun an umbrella turned
with the tongue, we knew

patience as our sentence, patience for color
drinking through color, for furniture billowing
in the backyard brush, something for which we
were already ready.

Rest Area

Across the divider lines and cracked asphalts of America,
the cottonwood, poppy, paintbrush bloom, iris
and interstate litter live without a past or future,
yet unfold into roadside history.

Here in the west we want to live loudly without a past,
counting on a future perfect with sensibly ordered signposts.
Highway-weary at a picnic table, rattled by wheels,
I'm of no account against confusion.

I want to drift like the leaves, freed from a calculable sense
of self, to imagine saving shapes rising on the horizon,
but it's difficult with the traffic.

I must be ready to walk among offices, among cynical
authorities determining time, among what pretends to live,
unlike cottonwood and poppy.

Two Poems by Thomas Sleigh

The Explanation

for Jared Baker, 1960-1992

Each time my mind comes back to it, the reasons
You gave me seem less substantial than before, to advance
Always less promise of an explanation

Of your father's house gone still, sulfur sour in the air, your
    broken
Brow like pieces of a mirror . . . Is it self-indulgence
Each time my mind comes back to it? — your reasons

Showing how alien my thinking is from your final action —
The barrel aligned, the trigger's blind insistence,
The bullet like the promise of an explanation

Not only for what *you* did, but for my fascination:
Exploding in the silence, is it your violence or the violence
Of my mind coming back to it which reasons

Against these words now offered in expiation
For risks never taken, words I somehow couldn't chance
— My silence hinting at failed promises, guilty explanations

Of that final moment's blast like an accusation
Whose echoes widen beyond your wound's circumference
And my mind coming back to it still hungry for your reasons,
Sifting like a lover unspoken promises and explanations.

Some Larger Motion

After she pieced together what was done to her,
And he too realized what was done to him,
With reaching hands they feel their fingers
Touch each other's bodies while the bodies
Hold inside the touch of hands that each one
Wanted and was shamed by.
                         All evening
They've longed to tell about those hands,
But others they've told shy away somehow;
As if to spare them this, the hands press
Hushing fingers to their lips, a touch
Conspiratorial, intimate as trust . . .
                           and so,
With those hands still vividly in mind,
After the small talk they touch each other,
Wreaking on each other what those hands once wreaked,
Uncontrollably repeating the cold rage
To be beyond that shame which keeps their bodies
Sealed off as if their flesh were numb:
                           Through her,
Her crippled father touches his body, through him,
His mother's cool, willful fingers touch her;
He shivers under the incapable hands
That timidly touch him, she shrinks from
The ravages she senses in those fingers . . .

When they finish, arms and legs motionless on the bed,
As they drift between her fear, his dread,
Rousing from this moment comes a rigorous
Balance, each supporting the other,
His body nestled against hers in fragile
Equilibrium as they lie wrapped together,
Her head on his shoulders, his breath fanning
Her cheek, their opposed bodies one
In opposition:

　　　　　And in this — especially this,
They begin to feel some larger motion
Lifting them above the bodies tensed
To pull away, while deep inside the other
They sense those hands, urgent as a lover's,
Tugging at their fingers locked together.

NOTES ON CONTRIBUTORS

FICTION

A.S. Byatt's fiction includes *Sugar and Other Stories* and *The Matisse Stories* as well as the novels *The Game*, *Shadow of a Sun*, *The Virgin in the Garden*, *Still Life*, *Possession* and *Angels and Insects*. Her next book, *The Matisse Stories*, will be published by Random House in April.

Charles D'Ambrosio's work has appeared in *Story*, *The New Yorker* and the anthology *I Know Some Things* edited by Lorrie Moore. He is currently a James Michener Fellow and lives in Seattle, Washington. Little Brown will publish his first book, *The Point*, this spring.

Romesh Gunesekera grew up in Sri Lanka and the Philippines. He is the author of *Monkfish Moon*. His second book, *Reef*, from which the piece in this issue is excerpted, will be published this spring by The New Press. He lives in London.

POETRY

Nin Andrews's first book of poetry, *The Book of Orgasms*, was published last fall.

Artis Bernard is a native of South Dakota and lives in Houston, Texas.

Don Bogen is the author of *A Necessary Order: Theodore Roethke and the Writing Process* and a book of poetry, *After the Splendid Display*. He was awarded grants from the NEA and the Ingram Merrill Foundation. He teaches at the University of Cincinnati.

John Gery is the author of *The Enemies of Leisure*, a book of poetry that will be published in 1995 by Story Line Press. His book of criticism, *Ways of Nothingness: Nuclear Annihilation and Contemporary American Poetry*, will be published by the University Press of Florida in 1996. He is an associate professor at the University of New Orleans.

Lise Goett lives in Paris. In 1988, she received the James D. Phelan Award in Literature from The San Francisco Foundation and a fellowship from the Institute for Creative Writing from the University of Wisconsin at Madison.

Edward Hirsch teaches at the University of Houston. His fourth book of poems, *Earthly Measures*, was published by Alfred A. Knopf.

Philip Kobylarz's poems have appeared in *Epoch*, *The Denver Quarterly* and *The Michigan Quarterly Review*. He is currently translating selections from the French poet Jude Stefan.

Steve Kronen is the author of a book of poetry, *Empirical Evidence*, and lives in Miami, Florida, where he has worked as a licensed massage therapist for the last twelve years.

Rika Lesser is the author of a book of poetry, *Etruscan Things*, and the translator of *A Child Is Not a Knife: Selected Poems of Goran Sonnevi*.

Judy Longley won the 1993 Marianne Moore Prize from Helicon Nine Editions. She is the author of *My Journey toward You* and two chapbooks of poems, *Parallel Lives* and *Rowing Past Eden*.

Richard Lyons was the winner of the 1988 Devins Award for his collection of poems, *These Modern Nights*.

Mary Maxwell lives in New York City. She was awarded the "Discovery" — *The Nation* prize in 1990 and has been a fellow at the Camargo Foundation in Cassis, France. Her translations of Sulpilia appeared last spring in *Latin Lyric and Elegiac Poetry: An Anthology*.

Gardner McFall received the "Discovery" — *The Nation* prize in 1989. Her children's book, *Naming the Animals*, was published by Viking in 1994. She teaches literature at The Cooper Union in New York City.

Jim Moore is the author of a book of poetry, *The Freedom of History*.

Joyce Carol Oates is the author most recently of *Haunted: Tales of the Grotesque* and the novel, *What I Lived For*, both published by Dutton.

Alicia Ostriker is a professor of English at Rutgers University. Her most recent book is *The Nakedness of the Fathers: Biblical Visions and Revisions*.

Kathleen Peirce is the author of *Mercy* and *Divided Touch, Divided Color*, a chapbook published last spring by Windhover Press.

Thomas Pfau lives in Houston, Texas. His poetry has appeared in *Denver Quarterly*.

Marie Ponsot's two poetry collections are *The Green Dark* and *Admit Impediment*.

Bin Ramke teaches at the University of Denver. He is the editor of *The Denver Quarterly* as well as the Contemporary Poetry Series for the University of Georgia Press. His book, *Massacre of the Innocents*, will appear this spring.

Pattiann Rogers lives in Castle Rock, Colorado. Milkwood Editions recently published her book, *Firekeeper, New and Selected Poems.*

Goran Simic, a poet and playwright, lives in Sarajevo. He is the author of several books, among them *Vertigo, Mandragora, Selected Poems* and *A Step into the Dark.* His wife, **Amela Simic**, translated the selections that appear in this issue. Her translations into Bosnian include *The Dean's December* by Saul Bellow, *Children of a Lesser God* by Mark Medoff and poetry by Sylvia Plath.

Thomas Sleigh won an NEA grant for poetry in 1994. He is the author of *After One* and *Waking.* The University of Chicago Press will publish his latest book of poetry, *The Work*, in the winter of 1996.

Henry Sloss completed a one-year diary of poems on December 31, 1994. His long poem, "An Old World Setting," about the ten years he spent in Italy, appears in the winter issue of *Western Humanities Review.*

Jordan Smith is the author of three books of poetry: *An Apology for Loving the Old Hymns*, *Lucky Seven* and *The Household of Continuance.*

Terese Svoboda's third book of poetry, *Mere Mortals*, includes her long verse play "Faust" as well as the poem that appears in this issue; it will be published by the University of Georgia Press this spring.

Frederick Tibbetts's poetry has appeared in *The New Republic*, *Antaeus* and *The Yale Review.* He lives in Princeton, New Jersey.

David Wagoner has written ten novels and fifteen books of poetry, most recently *Through the Forest.* He is a professor of English at the University of Washington and the editor of *Poetry Northwest.*

Michael White's latest book, *The Island*, was published in 1992. He received an NEA fellowship in 1993 and now teaches at the University of North Carolina at Wilmington.

Marc Woodworth is an assistant editor at *Salmagundi* and a lecturer in the Department of English at Skidmore College.

INTERVIEWS

Jerome Brooks (Chinua Achebe interview) has taught at universities in Madagascar and Nigeria. He now teaches English at Bard College and the City College of New York, where he is also Deputy to the President.

Robert Faggen (Czeslaw Milosz interview) is an associate professor of literature at Claremont McKenna College. He is working on a book about Czeslaw Milosz and is a founding member of L.O.S.T.

ART

Nancy Brett lives and exhibits in New York City. She is represented by Victoria Monroe Gallery, and her work can currently be seen at K & E Gallery.

Flavia Gandolfo is a native of Peru and lives in Austin, Texas. She holds a continuing graduate studies fellowship at the University of Texas at Austin. Her work has been shown at Galeria Forum in Lima, Peru.

Robert Greene was born in New York City in 1953. His work is in the collections of the Metropolitan Museum of Art and the Whitney Museum. He is represented by the Robert Miller Gallery.

Ken Lum is a Canadian artist currently living in Paris. In New York City, his work is represented by the Andrea Rosen Gallery. His comments about the portfolio of portraits in this issue have been taken from a conversation between Lum and the curator Marnie Fleming, made available to us by Oakville Galleries.

The Paris Review is pleased to announce its 1994 prizewinners:

The Aga Khan Prize for Fiction has been awarded to Rick Moody for his story "The Ring of Brightest Angels around Heaven."

The Bernard F. Conners Prize for Poetry has been awarded jointly to Marilyn Hacker for "Cancer Winter" and Stewart James for "Vanessa."

The Paris Review Discovery Prize has been awarded to Vikram Chandra for his story "Dharma."

front. **EL5-8857**

back. **EL5-9307**

reservations . **PL9-1650**

55th & 3rd

**A *Paris Review* Collectible,
Celebrating the Fortieth Anniversary of
The Paris Review and its Editor-in-Chief,
G. Plimpton, Esq.**

Illustrations   *   Scandalous Tales
Photos from the "Thanks, George!" Revel
Haiku   *   Disclosures

A Festschrift!

With Contributions from George Bush, Charlie Smith, Fran Lebowitz,
Paul West, Allen Ginsberg, James Salter, Peter Matthiessen,
John Train, Rick Bass, Jill Krementz, Jay McInerney, Dan Stern,
Jonathan Dee, and other luminaries

The Paris Review
Booksellers Advisory Board

BACK ISSUES OF THE PARIS REVIEW